Human Rights in a
Globalised World

Human Rights in a Globalised World

An Indian Diary

Mukul Sharma

$\circledS$ **SAGE** www.sagepublications.com
Los Angeles • London • New Delhi • Singapore • Washington DC

First published in 2010 by

 SAGE Publications India Pvt Ltd
B1/I-1 Mohan Cooperative Industrial Area
Mathura Road, New Delhi 110 044, India
www.sagepub.in

SAGE Publications Inc
2455 Teller Road
Thousand Oaks, California 91320, USA

SAGE Publications Ltd
1 Oliver's Yard, 55 City Road
London EC1Y 1SP, United Kingdom

SAGE Publications Asia-Pacific Pte Ltd
33 Pekin Street
#02-01 Far East Square
Singapore 048763

Published by Vivek Mehra for SAGE Publications India Pvt Ltd, typeset in 10/12pt Sabon by Star Compugraphics Private Limited, Delhi and printed at Chaman Enterprises, New Delhi.

Library of Congress Cataloging-in-Publication Data

Sharma, Mukul, 1961–
    Human rights in a globalised world: an Indian diary/Mukul Sharma.
        p. cm.
    Includes bibliographical references and index.
    1. Human rights.   2. Human rights—India.   3. India—Social conditions—21st century.   I. Title.

JC571.S4527   323—dc22   2010   2010029665

ISBN: 978-81-321-0462-9 (PB)

The SAGE Team: Rekha Natarajan and Shweta Tewari

For a great teacher Radhakrishna Sahay
and
For my dear friends Chandresh, Anand V. Swamy,
Ramkripal Singh

Contents

Acknowledgements

I am sincerely thankful to N. Ram, Charu Gupta, Govind Singh, Parsa Venkateshwar Rao Jr, C. Rammanohar Reddy, A.G. Noorani, Sana Das, Ishaan Sharma, Devadass Gnanapragasam (Gnanam), Dr Srirak Plipat, Sauro Scarpelli, Brian Wood, Chiara Misto, Helen Hughes, Anil Pant, John Samuel, Usha Ramnathan, Ujjwal Kumar Singh, Yamini Mishra, Mahesh Rangarajan, Deepa Menon, Amita Baviskar, Praful Bidwai, Rekha Natarajan, Shubranshu Mishra, Joe Athialy, Apporvanand, Medha Patkar, Ashok Chowdhary, Babu Mathew, Mazhar Hussain, Amitabh Behar, Kamal Kishore, Madhuresh, Mamata Dash, Sudhir Pattnaik, Leban Serto, Md Mashkoor Alam, Javed Naqi, Vijay Pratap, Aditya Nigam, Subha Menon, Aseem Shrivastava, Babu John, Pankaj Singh, Praveen Jha, Rakesh Sinha, Roma, Anil Mishra, Aseem Prakash, Vinay Pratap Singh and Kishan Kaljayee.

My special thanks to the daily newspapers *The Hindu*, *DNA* and *Amar Ujala* who regularly published my articles that are included in this book.

I must mention non-commercial, alternative journals and magazines in English and Hindi, mainly *Economic and Political Weekly*, *Sab Log*, *Adhikaar* and *Kathan*. They have also been publishing my pieces on similar concerns with consistency and conviction.

I blog in *Kafila* and *Culture Unplugged* where these issues appear at regular intervals and the debates, point–counterpoints amongst the fellow bloggers are very enriching.

Introduction

All people are born free and equal in dignity and rights. This guiding principle of the Universal Declaration of Human Rights lives strong in the hearts and minds of millions of people, as the declaration celebrated its 60th birthday in 2008. In 1948 the Universal Declaration of Human Rights (UDHR) set out for the first time the fundamental rights which allow all of us to live in dignity, to which everyone is entitled. Its 30 articles cover the economic, civil, social, cultural and political areas of our lives. They range from the rights to life and security—such as water, food, health care, shelter and freedom from torture—to those that provide full participation in that life, such as freedom from discrimination, freedom of expression, education, work, association and religion. They cannot be partitioned or diluted. Their meaning is in their indivisibility. Nobody can arbitrarily choose which rights to allow people to access. They are universal. When any of them are threatened, they all are.

In the six decades since the Declaration was signed by the international community, the world has undergone dramatic changes. Some regions have been able to fly with the vision further than others. In May 1948, several months before the adoption of the UDHR, the Inter-American Conference adopted the American Declaration of the Rights and Duties of Man, the world's first general human rights instrument. The America region's crucial contribution to international human rights has been overshadowed in the intervening years by the military rule that dominated much of the region. From the 1960s to the mid-1980s, many Latin American countries endured years of military government characterised by widespread and systematic human rights violations. The end of military rule and the return to constitutionally elected governments have seen an end to the pattern of widespread and systematic violations of peoples' rights. Today, most constitutions in the region guarantee fundamental rights and most countries in the region have ratified key international human rights treaties. Representatives of several

Middle Eastern governments participated in the negotiations to adopt the UDHR. Egypt, Iran, Iraq, Lebanon and Syria were among the 48 states with the vision to adopt the Declaration. Indeed, it was only on 15 March 2008 that an Arab Charter on Human Rights took effect. Over the decades, the human rights framework in the African region has developed through various regional human rights treaties and institutions. In 1986, the African Charter on Human and Peoples' Rights entered into force and the 20th anniversary of the African Commission on Human and Peoples' Rights was celebrated in 2007. In July 2008 the AU Assembly adopted the Protocol on the Statute of the African Court of Justice and Human Rights (African Court). Within a decade of its continent's devastation by the Second World War, western Europe had laid the foundations of what would become a pan-European regional institutional architecture—set to create a human rights system. In that time, the Council of Europe drew up the first international legal instrument to protect human rights and created the European Court of Human Rights to enforce it. The economic communities established in the 1950s evolved into the European Union—embracing new member states—and into a self-proclaimed 'union of values', aspiring to place human rights at the heart of policy.

Many of the Asia-Pacific states that adopted the UDHR in 1948 had recently achieved independence from colonial rule. For them, a global commitment to a world where all are 'free and equal in dignity and rights' held special significance. 'Freedom from fear and want' were equally powerful aspirations for the citizens of the many Asia-Pacific nations. But Asia remains the only region that does not have an overarching human rights instrument. However, in a major development in November 2007, the leaders of the Association of Southeast Asian Nations (ASEAN) marked the Association's 40th anniversary by signing their first formal charter—including a commitment to establish a human rights body for the sub-region.

Global political and economic processes, unprecedented in scale, change in the balance of forces in favour of liberty and freedom, successes of peoples' movements, media, communication and technological progress, different by nature and consequences, in various socio-economic systems, impact of this progress on the individual, and the danger overhanging humanity on account of the terror and counter terror are making human rights a cardinal issue of political and ideological life. Human Rights has become one of the most influential and formative ideas of our time. Every country in the world has formally signed up to at least one core human rights treaty. Human rights have become a standard measure by which states judge each other's legitimacy. Today, few members of the international community would dare say they were against human rights: those who do, risk making themselves a pariah. The language of human rights is so central to legal, political and moral discourse within and between states that this has been described as 'the age of rights'.

But if the idea of human rights is so recognised, why is it that defending human rights can still be so dangerous? The killing of A.D. Babu and the arrest of Binayak Sen are not isolated cases. There are numerous documented cases of attacks on rights activists in India, South Asia and most countries around the world. These attacks take many forms, from continual low-level harassment and subtle attempts to disparage their work, to wrongful imprisonment, torture and even murder. If this is the age of rights, why is this not yet the age of the rights activists? Rights activists are at great risk because they are pointing to the reality behind the rhetoric. They are concerned with rights as they are actually experienced or denied at the level of people's lived experiences, rather than as promises proclaimed on paper. That gap continues to be as enormous today as it was when the UDHR was adopted in 1948. The creation of the an international and national systems of human rights protection may have been one of the greatest legacies of the 20th century, but the century ended as it began with genocide, wars of unprecedented devastation and millions dying from preventable disease and malnutrition, despite huge technical advances and vastly increased global wealth. While commitments to the rights may have become mainstream and commonplace, public policies that abide by those principles are still seen as radical and are all too rare. By focusing on what governments have actually done to implement rights beyond merely invoking them, rights activists are often purveyors of uncomfortable truths, truths which governments often make strenuous efforts to suppress. If rights activists are branded dangerous dissidents today in the eyes of many, it is because they are unlocking the transformative politics of rights, to bring about the profound changes needed to fulfill the radical vision of our constitution makers. Bringing about that vision necessarily means challenging the status quo and encroaching on vested interests, whether it is the interests of a particular government, or the police–military, economic or political elites that sustain them.

It is not only the battle against the static or restrictive under-standing of rights by the rights activists, but in recent years people have also had to guard against a more fundamental assault on the validity and relevance of the human rights framework. First, some governments, particularly the US and in Europe, have argued that 'the rules of the game have changed' since the attacks in the US on 11 September 2001 and subsequent attacks in other countries. They have called into question the extent to which human rights con-siderations should take precedence over the concern to protect their populations. This has led to attempts to justify torture and other ill-treatment in the name of fighting terrorism, and to the bypassing of fundamental due process guaranteed by holding thousands of suspects indefinitely without charge or trial. The practice of extraordinary renditions and the detentions in Guantánamo, Bagram, Abu Ghraib and other 'war on terror' black sites were officially established. Later, it became the chorus of countries of Asia and Pacific where the disappearances, encounters, illegal killings are justified at the cost of long-recognised ethical values at the heart of the human rights framework such as the complete and utter unacceptablity of torture, and the right of everyone—no matter what they are alleged to have done—to be treated with dignity and fairness by the state.

In the same era, globalisation's state apparatus has undergone anti-democratic evolutions. It includes processes such as:

- the fusion of the state apparatus with the neo-liberal, corporate and market forces, its centralisation and bureaucratisation; the growing strength of the corporate-bureaucratic machine; the caste/religious exclusiveness of the bureaucracy and police/army;
- the increasing powers of the administrative apparatus and the decline of the actual power prerogatives of representative agencies; replacement of parliament by its commissions; falsification of the will of the electorate; growth of 'legalised' and illegal corruption at all levels of the formation and func-tioning of state agencies;
- growth of the influence of the security complex and of the militarisation of the state structure; formation and elevation of the unconstitutional organs; growth of the powers of the punitive and repressive complex; extension of illegal forms

and methods of administration; lastly, the tendency of these processes towards the securitisation of the state mechanism (notably, the military, intelligence and punitive and repressive apparatus).

The aggravation of contradictions in democracy and the exacerbation of the crisis in day-to-day delivery of democratic functioning in some key areas of our life are accentuating its character as 'universal' democracy. Moreover, this is leading to the growth of the tangible benefits that the corporate gets from this form of (dys)functioning. Like the time of the cold war, the human rights are getting immune to the new polarisation of the world. On one side the achievement of the basic economic and social rights is presented as requiring a political commitment to the neo-liberal and marketism. On the other, civil and political rights are portrayed as a luxury that could only be afforded once war on terror has been won.

Thus, a system of surveillance of the population, political killings, persecution of progressive-minded figures and democratic organisations, unlawful arrests and searches, new torture methods, etc., become an openly admitted features of day-to-day life in our 'democratic' states. The Satyam affair, which revealed dishonesty, corruption, direct violation of the law in the highest echelons of company and government, is just a harbinger of an endless stream of scandals involving the government agencies, banks, investors and multinational corporations, which involves practically the entire governance system.

Violations of peoples' economic, social and cultural rights occur frequently. However, three types of violations can be identified: *(a)* **Retrogression**, which includes developing and implementing new policies that move further for the realisation of rights; large-scale disinvestment in social services not justified by a general economic downturn; the reallocation of resources away from economic, social and cultural rights to other areas, such as unwarranted or excessive security expenditure. *(b)* **Discriminatory non-fulfilment.** Non-discrimination is an immediate obligation that cuts across all obligations to respect, protect and fulfil rights. The adoption of laws, policies and practice that are inconsistent with the principle of non-discrimination. *(c)* **Failure to prioritise minimum core obligations,** particularly for the most vulnerable.

Resource allocation and policy prioritisation are the key areas in realising the rights. All too frequently, our states seek to justify the violation of rights on the ground that they lack financial, technical or human resources. Our states also show skepticism in the face of overwhelming statistics on deprivation, hunger and poverty. Can all 973 million people who do not have access to nutritionally adequate food be victims of human rights violations? Though judiciability and enforcibility of rights have taken new positive shapes within and outside the realms of law and judiciary, a state's violation of its obligations about resource allocation and policy prioritisation is not much explored. In adjudicating on such matters, courts in some countries have been reticent to intrude on the terrain of the executive or other public policy makers, or to issue rulings implying the redistribution of resources from one sector at the expense of another. However the standard of 'reasonableness', developed in the South African courts, is useful in setting a threshold for acceptable state conduct:

> A Court considering reasonableness will not enquire whether other more desirable or favourable measures could have been adopted, or whether public money could have been better spent. The question would be whether the measures that have been adopted are reasonable. It is necessary to recognise that a wide range of possible measures could be adopted by the State to meet its obligations. Many of these would meet the requirement of reasonableness. Once it is shown that the measures do so, this requirement is met. (Government of the Republic of South Africa and Others v/s Irene Grootboom and Others, Case CCT 11/00, para 41)

In applying this principle, the Constitutional Court of South Africa considered whether the policy or programme was comprehensive, coherent and coordinated; balanced and flexible; allowed for short, medium and long-term needs; was reasonably conceived and implemented; and was transparent. The Court considered that the obligation to fulfil the right to adequate housing was violated where housing policy did not prioritise the improvement of the housing condition of those living 'with no access to land, no roof over their heads, and who were living in intolerable conditions or crisis situations'.

The inadequacy of legality is another concern. Legality adopted to the stable forms of 'industrial society' can not catch up with the main trends of the highly volatile, mobile age of capital: global production and supply chain, differentiation of production and economic life and the associated decentralisation, the short-lived character and instability of capital phenomena, etc. In this situation, which gives rise to a diversity of unregulated business practice, the law is allegedly unable to perform its main function as society's control to exploitation and expropriation. Thus, Bhopal saga continues even after more than two decades.

Responsibility for denial of rights frequently lies not only with governments but also with individuals, groups and companies. Primary accountability rests with the state in whose jurisdiction the violation occurs. However, in situations such as domination of the non-state armed groups in a particular area or internal armed conflicts, the controlling power must be answerable for human rights abuses within that territory. States are also responsible for abuses by private individuals and other non-state entities, such as transnational corporations, where the state has jurisdiction over such individuals and enterprises, and where it fails to exercise due diligence in regulating their conduct. The largest 300 firms control about 25 per cent of the world's productive assets. Given this reality, there is an emerging international consensus, on the need to recognise corporate accountability for human rights abuses. While the primary responsibility lies with states, there is growing recognisation of duties of every organ of society, including corporations. There are moves to develop standards, policies and laws that would hold businesses to account for abuses of human rights directly resulting from their operations, and would recognise their duty to prevent such abuses within their sphere of influence. However, it is quite likely that efforts to establish international binding standards for corporate accountability for human rights are likely to suffer a setback as corporations and governments collude to avoid or water down international initiatives. States that provide international development assistance and cooperation should be held responsible for the human rights impact of their policies outside their borders. Donor states should ensure that their development cooperation policies are consistent with their human rights obligations, not only on paper but also in practice. Those receiving development assistance also have an obligation to ensure that this is used in a way consistent with human rights, including through devoting the maximum available resources towards the full realisation of economic, social and cultural rights. Human rights violations resulting from development projects are therefore the responsibility both of donor states—where they were aware or should reasonably have been aware of the implications of the project—and of aid recipient states—where they failed to exercise due diligence to ensure that the intervention was consistent with human rights.

While all these events are taking place, the mechanism of justice is approaching a state of near coma. Endless and unwarranted procrastination in the operation of courts compromises the basic legal rights of countless numbers of the citizens and undermines, little by little, the very foundations of the state and the government. Because the legal means of the protection of the rights of many citizens can be used only when they have, in the course of the time, lost their dynamism, they become nothing more than an empty form of justice. The most important place held by justice in the system of functions of a modern civilised state is determined by the fact that it should serve to protect citizens' rights and redress violated rights. No matter how these rights may look on paper, if they are not properly protected, there can be no talk about law and order. Further, a society consisting of 'self-policing communities', like Salwa Judum, could rely more and more on improvised, uninstitutionalised, illegal courts, sanctions and so forth.

Human rights are recognised as a result of popular struggles. It is people, not politicians, who claim rights, and it is their efforts that lead to official recognition. All significant advances in the protection of human rights have developed from social struggles, including those of organised labour, anti-colonialists, the women's movement and tribals. Campaigning by local, national and regional organisations against abuses of rights is not new. Their messages gained greater resonance during the 1980s and 1990s as global politics began to thaw and as concern grew at the collapse in social conditions and the prioritisation of economic development over human dignity. The human rights agenda has always been a dynamic and constantly evolving one, with activists and organisations applying the principles and tools of peoples' rights to different contexts and struggles. At different points in history, courageous and visionary people have sought to extend human rights protection to those outside its boundaries, whether it be people living in slavery, workers unprotected against exploitation or women denied the vote. We see a world in flux: a world in contest, confusion and, in far too many places, in conflict. But we also see an increasingly interconnected and interdependent world in which global problems require global solutions and in which there are both opportunities as well as challenges for promoting and upholding human rights.

There is political re-configuration: The moral authority of western governments is at an all time low, particularly in the Islamic world. The United States Administration, overstretched and overwhelmed by its military adventures and counter-terrorism strategy, is being challenged at home and abroad. The 2008 Presidential elections has brought about a change of Administration but whether that will lead to a significant change in direction remains to be seen. Hamstrung by the different views of its member states, the European Union is likely to continue to punch below its weight on human rights and foreign policy issues. Russia is increasingly reasserting its authority as it slips further into a retrogressive pattern on human rights. China, India and Brazil are emerging as global players, forging new political and economic alliances with nations from Asia, Africa and Latin America, but their allegiance to international human rights standards remains unclear and erratic. At the same time, the impact of the 'non-state' actor on human rights, whether corporate or extremist, is rising. While democratic elections are on the rise, good governance is undermined by corruption, conflict and the failure by governments to tackle poverty. The disappointments of democracy are apparent in parts of the former Soviet Union, South Asia and Latin America. However, the call for pluralism and greater transparency and accountability of governments is gaining ground around the world. Thus, the new political configurations require new approaches in countries such as India, China, Brazil and Russia with the recognition of the shifting power and roles of regional/super-state organisations like ASEAN, SAARC and the Arab League.

In 2008, the world reaches an invisible but significant milestone: For the first time in history, more than half its population, 3.3 billion people, is living in urban areas. By 2030, this is expected to swell to almost 5 billion. Between 2000 and 2030, the world's urban population is expected to increase by 72 per cent, while the built-up areas of cities of 100,000 people or more could increase by

175 per cent. As mega cities develop in countries experiencing rapid economic growth, large slums are becoming the visible symbols of disparity, desperation and human rights abuse. Sprawling urban spaces will also bring crime and violence. The affluent middle and upper classes wall themselves in and pay for private security that can itself be a source of increased violence and disrespect for human rights. Policymakers continue to work against rural–urban migration using tactics such as house destruction, forced displacement, eviction of squatters and denial of services. What happens to and in urban centres in the coming years will have a dramatic impact on human rights concerns and rights must be at the heart of efforts to make these sustainable.

Population movements, voluntary and involuntary, within countries and across regions, are on the rise, pushed by economic, social, environmental and political factors. As noted above, for the first time in the history of mankind, those living in urban areas have outnumbered those living in rural areas. As ease of travel and labour shortages generate ever higher levels of international migration, more and more countries are confronted with issues of multiculturalism and the challenges of integration, tolerance and diversity. Tensions between western secular values and Islam are aggravated by a resurgence of religious fundamentalism, identity politics and extremist political violence, on one side, and counter-terrorism strategies and refugee/migration policies that erode human rights and encourage discrimination, racism and xenophobia on the other. However, in many instances, culturally persecuted individuals and communities find little recourse in the existing framework of human rights protection and the tensions surrounding cultural relativism versus universal human rights persist. Predominantly young populations in the developing world (Middle, East, Africa, Asia and Latin America) contrast sharply with the aging demographic pattern in the global North and West. In some African countries, the large number of AIDS related adult deaths creates an unprecedented number of child-headed households and orphans, raising issues of social and political stability as well as child rights and welfare. These changing demographic patterns bring new challenges as well for mobilisation of human rights activists.

The world continues to undergo revolutionary changes in information and communication technologies (ICT), but the benefits of instant connectivity, communication and learning are empowering the best as well as the worst of us: civil society, business and governments, as well as, armed groups and criminals. 'Borderless' media carry voices, opinion and messages around the world at the speed of light. But for all the multiplicity of channels, the concentration of media ownership in the hands of a few limits the content of such messages. New opportunities for bearing witness to human rights abuses are multiplying through new technology. The uprising in Myanmar showed the power of citizenship journalism, where ordinary people, using telephone-based cameras, can record and disseminate evidence of atrocities in real time. Satellite technology offers new methods of exposing mass violations in remote, inaccessible areas, but also generates new threats to the right to privacy of individuals. As ICT empowers people, some governments, like China, Tunisia, Egypt and Iran, are responding with new restrictions, making the internet the new frontier in the struggle for freedom of expression. A marked 'digital' divide exists but it does not mirror the 'paper' divide and the trend is for the world's online population to become more nationally and culturally diverse. Societies with advanced communications will generally worry about threats to individual privacy while others will worry about the spread of 'cultural contamination.'

In a world drowning in a sea of information, floating one's own message to the top will become tougher. But the virtual network also creates a greater sense of global citizenship, cutting across national, ethnic, sectarian, or other divides. New technologies and communication tools are fast becoming essential infrastructure for activism enabling collaboration across distance and organisational boundaries unlike the past. In the field of science, new discoveries bring new opportunities but also ethical dilemmas. New advances in healthcare are bringing about demands for a more equitable distribution of its benefits. However, as biotechnology becomes more widely available, its potential misuse also increases with the risk of biological weapons and 'dirty' bombs. Comprehensive genetic profiling, is spurring grave ethical and privacy concerns, calling into question the 'human' in 'human rights.'

There are several pressing issues, to be addressed. Violations of people's economic, social and cultural rights can no longer be ignored. Hunger, homelessness and preventable disease can no longer be treated as though they were intractable social problems or solely the product of natural disasters. They are a human rights scandal. Governments hide behind the excuse of lack of resources to fail their people, to deny them the means to realise their rights, and to allow companies and others to act without restrictions, even where this means endangering the lives and health of the people. The evolution of rights will continue and new generation of rights activists will challenge orthodox interpretations of human rights and articulate new claims. Those alerting us to the impact of climate change on the sustainability of life on the planet, or to the implications of biotechnological and genetic advances on what it means to be human, are already pointing out to some of the issues which will feature increasingly on the human rights agenda of the future.

Section I

Human Rights in
Times of Terror

1

Counter Terror with Justice

Terrorism is an assault on people's fundamental human rights. The heinous terrorist attacks in recent years that have left thousands of civilians dead or maimed, are many. The deliberate targeting of civilians, whether through planting bombs in restaurants or public places or bringing down buildings killing thousands; killing constitute a serious abuse of fundamental human rights and runs counter to basic principles of humanity. Those who commit such atrocities must be brought to justice. Deliberately attacking civilians should never be justified. Violence and terror will only breed more violence and terror.

However, in the aftermath of the Jaipur serial blasts (on 13 May 2008, a series of bombs exploded across the city of Jaipur, Rajasthan, killing a large number of people) and the human sufferings, this is also the time to urge our governments and political leaders not to respond to terror with terror. We will be repeatedly exposed with the human rights violations committed in the name of security, as well as, measures that undermine fundamental rights, such as encounters, disappearances, mass graves, torture and cruel, inhuman or degrading treatments. It will provide an effective smokescreen for governments to authorise arbitrary and long detention, unfair trial, suppression of political dissent, and minority persecution, knowing that any criticism and discontent will be weakened. A narrow focus on 'terror' emphasising the likes of a new anti-terror law or tough methods will certainly lead to the neglect of the terror's root causes in the country. At a time when we are witnessing a new lease of life for new security measures and a backlash against the human rights issues, protecting our rights should be an essential component of protecting our security. Fight against terrorism should also not be used as an excuse to end investigations into the role played by the police and armed forces in committing human rights violations against thousands of people, often in collusion with or the acquiescence of the state authorities.

We have no agreed definition of terrorism, and anti-terrorist legislation adopted in countries including India contains crimes so broadly defined as to violate the principle of legality, which requires clarity and certainty in the definition of offences. In her most recent report on human rights and terrorism, the High Commissioner for Human Rights noted that:

> ... many States have adopted national legislation with vague, unclear or overbroad definitions of terrorism. These ambiguous definitions have led to inappropriate restrictions on the legitimate exercise of fundamental liberties, such as association, expression and peaceful political and social opposition... Some States have included non-violent activities in their national definitions of terrorism. This has increased the risk and the practice that individuals are prosecuted for legitimate, non-violent exercise of rights enshrined in international law, or that criminal conduct that does not constitute 'terrorism' may be criminalized as such... There are several examples of hastily adopted counter-terrorism laws which introduced definitions that lacked in precision and appeared to contravene the principle of legality... Particular care must be taken... in defining offences relating to the support that can be offered to terrorist organisations or offences purporting to prevent the financing of terrorist activities in order to ensure that various non violent conducts are not inadvertently criminalized by vague formulations of the offences in question....
> (UN Human Rights Council, 2008, paras 20–23)

We have disturbing examples all-over the world: In 2007, the Russian Federation amended a 2002 law on 'extremist activity'. These amendments broadened the definition of 'extremism', criminalised public justification of terrorism and slander of government officials, and threatened to restrict and punish the activities of civil society organisations and other government critics. The USA PATRIOT Act of 2001 contains a vaguely-worded definition of 'material support' to proscribed entities by persons 'engaged in terrorist activities'. By the end of the year 2001, the Criminal Law of the People's Republic of China was amended to 'punish terrorist crimes, ensure national security and the safety of people's lives and property, and uphold social order'. Jordan passed an anti-terrorism law in October 2001 that broadened the definition of terrorism, restricted freedom of expression, and widened the scope of the death penalty. In 2006 it passed the Prevention of Terrorism Act, which defines 'terrorist activities' so widely that non-violent critics of the government or others exercising their right to freedom of expression can be detained under its provisions. According to the wide-ranging definition incorporated in Algeria's Penal Code, terrorism includes not only threats to state security, but also damaging national or republican symbols; harming the environment, means of communication or means of transport; impeding the functioning of public institutions; and hindering free exercise of religion and public freedoms. Tunisia's Anti-Terrorism Law of 2003 criminalises 'acts of incitement to hatred or to racial or religious fanaticism, regardless of the means used', and acts seen as illegitimately 'influencing state policy' and 'disturbing public order'. These terms are so broad that they can cover legitimate forms of peaceful expression, association and assembly, and may violate the principle of legality.

Terrorism has many forgotten faces in India today. Across the country, many violent conflicts are taking a bloody toll. In Chattisgarh, more than 100,000 people have been displaced, more than 1,000 have died, thousands have been jailed under Salwa Judum (a controversial campaign supported by the Chhattisgarh state government to counter Maoist sympathisers and supporters), and the terror and counter-terror continue unabated. In Assam and Nagaland, people's distress, despair, fear and alienation have grown as government resolutely looked elsewhere. The civil society and human rights groups also failed to challenge grave violations by both sides during the last four years. The photographs of defenceless Muslims, humiliated and terrorised, in Gujarat shocked all of us when they were published in 2002. But the abuses they exposed were not an aberration. The images followed numerous allegations of torture and ill-treatment reported from police custody in Hyderabad, Mumbai and Calcutta. Datas collected by the Sachar Committee, but not included in the final report, showed Muslims in much higher numbers as prison inmates in several states.

We have a plenty of anti-terror laws and measures in the country. National Security Act, Armed Forces Special Power Act, Terrorist and

Disruptive Activities (Prevention) Act 1987, Prevention of Terrorism Ordinance 2001, Prevention of Terrorism Act 2002, Unlawful Activities (Prevention) Amendment Ordinance 2004, Maharashtra Control of Organised Crime Act 1999, Chhattisgarh Public Security Act 2005 are some of the prominent ones. Several state governments like Madhya Pradesh, Uttar Pradesh, Rajasthan and Gujarat are proposing the new anti-terror laws. However, these did not work either to stop terrorism or to make us safe. Nothing that has happened in the past one decade shows that the state counter-terror works.

Instead, authorities who have power over detainees and are allowed to inflict pain and suffering are becoming more brutalised that they begin to abuse their charges for their own sadistic awards in Jammu and Kashmir and Gujarat, or in retaliation for friends and colleagues lost in battle, or to conquer their own fears. What we have also seen in Gujarat, Maharashtra and Chhattisgarh that once the 'coercive' techniques are authorised in limited circumstances for a so-called relatively small number of people, in practice, the authorised techniques become more and more cruel, and the number of victims soar. TADA began with arrests of a few hundreds that turned into thousands and finally around 72,000 out of 77,000 detained under it were released without having been charged or tried. Similarly, around 3,500 persons from 18 states of India were held under POTA in three years of its existence. More than a decade after the TADA lapsed and many years after the repeal of POTA, hundreds are still under detention for offences under these Acts. The abuses does not remain confined to detainees from the terrorist organisations, but get also directed against a wider population associated with the 'enemy'. People suspected of ordinary crimes start receiving the same treatment as terror suspects. And once all this happens, no one is safe.

The only way people can be protected—both from governments and suicide bombers—is to treat every single human being as possessing fundamental rights that no government, group or individual may ever justifiably take away human rights are grounded in fundamental values that create 'no go areas'—actions that one human being must never do to another.

Our Central and state governments have a duty to take all reasonable steps to prevent acts of terror and to bring to justice those responsible for committing or planning such acts. New beginnings should be explored and experimented. The specific threat of international and cross-border terrorism requires law enforcement agencies to develop special skills and techniques in policing, investigation and intelligence, including international cooperation. Such techniques need to address the new characteristics of international terrorism, such as its use of the Internet and other new technology. That may require new forensic and other law enforcement techniques, but it cannot justify the use of old unlawful methods such as torture and ill-treatment. Human rights are not a luxury only for good times. They must be upheld always, including in times of terror and insecurity. Adherence to clear rules, laid down in international conventions and treaties, is also important during this time, because national jingoism and social conservatism are also at display abundantly in the country.

The banned Students Islamic Movement of India (SIMI) might or might not be involved in the terror attacks in the recent past. However, because of the actions of certain groups and individuals, entire community is being viewed with suspicion. The stigmatisation has been compounded by the communal profiling and detention of Muslims, previously in Hyderabad and now in Jaipur, and by some politicians and media outlets describing them as if they were all potential terrorists. Whipping up public fears in the interests of short-term political gains is a dangerous business. If governments abandon the rule of law and use methods of terror, then won't groups fighting governments feel justified using methods of terror themselves? If whole communities are antagonised and alienated by security forces using terror, aren't those communities more likely to respond by supporting the use of violence?

Counter terror with justice, not with revenge. Human rights activists are sometimes accused of not caring about the needs of victims of terrorist acts. 'How would you feel if your child's life was at stake?' they are asked. What we would do in a moment of such panic and desperation is difficult to predict, but it is a measure of the extent of our despair rather than a guide for moral behaviour. Maybe we would ourselves commit an atrocity if we believed it would save our loved ones—but it would remain an atrocity.

The argument that terror, violence, discrimination and exclusion are wrong was won many years ago at the time of the making of Indian constitution. This was not a minority view or 'liberal' position—political opinions around the country agreed, and wrote into constitution and law, emphasising fundamental rights and freedoms of all citizens. We should build a national consensus even in the time of terror.

(*The Hindu*, 27 May 2008)

Following the late November 2008 terror attacks in Mumbai, Indian government has passed two tough anti-terror laws in end-2008. One law, the National Investigation Agency (NIA) Act, seeks to establish a new police organisation to investigate acts of terrorism and other statutory offences. The other, the Unlawful Activities (Prevention) Amendment (UAPA) Act, radically changes procedures for trying those accused of terrorism, extends the periods of police custody and of detention without charges, denies bail to foreigners, and the reverses the burden of proof in many instances.

2

Victims of Terrorism

Multiple terror attacks in Mumbai are unprecedented and blatantly violate the most fundamental principles of law and justice. Regrettably, as Mumbai shows today, there is a huge gap between governmental counter terror rhetoric and the reality of human security observance on the ground. Much more needs to be done to mainstream counter terror strategy and action throughout the government security system and states must demonstrate the political will and promptness to translate human security and rights commitment into action.

Mumbai reminds us of such serious attacks in New York, Washington and Pennsylvania (US) in September 2001, which amounted to crimes against humanity; in Bali, Indonesia in October 2002; in Casablanca, Morocco, in May 2003; in Madrid, Spain, in March 2004; in Saudi Arabia in June 2004, in Bedlam, the Russian Federation, in September 2004; in London, the United Kingdom in July 2005; in Amman, Jordan, in November 2005; in Egypt in April 2006; in Mumbai, in India, in July 2006; in Afghanistan in April 2007, in Iraq in February and in Algeria in August 2008. There have been other serious terror attacks in Afghanistan, Israel and the occupied territories, Iraq and Sri Lanka in the past.

In the time of increasing peoples' insecurity we must demand that states have a duty to protect all those under their jurisdiction. Individuals, groups and states have a duty to respect the human rights of others. Attacks by terror groups which are indiscriminate or which deliberately target civilians, are grave human rights abuses and can also be crimes under international law. Certain conduct committed with the intention to destroy, in whole or in part a national, ethnical, racial or religious group can amount to genocide.

Such attacks can never be justified. In India today, terror or armed groups are committing grave human rights abuses. Various reports detail them. Their perpetrators must be brought to justice, in fair proceedings that meet international human rights standards.

When hundreds of Mumbai people are killed and injured and the citizens are suffering immensely, their rights to justice, truth and reparation should also be emphasised to heal the wounds. While state will focus on counter-terrorism policies, they must not neglect the needs and rights of victims. We have seen security forces dying to save the city, the police personnel getting killed or seriously injured in saving the citizens. Now, state should ensure, in law and in practice, the respect and protection of human rights of victims through dedicating adequate resources without discrimination on any ground prohibited by law.

How should the state deal with victims and their families with humanity, compassion, dignity and due respect for their privacy? How should the state acknowledge the status of victims to both, the direct victims of terrorist attacks and their families, as well as to people who have suffered harm in intervening to assist victims? How should the state ensure that emergency medical and psychological assistance is available and accessible to any person who has suffered mentally or physically following the terrorist attack? How should it also ensure the availability, accessibility and provision of necessary and appropriate continuing assistance, including medical, psychological, legal, social and material to victims of terrorist attacks as well as to their families?

Following this massive terrorist attack, states have the obligation to open a prompt, thorough, effective and independent official investigation, capable of leading to the identification of the persons and groups reasonably suspected of being responsible for such an act. Victims must have the right to present and challenge evidence and receive prompt information about the progress of the investigation, unless they specifically request not to. The methods, scope and results of the investigation should be made public. At all stages of the investigation and any subsequent proceedings, appropriate measures must be taken to protect the safety, physical and psychological well-being, dignity and privacy of victims and witnesses.

Victims of terrorism have a right to reparation, which include compensation, restitution, rehabilitation, satisfaction and guarantees of non-repetition. Mechanisms for reparations should be easily accessible, involve a simple procedure and allow for reparation to be provided for rapidly. In some cases, states should consider establishing reparations programmes to ensure that victims receive prompt, full and effective reparations.

Mumbai city and its citizens need healing touch for long. And for this to happen effectively, state must respect and protect the freedom of expression of citizens and civil society organisations. Such individuals and groups should be able to campaign and offer assistance without any hindrance from state authorities or others. There is also a need to check any kind of direct and indirect victimisations of minority communities which often suffer violence and harassments after an attack.

Following several terror attacks in the country, a wider range of counter-terrorism pronouncements and practices have came in place. Some political leaders have also claimed the security of some can only be achieved by violating the rights of others. The voices of human rights defenders, political opposition leaders, journalists, people from minority groups and others have also been stifled. Governments have rushed through problematic laws. States have used the climate of fear created by terrorism to enhance powers to suppress legitimate political dissent, to torture detainees, subject them to enforced disappearances. Mumbai reaffirms once again that there is no other way to counter terrorism than to strengthen the national security architecture by implementing the police reforms and promoting the rule of law, respect for human rights, effective criminal justice systems and non-partisan, non-discriminatory political decisions which should constitute the fundamental basis of our common fight against terrorism. We can call on states and security bodies, in consultation with citizens, NGOs and national human rights institutions, to evolve and implement counter terror strategy with a view to ensuring that the rights of victims are respected in a framework that ensures the protection of the human rights of all.

3

In Cold Blood: Abuses by Armed Groups

India, Pakistan, Sri Lanka, Nepal, Bangladesh, Afghanistan, Iraq, Saudi Arabia, Israel and the Occupied Territories, Indonesia, Egypt, Jordan, US, UK, Spain, Russian Federation, to name a few, are a testimony to the cruel attacks on civilians and other human rights abuses in the recent past by non-state armed groups, including the terrorist groups. They are showing utter disdain for the lives of civilians and others, continuing a pattern of serious crimes and crimes against humanity. They fail to abide by even the most basic standards of humanitarian law. The attacks and other abuses by armed groups are so frequent and the security situation so grave that it is impossible to calculate with any confidence the true toll upon the civilian population, let alone the long term consequences that so many people inevitably suffer. There can be no valid justification for deliberate killings of civilians, hostage-taking, and torture and killing of defenseless prisoners. Those who order or commit such atrocities place themselves totally beyond the pale of acceptable behavior. There is no honour or heroism in blowing up people going to pray or murdering a terrified hostage. Those carrying out such acts are criminals, nothing less, whose actions undermine any claim they may have to be pursuing a legitimate cause.

Many non-state armed groups claim to oppose the continuing violence of state, army, police in the country, and that these forces have themselves committed grave violations, including killings, disappearances and encounters of civilians. But abuses committed by one side do not and can not justify abuses by another. This is all the more the case when the principal victims are ordinary men, women and children attempting to go about their everyday lives. All sides to the ongoing conflict have a fundamental obligation to respect the rights of civilians or of those who are rendered defenceless. Those who breach this obligation, on which ever side they stand, must be made to stop and they must be held to account.

As such, there is an obligation on both the concerned government and the international community at large to ensure that the perpetrators of these crimes are identified and brought to justice. There can be no excuse for such abuses; several international and national humanitarian laws clearly distinguish certain acts as crimes irrespective of the causes of a conflict or the grounds on which the contending parties justify their involvement.

Non-state armed groups are operating mainly in Andhra Pradesh, Arunachal Pradesh, Asom, Bihar, Chhattisgarh, Jammu and Kashmir, Jharkhand, Karnataka, Maharashtra, Manipur, Meghalaya, Orissa, Tripura, West Bengal states in our country. They are Maoists, Naxalites, terrorists, ethnic-caste based groups. In north-eastern states, we have many like, United Liberation Front of Asom (ULFA), Karbi Longri North Cachar Hills Liberation Front (KLNLF), Dima Halam Daogah (Jewel Garlosa) or Black Widow, United Liberation Front of Barak Valley, All Adivasi National Liberation Army, Kuki Revolutionary Army, Hmar People's Convention (Democratic), Muslim United Liberation Tigers Front of Assam, Harkat-ul-Mujahideen, Kanglei Yawol Kanba Lup, National Liberation Front of Tripura. We can see a pattern of widespread acts of violence and terror by armed groups.

There have been indiscriminate attacks resulting in civilian deaths. Hundreds of people have been killed as a result of car/scooter bombs or suicide attacks. The deadliest attacks have also hit the police and the army establishments. The attackers have generally disguised themselves as ordinary civilians, and sometimes as members of the police or other security forces. They appear to have made little or no effort to distinguish between military targets and civilians, or to avoid disproportionate harm to civilians when directing their attacks at military targets. Individuals, religious and ethnic groups have also been targeted.

Scores of civilians as well as police personnel have been taken hostage by various armed groups. Many of the hostages were later killed. It is sometimes difficult to distinguish between armed political groups and criminal gangs when it comes to hostage-taking. In many cases armed political groups seem to have made the release of their victims conditional on payment of money even when they make political demands. Armed groups vehemently oppose to the holding of elections. Take for example, Jammu and Kashmir or Chhattisgarh, before the elections, voters received many threats, including that they would be killed, that their children would be abducted and that their houses would be burned down.

In Maoist-controlled areas of country, the Maoists are employing quasi-judicial bodies charged with dispensing 'justice'. Some locals, disillusioned with the official state system, turn to these 'courts' which they view as fairer and less corrupt than state justice system. Although information concerning the charges against individuals is limited, the majority of people who have come before such courts are being 'charged'. Many of those who come before such bodies have been abducted by the Maoists. In many cases harsh punishments have been issued and carried out. Few details about the nature of proceedings are known.

Armed group's oppressive treatment of women has been well documented. Under their hardline rule, women are discriminated in all walks of life, including the denial of education, employment, freedom of movement and political participation and representation. They are excluded from public life and prohibited from studying, working or leaving the house without being chaperoned by a male blood relative. The severe restrictions on their freedom of movement virtually confine women to the home. The effects of these restrictions are particularly hard on widows. Many forms of gender-based violence are also perpetrated. Women aid and health workers, election candidates, teachers, women's rights activists and other human rights defenders are specially subjected to threats and attacks, in some cases resulting in death.

Afghanistan is the burning example of the operation of the armed groups. The human rights abuses by the Taleban, include threats, intimidation and attack targeting civilians and indiscriminate attacks, including suicide bombings attacks on schools, abductions and unlawful killings of captives. The make-up of the insurgency in Afghanistan is diverse and complex and it is not always clear who is behind the violence. Many armed groups are said to be operating in Afghanistan, including al-Qa'ida, Jeysh-e-Mohammadi, Lashkar-e-Tayyiba and the armed political group, Hezb-e-Eslami. The term 'Taleban' has often served as a catch-all tag for armed groups or elements hostile to the central government and foreign forces. As a result, some attacks attributed to the Taleban by the media may have been carried out by al-Qa'ida, or the armed political group Hezb-e-Eslami, headed by Gulbuddin Hekmatyar, Hezb-e-Eslami and al-Qa'ida. Other elements attributed to the Taleban might include local warlords, criminal gangs involved in the drugs trade or private individuals. Financial support for the Taleban flows in from supporters in the region but is also thought to come from wealthy donors from the Persian Gulf states. Other sources of income are derived from the illegal drugs trade, kidnappings in which ransoms are demanded and the smuggling of goods. The Taleban also receive money and support in strongholds in southern Afghanistan either by coercion, for example, by the demanding of food and shelter, or by Zakat (the religious obligation of Muslims to make an annual charitable donation as defined by the Qur'an).

There is a Taleban military rulebook, or Layeha, containing 30 rules. Some rules explicitly sanction the targeting and killing of civilians. Rule 25 states that a teacher who ignores warnings from the Taleban and continues to teach 'must be beaten' and should they 'continue to teach contrary to the principles of Islam, the (Taleban) district commander or a group leader must kill him'. Rule 26 suggests that NGOs and humanitarian workers may be targeted: 'Those NGOs that come to the country under the rule of the infidels must be treated as the government is treated…we tolerate none of their activities, whether it be building of roads, bridges, clinics, schools, *madrassas* or other works'.

Much of the strength and support for the Taleban can be linked to Pakistan's apparent tolerance of Afghan Taleban and local Taleban fighters in its border regions, notably the Northwest Frontier Province, the Federally Administered Tribal Areas and parts of Baluchistan. Twenty four Taleban fighters—local and Afghan—have reportedly regrouped and re-supplied from bases in these regions, directing attacks in Afghanistan from these strongholds, in many instances with little interference from the Pakistani authorities.

Many non-state armed groups in our country and outside condemn terrorism, but they brand their violent struggle against the oppression and occupation legitimate. They ask us to differentiate between terrorism and the struggle against the state, feudal and corporate agencies sanctioned by the tenets of the political and ideological convictions. Contrary to these assertions, attacks on civilians, killing, and hostages are not permitted under any recognised standard of law, whether they are committed in the context of a struggle against oppression or any other context. Not only are they considered murder under general principles of law in every national legal system, they are contrary to fundamental principles of humanity which are reflected in the foundations of every human society. In the manner in which they are being committed in India or in any other country, they also amount to crimes against humanity.

Whatever noble may be the cause, whenever armed force is used the choice of means and methods are not unlimited. The principles of rule of law must set out standards of humane conduct applicable to both state forces and armed groups. Regardless of the formal legal categorisation of the situation in any region, the non-state armed groups remain bound by fundamental principles of humanity, which are reflected in the rules of international humanitarian laws outlined. In cases not expressly covered by our present systems, both 'civilians' and 'combatants' remain under the protection and authority of the principles of international law derived from established custom, from the principles of humanity and from the dictates of the human conscience. Armed Groups in our country should remember Professor Edward Said saying in May 2002 that

> [Suicide bombings have] disfigured and debased the Palestinian struggle. All liberation movements in history have affirmed that their struggle is about life not about death. Why should ours be an exception? The sooner we educate our Zionist enemies and show that our resistance offers co-existence and peace, the less likely will they be able to kill us at will, and never refer to us except as terrorists.

4

How Not to Fight Terrorism

The response of governments to the threat of terrorism is one of the fundamental challenges of our times. Since the 11 September 2001 attacks on the US and in other countries since then, a wide range of counter-terrorism laws, policies and practices have come into being. While counter-terrorism policies in numerous countries had led to human rights violations well before 2001, the 'war on terror' launched by the US has had worldwide repercussions. It has undermined the rule of law, and poses significant challenges to the protection of rights worldwide in numerous countries of the world today. The US has taken on the role of the global leader, and in the name of fighting terrorism, the US government has subjected people who have not been charged with, or convicted of, any crime to torture, abductions; illegal and indefinite detentions in Guantánamo, other US facilities and secret CIA sites; and denial of basic legal rights, including habeas corpus. Additionally, the US government has employed private companies that are implicated in cases of killings, torture and rape. The war on terror in Iraq, Afghanistan and Pakistan and other parts of the world continues, with disastrous consequences.

After the November 2008 multiple attacks on the Mumbai city, comparisons have variously been made between September 2001 and November 2008. Suggestions have been made, directly and indirectly, that India should learn positively from the US ways of fighting terrorism, and take measures accordingly within and outside the country. Even Israel is being suggested as a model to fight terrorism. Many Indians, understandably angry and seeking some manner of revenge after the vicious attacks of November, have fallen prey to the proposition that new draconian laws, tit-for-tat approach, counter-terror against terrorists and their supporters, and excessive physical pressures are necessary to root out terrorists and terrorism.

The government has rushed through the problematic 'Unlawful Activities (Prevention) Amendment Bill 2008', and there are calls for tougher measures on the lines of the US. Passing anti-terrorist laws is nothing new. Long-standing experiences, for example, in Northern Ireland, Israel and Malaysia show that they invariably trigger off more violence and violations. Thus, this is the time for us to take stock of the key elements of the US' war on terror. In this chapter, I conduct a brief review of the type of human rights violations committed in the pursuit of counter-terrorism measures by the US regime, citing a range of less-reported issues. As this experience shows, using the climate of fear created by terrorism to enhance powers that suppress legitimate political dissent, to torture detainees, subject them to enforced disappearances, or launching war or attacks against a country, will certainly be a failure. International law and practice of counter-terrorism under the US dictates has been distorted or misapplied in ways that undermine its legitimacy. The perpetrators are virtually never brought to justice, nor do the victims receive justice and truth.

Habeas Corpus

President George Bush tried to suspend habeas when he issued a military order in 2001 entitled *Detention, Treatment and Trial of Certain Non-Citizens in the War Against Terrorism.* He declared the right to indefinitely detain individuals that, he claimed, were suspected of having links to terrorism as 'unlawful enemy combatants'. He asserted that these detainees could be held forever without legal counsel, without knowing what they were accused of doing, and without ever seeing the inside of a courtroom.

Habeas corpus, also known as 'The Great Writ' refers to a centuries-old legal concept, fundamental in any democracy. This Latin term, literally meaning, 'holding the body', refers to a legal action that a person can bring in order to seek relief against arbitrary and unlawful detention. Habeas corpus represents the idea that the king or the President, may not, at his whim, detain whomever he wants without allowing the detainee the opportunity to stand before a fair court to hear the charges against him or her and to have an opportunity to answer the charges. Filing a petition for a writ of habeas corpus is a legal challenge to the government's ability to detain an individual. It is brought against the person(s) responsible for holding a detainee and requires that s/he produce the detainee along with the reasons that this person is being held. As a legal concept, habeas corpus is centuries-old. Habeas rights are typically traced back to the Magna Carta of 1215 and have since become a cornerstone of democratic governance. In the US, the Constitution requires that habeas rights can only be suspended under very limited circumstances: 'the Writ of Habeas Corpus shall not be suspended, unless when in Cases of Rebellion or Invasion the public Safety may require it.'

However, contrary to all this, under the military order, a Combatant Status Review Tribunal (CSRT), an executive body is established, to determine whether the detainees held in the base were 'properly detained' as 'enemy combatants'. The CSRT consists of panels of three military officers who can consider any information, including information that is hearsay, classified, or that has been obtained under torture in making their determinations. Under the Detainee Treatment Act (DTA), enacted in December 2005, judicial review is limited to a single court, the US Court of Appeals for the District of Columbia (DC) Circuit, and to review of the CSRT's 'propriety of detention' decisions. The decision of a CSRT represents a potential life sentence for a detainee.

The CSRTs lack independence from the executive, the branch that entirely controls the detentions and applied the 'enemy combatant' label to the detainees in the first place. Some detainees initially found not to be 'enemy combatants' had that determination reversed after Pentagon authorities sent their cases back to the CSRT for reconsideration; the CSRTs are not a competent tribunal as they lack the power of remedy, including release. Indeed, detainees have been held for as long as 20 months after a CSRT finding of 'no longer enemy combatant'; there is no meaningful way for the detainee to challenge the government's information. He has little or no access to witnesses, no access to classified information used against him, and little way of challenging hearsay information; the detainee is denied access to a lawyer for the CSRT process. He is merely assigned a 'personal representative', a US military officer; the CSRT considers the status of 'enemy combatant' as synonymous with 'lawfully held', and the detainee has no meaningful opportunity to challenge this; the CSRT is a procedure that is applied only to foreign nationals, in violation of the prohibition against discrimination; the CSRTs were conducted after an unreasonable delay of more than two years after the detentions began. Once started, they were conducted with undue haste.

Over the course of years, the US administration held hundreds of such designated 'unlawful enemy combatants' on a US detention camp in Guantánamo Bay, Cuba. All the while, in American court rooms, a vigorous legal battle over the legality of the detentions had ensued. Finally in June 2008, the US Supreme Court in Boumediene v Bush, held that those held at Guantánamo Bay have the right of habeas corpus and can bring such claims in US federal court. The Court also ruled that the system the Bush administration and Congress have put in place to review classification of the detainees as 'unlawful enemy combatants' is inadequate. The Court resoundingly rejected the arguments put forth by the US administration that non-US nationals, held outside the sovereign territory of the US are beyond the reach of this fundamental legal protection. The Court concluded that

> The laws and Constitution are designed to survive, and remain in force, in extraordinary times. Liberty and security can be reconciled; and in our system they are reconciled within the framework of the law. The (Constitution's) Framers decided that habeas corpus, a right of first importance, must be a part of that framework, a part of that law.

Instead, President Bush's response to the judgement was to side with the four Justices who dissented from the majority opinion. The President stated that the dissenters had been concerned about national security, and that the administration would 'study this opinion, and we'll do so with this in mind, to determine whether or not additional legislation might be appropriate, so that we can safely say, or truly say to the American people: We're doing everything we can to protect you.' The US Justice Department has also expressed its disappointment with the Boumediene decision.

Extraordinary Rendition, 'Disappearances' and Secret Prisons

The United States has implemented a global system of unlawful rendition with the collaboration, complicity and acquiescence of other governments. Rendition is the process of transferring an individual from one country to another by means that bypass all judicial and administrative due process. In the 'war on terror', the US has also used 'extraordinary rendition', a practice whereby prisoners captured or detained by the US government are transferred for interrogation or detention to countries known to use torture. The aim is to use whatever means necessary to gather intelligence, and to keep detainees away from any judicial oversight. This system puts the victim beyond the protection of the law and sets the perpetrator above the law. The US administration has acknowledged it uses 'rendition', maintaining that the practice is aimed at transferring 'war on terror' detainees from the country where they were captured to their home country or to other countries where they can be questioned, held or brought to justice. It has contended that these transfers are carried out in accordance with US law and treaty obligations.

This system of covert prisons were referred to in classified documents as 'black sites', a term first revealed by the Washington Post in November 2005. These 'black sites' or secret detention centres are in Afghanistan, Guantánamo Bay in Cuba, Iraq, Jordan, Pakistan, Thailand, Uzbekistan and other unknown locations in Europe and elsewhere, including on the British Indian Ocean territory of Diego Garcia. Based on the available evidence, the number of people held in 'black sites' is likely to be in the thousands. However, given the secrecy surrounding the transfer and detention of victims of 'rendition', who are kept beyond the reach of the law, the scale and scope of the practice is extremely difficult to estimate. The New York Bar Association estimated in 2005 that about 150 people had been subjected to 'rendition' to other countries since 2001. This estimate is likely to be conservative, as the Egyptian prime minister noted in 2005 that the US has transferred some 60–70 detainees to Egypt alone, and a former CIA agent with experience in the region believes that 'hundreds' of detainees may have been sent by the US to prisons in Middle Eastern countries.

Extraordinary rendition involves multiple human rights violations. Most victims were arrested and detained illegally, some were abducted, and all were denied access to any legal process, including the ability to challenge the decision to transfer them because of the risk of torture. There is also a close link between extraordinary rendition and enforced disappearances. Dozens have 'disappeared' in the US custody, some reappearing months or years later in the detention facilities at Guantánamo Bay. The detention regime and practices in US-run places of detention are aimed at inducing maximum disorientation, dependence and stress in the detainees. Hooding, cuffing and shackling, isolation and 'white noise' impair an individual's sight, hearing and sense of smell, lead to disorientation and an increased sense of vulnerability, and cause mental and physical suffering. Prolonged isolation has been shown to cause depression, paranoia, aggression, hallucinations and suicide. Former 'war on terror' detainees consistently underline the mental suffering caused by prolonged isolation and uncertainty about their fate, and many have said it was worse than the physical abuse they suffered.

It has been reported that the CIA, often using covert aircraft leased by front companies, has flown individuals to countries including Egypt, Jordan, Morocco, Pakistan, Saudi Arabia and Syria. Most of the states to which the US transfers these individuals are known to use torture and other ill-treatment in interrogations. It is alleged that states which are known to be practising torture have been specifically selected to receive detainees for interrogation. Concerns about European involvement and the use of European facilities in 'rendition' have prompted the Council of Europe to launch inquiries into alleged CIA activities in Europe. The Committee on Legal Affairs and Human Rights of the Parliamentary Assembly of the Council of Europe (PACE) is looking into the alleged existence of secret detention centres in Council of Europe member states and flights which may have transferred prisoners without any judicial involvement. Dick Marty, Chairperson-Rapporteur of the Committee, said to the press that the information received so far had 'reinforced the credibility of allegations concerning the transfer and temporary detention of individuals, without any judicial involvement, in European countries'.

The Military Commissions Act

In October 2006, Congress passed and President signed the Military Commissions Act. The MCA established a system of military commissions that would try 'unlawful enemy combatants' or persons pending that designation. Aside from setting up the military commissions at Guantánamo, the MCA established many draconian provisions. It broadly defines 'unlawful enemy combatant' to refer to anyone 'engaged in hostilities or who has purposefully and materially supported hostilities' against the US The MCA gives retroactive and future immunity to US perpetrators of certain war crimes.

The MCA is most infamous for setting up the fatally flawed military commissions system at Guantánamo. Notably, it strips the right to a speedy trial, permits the use of evidence obtained through compulsory self-incrimination, and restricts defense access to materials used to prosecute the defendant. There is no right to confront accusers, no exclusion of evidence based on the failure to obtain a warrant, and hearsay evidence is permissible. Military commissions violate standards for fair trials in a number of ways: The prosecution may use as evidence statements obtained through coercion and torture. The defendant can face secret evidence which the defense will be unable to rebut—this includes preventing the defendant from seeing some witnesses testify and from learning the content of their testimony. The defendant can be excluded from certain parts of his own trial. Hearsay is permissible. Under the act, the prosecution is permitted to withhold classified evidence which prevents the defense from seeing evidence that points to innocence. The prosecution can introduce verbal confessions by the defendant without any corroboration. The right to appeal to an independent and impartial tribunal is severely restricted.

In this system, created to decimate a defendant's right to a fair trial, a penalty of death can be imposed. Even if a defendant is found not guilty of all charges, he can still spend the rest of his life in detention based on the US' assertion of the power to hold detainees for the duration of the 'war on terrorism'. The MCA also sought to strip the federal courts of the jurisdiction to hear habeas corpus or other suits brought by or on behalf of the detainees.

Military Outsourcing in the 'War on Terror'

As the United States conducted the 'global war on terror', the US government outsourced key security and military support functions, particularly in Iraq and Afghanistan, to private companies. Their civilian employees carry out work ranging from logistical support, training military personnel, operating and maintaining weapons systems and rebuilding infrastructure, to more sensitive roles, such as interrogation and translation during questioning of detained persons and provision of static and mobile security. Allegations have surfaced of US contractor involvement in hundreds of incidents of shootings and killings of Iraqi civilians, as well as torture and abuse of detained persons, including at Abu Ghraib. Private military and security contractors (PMSCs), many with multi-million dollar government contracts, have been accused of engaging in sexual abuse and torture.

The use of PMSCs is growing to an unprecedented extent. According to Brookings Institute scholar Peter Singer, the ratio of military personnel to contractors was 50:1 in the 1991 Gulf War. Today, contractors working for the US government and military outnumber US troops in Iraq. The Department of Defense (DOD) testified in front of the Senate in February that for the first quarter of fiscal year 2008, the US Central Command had 163,590 contractor personnel in Iraq (and another 36,520 in Afghanistan).

There is a murky contract system: Only 40 per cent of Pentagon contracts were awarded under full and open competition during this period, according to the Center for Public Integrity, which examined contracts totaling $900 billion. Of 60 publicly available Iraq contracts that University of Connecticut Law Professor Laura A. Dickinson examined, none required contractors to obey anticorruption or transparency norms. Senators Jim Webb and Claire McCaskill added a provision to the 2008 National Defense Authorization Act to create a bipartisan Commission on Wartime Contracting with the purpose of investigating allegations of waste, fraud and abuse in relation to federal agency contracting for reconstruction and logistical support of coalition forces, and misconduct by security and intelligence contractors in Iraq and Afghanistan. President Bush opposed the creation of the commission in a signing statement.

There are many scattered cases, but hardly acknowledged by the government. The US Army's Fay/Jones and Taguba reports implicated employees of two companies in the torture committed at Abu Ghraib. According to the Fay/Jones report, 35 per cent of contracted interrogators did not have formal training in interrogation policies and techniques. Twenty-four known cases of abuse allegedly committed by civilians been forwarded to the Department of Justice (DOJ) by the Department of Defense (DOD) and CIA Inspector General for investigation and prosecution. The alleged violations include torture and sexual abuse, and at least four detained persons have died, two each in Iraq and Afghanistan, in the custody of civilian contractors.

After repeated inquiries beginning in 2005, there was a response from the DOJ in February 2008, which stated that of a total of 24 cases referred to it, 22 had been declined and two were pending. The DOJ did not transparently or publicly disclose detailed reasons for its decisions to decline prosecution of the cases. Most recently on 16 September 2007, Blackwater security personnel accompanying a US Department of state convoy shot and killed 17 civilians and injured many more in Nisour Square, Baghdad. The circumstances of the incident are disputed; currently the FBI is conducting an investigation of the alleged excessive and undue use of force and a grand jury has been convened, although charges have yet to be filed.

Torture

The UN Convention Against Torture defines torture as '...the intentional infliction of severe physical or mental pain or suffering for purposes such as obtaining information or a confession, or punishing, intimidating or coercing someone'. Torture is always illegal. 'No exceptional circumstances whatsoever, whether a state of war or a threat of war, internal political instability or any other public emergency, may be invoked as a justification of torture.' Abuse of prisoners doesn't have to be torture to be illegal. Cruel, inhuman, and degrading treatment (CID) is also illegal under international and US law. CID includes any harsh or neglectful treatment that could damage a detainee's physical or mental health or any punishment intended to cause physical or mental pain or suffering, or to humiliate or degrade the person being punished.

In the years since 9/11, the US government has virtually legalised torture and CID in the name of fighting terrorism:

- The Administration decided the Geneva Conventions would not apply to detainees held in Guantánamo Bay (a decision later overturned by the US Supreme Court);
- The Justice Department's Office of Legal Counsel produced a series of 'torture memos', which mutilated the law so as to restrict the definition of CID and to make certain torture practices seem legal under US law;
- US interrogations of suspects in the 'war on terror' have included techniques as prolonged isolation and sleep deprivation,

intimidation by the use of a dog, sexual and other humiliation, stripping, hooding, the use of loud music, white noise and exposure to extreme temperatures;

- The CIA used waterboarding—illegal as torture under international and US law—to interrogate 'high-value' detainees;
- The US began to send detainees for interrogation to countries known to use torture;
- The administration admitted that several high-level officials of the administration met secretly to authorise specific interrogation methods otherwise prohibited.

Several measures reveal that the US has seriously undermined the fight against terrorism, and shown itself to be far from the global anti-torture champion it claims to represent. They have not been able to feel or make themselves safer and peaceful within and outside their country. Thus, our national counter-terrorism strategies and international cooperation must include measures to prevent the spread of terrorism, and must also include measures to prevent regional, religious or other discrimination, political exclusion and socio-economic marginalisation, as well as measures to address impunity for human rights violations.

(*Economic and Political Weekly*, Volume 44, No. 5, 31 January 2009)

5

Guantánamo Bay:
A Legal Black Hole

I

For as in absolute governments the king is law, so in free countries the law ought to be king, and there ought to be no other. (Thomas Paine, 1776)

On 11 January 2007, the Guantánamo detention centre—the unlawful detention of 'enemy combatants' at the US Naval Base at Guantánamo Bay, Cuba—will be five years old. Hundreds of people of around 35 different nationalities remain held in effect in a legal black hole, many without access to any court, legal counsel or family visits. Many of them allege they have been subjected to torture or other cruel, inhuman and degrading treatment. Three detainees have died at the camp, after apparently committing suicide. Others have gone on prolonged hunger strikes, being kept alive only through painful force feeding measures. Guantánamo Bay is a symbol of US abuse and injustice. Outraged by this, human rights activists worldwide have joined together on an International Actions Day on 16 December 2006 in solidarity with the detainees and their families, to demand once more that the US government close Guantánamo. This date also marked the start of one month of activism against the detention centre that will be culminated on 17 January this year.

In January 2002, the US authorities transferred the first 'war on terror' detainees —hooded and shackled—to the Guantánamo Bay. Many of those were captured during the international conflict in Afghanistan. Others were picked up outside any zones of armed conflict in countries as diverse as Gambia, Bosnia, Egypt, Indonesia and Thailand. They were the first of more than 750 detainees of some 45 nationalities. They have included children as young as 13, as well as elderly. They have included people who were simply in the wrong place at the wrong time. They have included scores of individuals handed over to the US by Pakistan or Afghanistan agents in return for bounties of thousands of dollars. In his recent memoirs, Pakistan President Musharraf wrote that CIA had paid million of dollars in 'bounties' and 'prize money' for 369 suspects handed over by Pakistan to the United States. In early September 2006, US authorities transferred to Guantánamo 14 men who had been held in secret CIA custody. President George W. Bush finally admitted that, in the 'war on terror', the US has been resorting to secret detentions and enforced disappearance, which is a crime under international law.

Released detainees and others still in the camp have alleged that they have been subjected to torture and other cruel, inhuman and degrading treatment while detained by US authorities at Guantánamo or elsewhere. Some of the detainees are still held in maximum security blocks, sometimes for up to 24 hours a day and with very little out-of-cell exercise time. The detainees have also been subjected to repeated interrogations sometimes for hours at a time and without the presence of a lawyer, raising fears that statements may have been extracted under coercion. The International Committee of the Red Cross (ICRC) is still the only non-governmental organisation allowed access to the detainees.

With the prospect of indefinite detention without a fair trial in such conditions, the potential psychological impact upon those held and their loved ones is a major concern. The camp is condemning thousands of people across the world to a life of suffering, torment and stigmatisation.

None of the Guantánamo detainees have been convicted of any criminal charge. Hundreds of them have been released from the base without charge or any form of compensation for the many years they were illegally detained at Guantánamo. Yet the US authorities still label those held as 'enemy combatants', 'terrorists', or 'the worst of the worst', flouting their right to be presumed innocent and illegally justifying the denial of many of their most basic human rights. None of the Guantánamo detainees have been granted prisoner of war status or brought before a 'competent tribunal' to determine his status, as required by international law. The US government refuses to clarify their legal status.

In November 2001, President Bush signed a Military Order establishing trials by military commission which had the power to hand down death sentences and against whose decision there was no right of appeal to any court. On 29 June 2006, the US Supreme Court ruled that US President George W. Bush had overstepped his authority in ordering Military Commissions trials, and maintained that the proposed commissions violated the US law and the Geneva conventions. The decision was based on the case of Salim Ahmed Hamdan, a 36-year-old Yemeni national who has spent four years in the US detention centre. The ruling was a victory for the rule of law and human rights and human rights organisation called on the US government to use it as a springboard for bringing all its 'war on terror' detention policies into full compliance of the US and international law. Instead, on 29 September 2006 the US Congress gave its stamp of approval to human rights violations committed by the US by passing the Military Commissions Act, a new legislation to try foreign nationals held in Guantánamo. President Bush signed the Act on 17 October 2006.

The Military Commissions Act leaves the US squarely on the wrong side of international law. The Act is discriminatory because it provides for trials of the 'enemy' in front of military commissions using lower standards of evidence than apply to US personnel. It also grants the US President the power to hand down death sentences. Whether charged for trial or not, those detained by the US as 'enemy combatants' will not be able to challenge the lawfulness or conditions of their detention in habeas corpus appeals.

Human rights are under threat. The ban on torture and other cruel, inhuman and degrading treatment—the most universally accepted of human rights—is being undermined. In the 'war on terror', governments are not only using torture and ill-treatment; they are making the case that this is justifiable and necessary. Those who claim to set their human rights standards high are at the forefront of this assault. The US is one such government. Their conduct influences governments everywhere, giving comfort to those who commit torture routinely and undermining the very values the 'war on terror' is supposed to defend. Several reports suggest that the US during the 'war on terror' using all the torture methods— abduction, forced to walk barefoot on barbed wire, blindfolding, burking, chemical spray, electric shocks, claustrophia—including techniques, forcible injections, physical assault, sexual assault, threat of rape, secret detention, *et cetera*.

They speak of 'coercive interrogation' but when the door to torture is opened, the pressure is always upward. If one slap doesn't work, then a beating will follow. If a beating doesn't work, what comes next? See the photographs or hear the testimonies that are available for few. It is cruel, inhuman; it degrades us all.

Moazzam Begg was unlawfully detained in Pakistan, Afghanistan and Guantánamo Bay for 3 years, and eventually released without charge Moazzam Begg spoke in September 2006: 'The biggest suffering everybody has in Guantánamo Bay, I think at this point, is the sheer lack of any ability to prove your innocence because you remain in legal limbo, and have no communication at all, no meaningful communication with your family.' He charged, 'From being in isolation and practically being stripped naked apart from a pair of shorts ... in isolation the air-conditioning was left on so it was particularly cold at night. I wasn't able to sleep and had to do exercises throughout the night periodically, I kept waking up because of the cold.' Abdel-Jabbar Al-Azzawi was detained and tortured by the US forces and civilian interrogators hired by the US government in Iraq. He said,

> They made me lie on a wooden board. Then they tied each of my hands to a winch. Then they placed me like this. They started taking photos of me. With every question they asked they would tighten the winch until I was stretched flat. They threatened to bring my wife and my eldest son and rape them in front of me.

The continuing pursuit of unchecked executive power is unparallel. The assaults on rights, freedom, laws are unimaginable. The laws, justice systems, institutional arrangements, power have been stretched to give cover for abhorrent policies. In this so-called 'nation of laws', this is not the rule of law. As John Locke said four centuries age, this is the first step towards tyranny.

II

Rights-free Zones

'O Father, this is a prison of injustice.
Its iniquity makes the mountains weep.
I have committed no crime and am guilty of no offence.
Curved claws have I,
But I have been sold like a fattened sheep.'

—Abdulla Thani Faris al Anazi, a Guantánamo detainee since 2002, arrested in Afghanistan, and turned over to the US forces by bounty hunters.

11 January 2008 marks 6 years since the first detainees were transferred to Guantánamo Bay. Guantánamo Bay is a rights-free zone, for the detention, treatment and trial of certain people in the 'war on terror'. Here the Pentagon is authorised to hold non-US citizens in indefinite custody without charge; here detainees are barred from seeking any remedy in any proceedings in any US, foreign or international court; here if any detainee were to be tried, the trial would be by military commission—an executive body, and not an independent or impartial court. A memorandum from the Justice Department to the Pentagon advises that because Guantánamo Bay is not a sovereign US territory, the federal courts should not be able to consider habeas corpus petitions from 'enemy aliens' detained at the base.

Most Guantánamo detainees are housed in conditions amounting to cruel, inhuman or degrading treatment. Most spend 22 hours a day in total isolation, and suffer other forms of sensory deprivation. Majority of them have been held for nearly six years, with no prospect of a fair trial, no direct access to their families and no access to a lawyer. These conditions have had a shattering impact on the psychological and physical health of many detainees.

International campaigns in the last six years have raised many issues regarding this: closing down of Guantánamo Bay and ending the US secret detention programme, wherever it is based; releasing all detainees held in the 'war on terror', including those held at Guantánamo, unless they are to be charged and given a fair trail; stopping secret detention, unlawful transfer of detainees between countries (rendition) or enforced disappearance in counter-terrorism operations; repealing of the Military Commissions Act 2006; and providing prompt and adequate reparation. The fifth anniversary of the first transfers to Guantánamo was marked by activists around the world staging demonstrations and other activities. The UN Secretary General Ban Ki-Moon, UN Committee against Torture, former the US Presidents Carter and Clinton, heads of States from Europe and elsewhere, human rights and legal organisations, and many more have supported various calls for Guantánamo to be closed. The US Supreme Court ruled against the government in two Guantánamo cases, decided in 2004 and 2006, and is now considering whether the detainees should have access to the courts—right to habeas corpus—to contest their detention.

Yet, Guantánamo has not been closed, and it has thrown up a huge challenge for the international community. A model like Guantánamo signifies the abandoning of basic principles of human rights. It delegitimises us. As Archbishop Desmond Tutu said on 17 February 2006, 'It is disgraceful. I never imagined I would live to see the day when the United States and its satellites would use precisely the same arguments that the apartheid government used for detention without trial.'

It would have been virtually impossible for Guantánamo to continue without a global war paradigm, which has been constructed under the rubric of 'war on terror'. Using this, parts of international humanitarian laws, selectively interpreted, are deemed to apply, and human rights laws are generally disregarded. The administration repeatedly claims that they do not hold ground in armed conflicts. There are thus new rights-free zones, like Guantánamo, in different parts of the world, where detainee can be subjected to cruel, inhuman and degrading treatment or punishment, including prolonged solitary or cellular confinement in conditions of reduced sensory stimulation. Here we have secret, incommunicado and unacknowledged arrests and tortures, where all those who have been subjected to enforced disappearances and encounters are not provided access to effective remedy and justice, including compensation. Here we have anti-terror, so-called security laws, which suggest humane treatment as a matter of choice, rather than law, and which exclude the security officials even from that choice. These occurrences have also to been seen within the context of a dominant development paradigm, where Exclusive Economic Zones, Special Economic Zones, and industrial projects in the tribal heartlands can be implemented, without free, informed and prior consent of people. Human rights activists in the rights-free zones are subjected to death threats persecuted through the use of the judicial system and silenced through the introduction of security laws. Going through unfounded investigations and prosecutions, many even disappear or are murdered.

Europe often presents itself as a beacon of human rights. However, the uncomfortable truth is that without Europe's help, some men would not now be nursing torture wounds in prison cells in rights-free zones, including Guantánamo. The revealing report of Dick Marty, Rapporteur of the Committee on Legal Affairs and Human Rights of the Parliamentary Assembly of the Council of Europe, concludes:

The body of information gathered makes it unlikely that European states were completely unaware of what was happening, in the context of the fight against international terrorism, in some of their airports, in their airspace or at American bases located on their territory. Insofar as they did not know, they did not want to know. It is inconceivable that certain operations conducted by American services could have taken place without the active participation, or at least the collusion, of national intelligence services. (Dick Marty, 2006, para 230).

In Asia and Africa, a large number of people in Pakistan, Kenya, Somalia and Ethiopia became victims of rendition transferred in secret from one country to another, and to Guantánamo, through their governments.

Facts and figures on Guantánamo, released recently, at the end of 2007, by Amnesty International are an eye-opener: nearly 800 detainees have been held here. Approximately 300 detainees of around 30 nationalities were still held without charge or trial in November 2007. Only one Guantánamo detainee, David Hicks, has been convicted by the military commission in March 2007. He pleaded guilty to 'providing material support for terrorism' under a pre-trial agreement that ensured his release from the US custody after five years, and return to his native Australia to serve a nine-month prison term. Only three detainees had been charged for trial by the military commission. Between 2002 and November 2007, around 470 detainees had been released to other countries. At least four of those still held were 18 years old when taken into custody. Detainees had been taken into custody in more than 10 countries before being transferred to Guantánamo, without any judicial process. An analysis of around 500 of the detainees concluded that only five per cent had been captured by the US forces; 86 per cent had been arrested by Pakistan or Afghanistan based Northern Alliance forces and turned over to the US, often for a reward of thousands of US dollars.

All rights-free zones are in violation of international and national human rights laws. Each detainee being held here or every act of appropriation of natural resources in these zones is illegal and unjust. Treating all people deprived of their liberty with humanity, and with respect for their dignity, is a fundamental and universally applicable rule. It must be applied without distinction of any kind. Rights-free zones, like Guantánamo, should be closed not tomorrow, but this morning. In general, most countries and their people have simply not taken a stand till now. They seem to believe that this is not their problem. They think that they did not contribute to Guantánamo, and therefore they do not have to be a part of the solution. We the people and the governments around the world can play a positive role in ending illegal US detentions in the name of 'war on terror'. Among other things, we and our governments can protest to the US authorities about illegal detentions, provide lasting protection for detainees released from Guantánamo and elsewhere, and oppose all unlawful transfers of detainees between countries.

III

Time for Real Change: Guantánamo and Illegal US Detentions

The United States detention facilities at Guantánamo Bay, Cuba—seven years old in early January 2009—have become emblematic of the gross human rights abuses perpetrated by the US Government in the name of fighting terrorism. Though the US President Barack Obama has pledged to close down the Guantánamo Bay, there are undoubtedly substantial challenges to closing. Every day that Guantánamo is kept open is another day in which hundreds of detainees and their families are kept in the legal shadows. Distressing to the individuals concerned and destructive of the rule of law, the example it sets—of a powerful country undermining fundamental human rights principles—is dangerous to us all. It would be no less dangerous, and no less unlawful, if the US were simply to transfer the problem it has created at Guantánamo to another locations.

The detention facility at Guantánamo Bay isn't the only prison where the United States is holding detainees from the 'war on terror'. At Bagram Air Force Base in Afghanistan, Camp Bucca and Camp Cropper in Iraq, and many more—some known and others secret—are used to detain those captured by the US military. Camp Bucca alone has at times held 20,000 prisoners, most of whom live in groups of tents surrounded by wire. Most detainees are held unlawfully, without warrant or charge, and without recourse to challenge their detention. Even when Guantánamo is closed, the need to push for detainee human rights will continue.

The past one year has been more embarrassing for the US Government: In *Rasul v. Bush* (2004) the US Supreme Court ruled that federal courts had jurisdiction over detainees in Guantánamo, allowing detainees to file petitions seeking habeas corpus—the centuries old right to challenge the legality of one's detention. In *Hamdan v. Rumsfeld* (2006) the Court found that Article 3 common to the four Geneva Conventions applied to Guantánamo detainees. In 2006, Congress passed the Military Commissions Act (MCA), which stripped federal courts of the right to hear habeas corpus cases by or on behalf of any Guantánamo detainees. But on 12 June 2008, the US Supreme Court ruled in *Boumediene v. Bush* that detainees held at Guantánamo are entitled, under the US Constitution, to habeas corpus. More than seven years after the first detainees were transferred to Guantánamo, only two people have had their cases adjudicated. One pleaded guilty in 2007 in exchange for a light sentence to be served in his native Australia. Another was convicted in August 2008 of some of the charges against him (though he was acquitted of the most serious charges) and will have completed his sentence by the start of 2009. Fewer than 25 others have even been charged. The hundreds who remain, some of whom are in their seventh year of detention, have been subjected to a wide range of interrogation tactics that constitute ill-treatment, including stress positions, sensory deprivation, prolonged isolation, the use of 20-hour interrogations, hooding during transportation and interrogation, stripping, forcible shaving, and 'using detainees individual phobias (such as fear of dogs) to induce stress'. The indefinite and arbitrary nature of their detention has led to a steep decline in the mental health of many incarcerated at Guantánamo. There have been numerous suicide attempts and hunger strikes. In June 2006, after the apparent suicides of three inmates, many detainees were moved to isolated cells in 'supermax' facilities known as Camp 5 and Camp 6. There, they lost the ability to eat or exercise communally. They have very limited contact with anyone but their jailers and almost no access to sunlight or fresh air. A fourth detainee died of an apparent suicide in March 2007.

There must be a clear framework for an end to Guantánamo Bay. There are many calls for the some key points to be included in any strategy pursued: closing Guantánamo or other facilities must not result in the transfer of the human rights violations elsewhere. All detainees in the US custody must be treated in accordance with international human rights law and standards, and, where relevant, international humanitarian law. The responsibility for finding a solution for the detainees held in Guantánamo and elsewhere rests first and foremost with the US. The US government has created a system of detention in which detainees have been held without charge or trial, outside the framework of international law and without the possibility of full recourse to US courts. It must redress this situation in full compliance with international law and standards. All detainees must be able to challenge the lawfulness of their detention in an independent and impartial court, so that that court may order the release of anyone whose detention is not lawful. The Military Commissions Act should be repealed or substantially amended to bring it into conformity with international law, including by fully ensuring the right to habeas corpus. Those currently held in Guantánamo should be released unless they are to be promptly charged and tried in accordance with international standards of fair trial. No detainees should be forcibly sent to their country of origin if they would face serious human rights abuses there, or to any other country where they may face such abuses or from where they may in turn be forcibly sent to a country where they are at such risk.

There is great demand of transparency pending closure. The human rights organisations have asked that the US should invite at least the five UN experts who have sought access—the Special Rapporteur on torture and other cruel, inhuman or degrading treatment or punishment, the Special Rapporteur on the independence of judges and lawyers, the Special Rapporteur on freedom of religion or belief, the Special Rapporteur on the right of everyone to the enjoyment of the highest attainable standard of physical and mental health, and the Chairperson-Rapporteur of the Working Group on Arbitrary Detention—to visit Guantánamo without the restrictions that led them to turn down the US' previous invitation.

Even after seven years, the European governments are in a state of denial. Their involvement in renditions and secret detention runs in stark contrast to their claims to be responsible actors in the fight against terrorism. Many reports highlighted the cases and detailed the involvement of European states. These include allowing Central Intelligence Agency (CIA) flights headed for rendition circuits to use European airports and airspace to hosting secret detention facilities, or 'black sites'. Along with Guantánamo Bay, there are demands for ending European involvement in renditions and secret detention that calls on states to condemn such activities; initiate independent investigations into all cases implicating European agents or territory; bring the perpetrators to justice; ensure oversight of intelligence agencies; refuse to carry out or facilitate the transfer of any detainee to another state without appropriate judicial supervision; and provide reparations for victims.

Guantánamo Bay should also make other countries, who are victims of terrorism, learn that justice cannot be achieved in a rule-of-law vacuum. To hold people in secret custody or indefinite, virtually incommunicado, detention without charge or trial, while labeling them as 'terrorists', 'killers' and 'bad people', is to jeopardise the possibility that the lawlessness and violence can be brought to an end. To undermine the prohibition against torture and other ill-treatment in the name of national security makes bringing to justice any detainee who bears the brunt of such a policy more difficult because it calls into question the admissibility of any information obtained under such conditions. And the longer this goes on, the more distant the prospect for justice becomes. In other words, a government which resorts to such tactics facilitates impunity and denies justice to the victims of crime, including terrorism.

There is no doubt that the detainees would face significant challenges in adjusting to life outside Guantánamo after years of harsh and indefinite detention. However, providing a safe place for them to live is the only way to end the human rights violations that they have endured, and finally close Guantánamo. Wherever they are accepted, the detainees require guarantees of both their physical and legal safety in order to begin rebuilding their lives in dignity. Other governments able to offer a lawful, humane and sustainable solution to what has become an international scandal should also act immediately.

(This is a subsequently expanded and revised version of the articles published in *The Hindu* on 6 January 2007 and 4 January 2008.)

On 22 January 2008, the US President Barack Obama signed an executive order stating that Guantánamo 'shall be closed as soon as practicable, and no later than one year from the date of this order.'

6

Europe and Counter-terrorism

Amid the flurry of counter-terrorism initiatives both in the European Union (EU) and beyond, the concept of human rights and the rule of law as the basis for genuine security has been lost all but in the rhetoric. In its policies and legislation on counter-terrorism, the EU has failed to properly address the serious issue of the protection of fundamental rights. While one element of the creation of the EU's Area of Freedom, Security and Justice is the promotion and protection of fundamental rights, this aspect has not been manifest in concrete proposals on counter-terrorism. The language adopted in the area of judicial and police cooperation within the EU to combat serious and organised crime including terrorism, speaks of mutual trust and shared values. But in practice, the fight against terrorism often is being used as justification for compromising those values or turning a blind eye to the questionable practices and legislative frameworks on counter-terrorism in many EU member states. As far as cooperation with third countries in the fight against terrorism is concerned, the EU and its member states too often are prepared to remain silent on the issue of rights protection. While there is a general assumption that the human rights of terrorist suspects will be protected within the European Union, little attention is given to credible concerns that serious human rights abuses occur when those suspects are transported to some countries outside the borders of the Area of Freedom, Security and Justice.

The EU and its Member States

The EU has not been slow in responding to the threat of international terrorism even though its structure and the powers conferred on the

EU by member states create a unique and complex framework for measures in this field. The EU anti-terrorism roadmap, produced within weeks of 11 September 2001, covered a broad range of areas that could have an impact on the fight against terrorism and the root causes of terrorism, from criminal law initiatives to the safety of air transport to relations with third countries and aid. The areas covered by the fight against terrorism span the three 'pillars' of the EU: the first (or Community) pillar which includes issues such as the free movement of persons, asylum and immigration and judicial cooperation in civil and commercial matters; the second pillar (which is intergovernmental) covering the Common Foreign and Security Policy (CFSP); and the third pillar (also intergovernmental) covering criminal law issues of justice and home affairs, in particular police and judicial cooperation in criminal matters. The powers of the EU to act and the ways in which measures are taken vary considerably depending on which of the three pillars the subject matter is governed by. Here I will concentrate primarily on EU measures taken under the third pillar in the field of judicial cooperation in criminal matters. It will also look at the interaction between extradition and asylum procedures.

Article 6 of the Treaty on European Union (TEU) provides that 'The Union is founded on the principles of liberty, democracy, respect for human rights and fundamental freedoms, and the rule of law, principles which are common to the Member States.' and 'The Union shall respect fundamental rights, as guaranteed by the European Convention for the Protection of Human Rights and Fundamental Freedoms signed in Rome on 4 November 1950 and as they result from the constitutional traditions common to the Member States, as general principles of Community law.' Article 7 provides a mechanism whereby the EU can suspend certain membership rights relating to a member state where the existence of a serious and persistent breach of the principles of Article 6. These articles constitute the legal and political basis of the collective responsibility of the EU for the protection of human rights and fundamental freedoms throughout its territory.

There are worrying trends in the EU in relation to the fight against terrorism. Disturbing legislative developments in member states have led to incommunicado detention in Spain; the UK has derogated from the European Convention on Human Rights and Fundamental Freedoms (ECHR) to allow for indefinite detention without trial and the use in court of secret intelligence evidence, potentially extracted through torture. The Secretary-General of the Council of Europe condemned UK anti-terrorist legislation (Anti-Terrorism, Crime and Security Act of 2001) following a judgement from the House of Lords that the legislation was incompatible with human rights.

There are cases where member states—the UK and Sweden—may have been complicit in the 'extraordinary rendition' of suspects without due process to countries where they are at a grave risk of torture and a flagrant breach of their fair trial rights. Removals of people suspected of terrorism show a worrying tendency to reduce or ignore the rights of suspects, justified by the interests of swift procedures. Furthermore, racism and discrimination are a significant problem in Europe and this is a serious concern that the fight against terrorism is fuelling discrimination by states and non-state actors against certain groups in society. Statements such as that by the UK's Minister for Counter Terrorism, Hazel Blears, that Muslims must face the reality that the police would target them because of the threat from an extreme form of Islam are very worrying and encourage discriminatory policing which exacerbates feelings of alienation in the Muslim population. This trend to equate terrorism with Islam risks undermining the commitment to fight racism and xenophobia.

Despite these problems which appear across the EU, the EU itself has paid no more than lip service to the question of protecting human rights in the context of the fight against terrorism. In the rush to take action in the political climate following 11 September 2001, the key EU level measures aimed at combating terrorism in the criminal law sphere were drafted with little consideration being given to procedural safeguards or to legal certainty. The negotiations on certain procedural rights for suspects in criminal proceedings throughout the EU have included debates about excluding terrorist suspects completely from the application of procedural rights to reflect current national practices in some member states, a suggestion which not only runs contrary to the principle of the universality of human rights but potentially also undermines the possibility of effective prosecutions and cooperation between member states to combat terrorism.

The EU as a Separate Legal Framework

In a global environment where there is an increasing tendency to categorise certain acts as 'terrorist' and to base levels of cooperation between states and types of legislation on this categorisation it is important to know precisely what is meant by 'terrorism'. The consequences of an offence being categorised as 'terrorist' can be very serious in terms of limitations on certain rights. For example, in some member states, the classification of proceedings as relating to 'terrorism' can result in curtailment of the right of access to a lawyer, inclusion on public lists identified as a terrorist, invasion of privacy, the use of secret evidence and incommunicado detention. When states cooperate with each other on counter-terrorism, the difference in treatment and procedures in 'terrorist' cases as well as very different approaches to the classification of groups as 'terrorist' makes it crucial for states to understand what each one means by the term.

While the existence of legislation and special procedures relating to 'terrorism' demand a clear definition of terrorism to ensure legal certainty and the effectiveness of a counter-terrorism strategy, what is not clear is the added value or justification of treating 'terrorism' as an issue which is separate from the underlying criminal acts to be prosecuted such as murder or kidnapping which can be found in the regular criminal justice systems of member states. While the general threat of terrorism is put forward as a justification for the limitation of fair trial rights and intrusions into private life, among other things, there has been no serious discussion as to whether these limitations are in fact necessary in relation to terrorism as opposed to other forms of serious violent and/or organised crime. The right to a fair trial, for example, is a fundamental concept of justice and the rule of law, its function being to protect against miscarriages of justice which are prejudicial both to the individuals concerned and to society as a whole. It is hard to see what benefit there can be in increasing the risk of miscarriages of justice in highly sensitive terrorism cases by limiting the right to a fair trial. A miscarriage of justice not only gives impunity to the real perpetrators of acts of terrorism but also undermines the public faith in the state's ability to guarantee freedom, justice and security. It may also alienate minorities who are perceived as a higher 'risk factor' for generating terrorist activity and who are therefore more likely to suffer from potential abuses of human rights connected to the fight against terrorism.

The Definition of Terrorism

The international community has found it very hard in the past to come up with a consensus on what exactly is meant by 'terrorism' due to ideological clashes between states. The Council of Europe Convention on the prevention of terrorism, as adopted on 3 May 2005, requires states parties to criminalise provocation of and recruitment and training for terrorism. It does however not include a precise definition of terrorism for the purpose of the treaty, thus effectively creating subsidiary offences while the primary offence of terrorism remains undefined. While existing UN conventions refer to terrorism, they prohibit certain crimes without defining terrorism as such. The UN High Level Panel on Threats, Challenges and Change in December 2004 suggested the following definition of terrorism be adopted: 'Any action constitutes terrorism if it is intended to cause death or serious bodily harm to civilians or non-combatants with the purpose of intimidating a population or compelling a government or an international organisation to do or abstain from doing any act.'

The EU Council Framework Decision on combating terrorism, however, which was agreed in record time in December 2001 is broader than this, including in the acts covered 'causing extensive destruction to a government or public facility, including an information system, a fixed platform located on a continental shelf, a public place or private property likely to endanger human life or result in major economic loss'; and a threat to commit any of the acts listed in the Framework Decision, thus extending the notion of terrorism beyond actual violent acts designed to cause death or serious bodily harm or attempts at such acts. The Framework Decision on combating terrorism was one of the key elements of the EU's response to 11 September 2001 along with the European Arrest Warrant. At the time of negotiation it was felt that a common definition of terrorism was necessary to ensure effective cooperation between member states to combat terrorism as some member states did not have 'terrorism offences' as such in their legislation and this undermined the possibilities for extradition or other forms of judicial cooperation which required double criminality (that is that the offence concerned is an offence both in the requesting and requested country).

During the negotiations of the Framework Decision on combating terrorism, a number of member states, as well as NGOs, raised concerns that the definition contained in the Commission proposal was not sufficiently precise as to guarantee legal certainty and that the breadth of the proposed definition could threaten the right to freedom of association and legitimate protest. Requiring criminalisation of 'terrorist' acts, it allowed for prosecution for offences such as 'unlawful seizure of or damage to state or government facilities, means of public transport, infrastructure facilities, places of public use, and property', and 'promoting of, supporting of or participating in a terrorist organisation'. Without clearly defining the terms this could lead to criminalisation of activities which are unrelated in any way to acts of violence. In response to some member states' concerns that the still relatively broad definition finally adopted would threaten the right to legitimate protest, a declaration attached to the Framework Decision provides that the Framework Decision 'should not be understood to criminalise on terrorist grounds persons who exercise their legitimate right to manifest their opinions, even if they commit criminal offences while exercising this right'. This declaration though, remains ambiguous, has no legal status or effect and does not cure the vagueness of the definition itself.

The Framework Decision contains nine specific acts mostly concerning attacks on persons or weapons-related acts although some are less clearly related to violence. The act committed must fall under one of three categories of objectives in order to qualify as a 'terrorist act'. Those objectives are: to seriously intimidate a population, or unduly compel a government or international organisation to perform or abstain from performing any act, or seriously destabilise or destroy the fundamental structures of a country or an international organisation. The definition contained in the Framework Decision on combating terrorism is important in that it establishes the parameters for other counter-terrorism initiatives at EU level such as the establishment of lists of organisations and individuals involved in terrorism. While this definition, vague as it is, exists at EU level, the development of the European Arrest Warrant (EAW) has further exacerbated the lack of legal certainty in the definition of 'terrorism' in practice. As the EAW removes the requirement for double criminality in relation to 'terrorism' and membership of a proscribed organisation, the definitions which apply in the application of the EAW are those which apply in national law, not commonly agreed definitions. National definitions are thus extended across the EU without a clear picture of what those definitions might be. The Framework Decision on combating terrorism establishes a basic set of acts and objectives, but member states are not prevented from going further than these acts and objectives in their national legislation. The vagueness of the definition contained in the Framework Decision on combating terrorism is primarily of concern in that it provides a basis for further measures such as the establishment of terrorist lists.

Who is a Terrorist?

The difficulties encountered in identifying what terrorism is become more acute when people or organisations are identified as 'terrorist'. In a climate where identification as a 'terrorist' has such serious implications for the enjoyment of rights (in particular on the right to freedom of assembly and association, freedom of expression, the right to respect for private and family life, the right to basic public services and on the right to liberty and the right to a fair trial) it is crucial that such identification must be based on clear evidence that is capable of being challenged. In implementing UN Security Council resolution 1373 the EU introduced a series of legislative measures which created EU terrorist blacklists building on the UN lists. The EU lists comprise 'persons who commit, or attempt to commit, terrorist acts or who participate in, or facilitate, the commission of terrorist acts' and 'groups and entities owned or controlled directly or indirectly by such persons; and persons, groups and entities acting on behalf of, or under the direction of, such persons, groups and entities'.

The definition of terrorism in these instruments is the same as that in the EU Framework Decision on combating terrorism, although it goes beyond that definition in that it is not limited to acts by or against EU citizens/residents or on EU territory. The legal effect of these EU lists is unclear which leads to an absence of legal certainty as to their impact on the rights of persons and organisations included on the lists. There was practically no democratic scrutiny related to the establishment of these lists and there is no judicial supervision regarding inclusion on them, which further undermines their legitimacy, and indeed their practical usefulness in their stated aim of combating terrorism. In December 2001 a number of measures were adopted by the Council within the context of the fight against terrorism: Council Regulation on specific restrictive measures directed against certain persons and entities with a view to combating terrorism, Council Decision establishing the list, Council Common Position on combating terrorism, Council Common Position on the application of specific measures to combat terrorism. Once again, the haste and timing of the adoption of these instruments along with the choice of instrument meant that there was little opportunity for scrutiny or debate on the content or potential impact of the measures.

Groups and Individuals External to the EU

In addition to an obligation to enhance police and judicial cooperation in relation to many of the groups and individuals included on the list, provisions relating to asset freezing apply to many as well and the consequent financial implications for them mean that there is a Community (first pillar) effect which gives the ECJ a degree of competence on related issues. As in relation to the UN lists, there are concerns that the manner in which numerous individuals have been placed on such lists with extremely short notice and without the possibility of review or appeal raises indeed, as the UN High Level Panel suggests in the case of 'terrorist lists', 'serious accountability issues and possibly violate fundamental human rights norms and conventions' (recommendations 40 and 52). One case currently before the ECJ is that of the Philippine national José-Maria Sison who was included in the list. Mr Sison contests his inclusion in the list and any link to terrorism. The impact of inclusion on the list was that Mr Sison, resident in The Netherlands, among other things had his social benefits terminated and his bank account frozen. A request from his lawyers to the General Secretariat of the Council of the EU for information on the justification of his inclusion on the list was refused and this decision was upheld by the Court of First Instance (CFI) that rejected the application for access to documents. The inability to gain access to documents relating to the decision to include a person on the list has the effect of undermining the practical possibility of challenging that inclusion. It is impossible to contest inclusion if the reasons for it remain unknown. The complexity of EU law may create a smokescreen to prevent the effective protection of rights.

Prosecuting Terrorists across Borders: Extradition and Surrender between EU Member States

In the international approach to combating terrorism, it has become increasingly clear that while prosecutions and investigations may cross borders, adequate protection of human rights does not go with them. The crossing of borders in terms of preventing, investigating and prosecuting terrorism-related offences can be divided into two parts in relation to the EU: cooperation between member states and cooperation with third countries. Two major planks of the EU roadmap to combat terrorism post 11 September 2001 were developed at EU level: the European Arrest Warrant adopted in 2001 and the EU-US agreements on extradition and mutual legal assistance concluded in 2003. Aside from these two EU-level developments, there has been a worrying trend in the methods for removing terrorist suspects from EU jurisdictions through deportation, 'rendition' and even abduction.

The two categories raise quite different issues for EU policy and the protection and promotion of rights. On the one hand, cooperation between member states can only be facilitated by ensuring that there is a level playing field of rights protection, in particular in relation to fair trial and other procedural rights, across the territory of the EU. It is only on this basis that the principle of mutual trust can develop, enhancing cooperation based on a well-founded belief that miscarriages of justice are unlikely within the European judicial space. On the other hand, cooperation with third countries must not result in an erosion of the level of rights protection found within the EU. How can one feel a sense of 'a high level of security' where people may be taken off the street and flown out of the jurisdiction of EU member states without even a nod to due process? The idea of an Area of Freedom, Security and Justice seems particularly thin when the EU is not prepared to use its external borders as a means of ensuring that the rights and principles enshrined in its Treaty are applied to all within its territory, including those who may be facing extradition, expulsion or other forms of removal from that territory.

There are several problematic provisions now in laws of European countries. For example, in France, a 96-hour special custody regime was extended to a wider range of offences since 2004. Moreover, under this law, persons suspected of terrorism or drug trafficking can be held incommunicado for the first 48 hours without access to a lawyer. In Spain, concern has also been raised about the lack of prompt access to a judge or lawyer and the incommunicado detention of persons suspected of terrorism-related offences. Among other things, such suspects can be held in police custody for five days before being brought before a judge. Furthermore, the judge can extend the period of incommunicado detention for up to 13 days. During incommunicado detention, a suspect is denied access to a lawyer of their choice. In addition, although the suspect is provided with an appointed legal aid lawyer, the role of the lawyer is so restricted as to deny the suspect's right to legal assistance. The suspect is denied that right at the outset of detention, and the lawyer is only present when the suspect gives an official police statement, which may be several days after detention. Furthermore, throughout this time, before and after statements are given, as well as during hearings before judges, the legal aid lawyer may not communicate in private with the detainee. Moreover, the judges can impose secrecy (*secreto de sumario*) on the investigation and on judicial proceedings, either in whole or in part. Under *secreto de sumario*, suspects and their lawyers are denied access to critical information regarding the charges or the evidence, and this denial could be maintained until the investigation phase of the legal process is almost concluded. Thus the suspect is denied any effective legal assistance throughout this period of detention. In February 2004 the UN Special Rapporteur on Torture issued a report on a visit to Spain in October 2003. The aim of the visit was to study the various safeguards for the protection of detainees in the context of anti-terrorism measures. The Rapporteur noted that 'the degree of silence that surrounds the subject and the denial by the authorities without investigating the allegations of torture has made it particularly difficult to provide the necessary monitoring of protection and guarantees'. He concluded that 'in the light of the internal consistency of the information received and the precision of factual details…these allegations of torture cannot be considered to be fabrications'. Although not a regular practice, 'their occurrence is more than sporadic and incidental'. Under Part 4 of the UK Anti-Terrorism, Crime and Security Act 2001 (ATCSA), which expired in March 2005, the Secretary of State was able to certify non-UK nationals as 'suspected international terrorists' and detain them indefinitely without charge or trial.

In the discourse surrounding counter-terrorism and human rights in the EU, a distinction is often made between the requirements of freedom and justice and those of security. This distinction is misplaced: the protection of human rights and respect for the rule of law are fundamental elements of genuine security rather than competing interests. If the EU is to be successful in creating an Area of Freedom, Security and Justice it cannot afford to be complacent but rather must strive to reinforce these elements as part of an effective security strategy.

7

50 Years of a Law

Come September 2008, and the Armed Forces Special Power Act (AFSPA) is now 50 years old in our country. It is a law in force in large parts of the northeast that gives armed forces special powers in a locality declared as 'disturbed area'. However, while AFSPA is considered necessary by the state and army officials to protect the state against internal disturbances, to uphold the integrity of nation, to fight against terrorism and insurgency, and to protect sensitive border areas, it is being vehemently opposed and discarded by human rights groups, women's organisations and political groups, as it is seen as facilitating grave human rights abuses, impunity, rape and torture, and silencing of democratic dissent. The Act has long been challenged internally through country-wide campaigns, coalitions, self-immolation, fast until death and naked protests. It is also regularly referred to internationally, for example, in the recently concluded UN Human Rights Councils' Universal Periodic Country Review or in the previous Human Rights Committee, as an issue of serious concern. Several Indian and international voices like Administrative Reforms Committee headed by Veerappan Moily (2007), Working Group on Confidence Building Measures in Jammu and Kashmir headed by Mohammad Hamid Ansari (2007), Centre's interlocutor in the Naga peace talks, K. Padmanabhaiah (2008), B.P. Jeevan Reddy Committee (2005), UN Special Rapporteur on extrajudicial, summary or arbitrary executions (2006), UN Committee on the Elimination of Discrimination against Women (2007), Committee on the Elimination of Racial Discrimination (2007) have called for its repeal.

Laws of human rights apply at all times. Some human rights, including the right to life (of which extrajudicial executions are a violation), freedom from subjugation, freedom from torture and other cruel, inhuman or degrading treatment or punishment, should not be derogated from even during extreme conflict situations, including wars. Other rights may be derogated from only to the extent necessitated by the situation and only for a limited period. If 50 years of a law could not control the conduct of parties to armed conflicts, if it could not protect civilians and citizens not participating in hostilities or civilian and military objects, if it could not bring peace and tranquility, then it is again an appropriate time to ask for a swift repeal of the AFSPA. The government repealed the Prevention of Terrorism Act (POTA) after recognising 'concerns with the manner in which POTA had been grossly misused'. Similar concerns exit with regard to the AFSPA.

It is a time to remind the Prime Minister, Dr Manmohan Singh, of his promise that the 'government would consider replacing the Act with a more 'humane' law that would seek to address the concerns of national security as well as rights of citizens'. It is a time to implement the key recommendation of the Government of India's constituted five-member panel, led by former chairperson of the Law Commission, Justice B.P. Jeevan Reddy. It is also a time of a new beginning, where the citizens' voices, who are taking no part in hostilities, shall in all circumstances be treated humanly in the so-called disturbed areas, without any adverse distinction founded on their religion, faith, sex, birth, or any other similar criteria.

Security is a shared responsibility. In order to give effect to the state's responsibility for the maintenance of borders and order in our territory requires some insight on its part on the levels of 'order' within the country. We may argue that to achieve this in a conflict-ridden or terror-affected areas, it is required to measure the nature and volume of crimes committed by the non-state armed groups, and use this as an indicator of how secure society is. However, doing so ignores the fact that people's sense of security is affected by more factors than insurgency alone. In order to develop an effective security policy in disturbed areas, some insight into both objective terror threats, as well as people's sense of security is required. AFPSA has miserably failed in making either the state safe or the people secure. North eastern people are aspiring for a community safety 'on the ground'.

In the case of AFPSA, the 'local perspective', as opposed to the national perspective, is all the more relevant, as it has become clear in the past fifty years of the implementation of the law that states of the disturbed areas are not successful in their ability to ensure peace and order. Even with such sweeping powers, states' capacity to intervene in conflicts of all sorts, and influence non-state actors, has erased considerably and is often biased in favor of parochial and specific interests. If Indian security forces would not be able to function without the AFSPA, as is being stated by our Defence Minister, then what to do with the majority of the affected citizens who do not want to live with it. Ensuring area safety requires cooperation and confidence amongst all the relevant entities involved as well as the civil society. Our states are required to protect peoples' rights but they have to also support their empowerment, so as to enhance their potential for self-protection. States must acknowledge the indivisibility of security, economic development and human freedom.

There are numerous reports of illegal detentions, extrajudicial killings, arbitrarily open firing and killing of civilians, disappearances, torture and many more in the disturbed areas, operating under the AFSPA, and its equivalents in Jammu and Kashmir. The cases have surfaced at regular intervals, but they are far from a complete picture of the human rights situation in areas under AFPSA. The lack of access to some areas and the denial of information and communication rights, combined with factors such as fear of reprisal by security forces, have made it very difficult to even know or verify the facts. In fact, the recent spurt of activism against the Act came after an alleged sexual assault and death in custody of a woman Thangjam Manorama in Imphal, Manipur, in July 2004. Do's and don'ts, directed by the Supreme Court in 1997, were a response to the atrocities by the security forces in these areas. At the same time, ironically, 'no prosecution, suit or other legal proceeding shall be instituted, except with the previous sanction of the Central Government, against any person in respect of anything done or purported to be done in exercise of the powers conferred by this Act' (Section 6, AFSPA). An example of the powers of the officers is to 'fire upon or otherwise use force, even to the causing of death' not only in cases of self-defense, but against any person contravening laws or orders 'prohibiting the assembly of five or more persons' (Section 4).

The everyday practice of insurgency and counter-insurgency under regimes like the AFPSA dehumanises all, and leads to massive human rights violations. This is because it negates the basic demo-cratic norms of behaviour within and between groups, by making security forces all mighty and powerful. It is a historic fact that militarised states tend to be less responsive to community needs and demands (as a consequence of culture as well as methods), and they cannot establish just and humane relationships with the public. Militarisation, its associated hierarchical structures, discipline and denial of rights, quite often become the breeding ground for unleashing more brutality, and ensuring a degree of perpetual public insecurity.

AFPSA originally came up in select regions of Northeast, in response to the armed political activity in that region, and was to remain in force for one year. However, it not only continued but was extended to more regions. Instead to being a one time measure in some emergency, it became a regular regime for all times. Indian democracy has continued to grow and gain strength in the past fifty years. However, the brutal and black AFPSA, and the regions under it, have been left in the dark, silenced and suffering. The maintenance of order against disorder and peace against disturbance are not neutral concepts. They are hollow notions if not aligned with human rights principles of rule of law, leading to human beings being free and enjoying all their rights. In fact, in these times of India's economic prosperity, people's rising aspirations and political power, the unrest within the AFPSA regions will be more. If order and peace regimes have also the connotation of suppression and maintenance of the status quo, if it brings about fear, revenge and the preserving of an inequitable distribution of power and resources, then it is better to change it now with the repeal of its main tool, that is, a 50 years old repressive law.

(This was published in *DNA*, 25 September 2008. It has been expanded and revised subsequently.)

8

Laws without Justice: In the Name of Public Security

In the context, and under the pretext, of rising terrorism, violence and insecurity, our state and central governments around the country have been openly flouting the absolute ban on torture and other cruel, inhuman or degrading treatments, fake encounters and disappearances. Gujarat chief minister's defence of unlawful killings and encounters is a new case in point. In Chhattisgarh, evidence of large-scale violence and killings by the state, or its supported forces, named Salwa Judum, as well as the arrest of human rights activists, continue to haunt us. In states like Bihar and Jharkhand, where cruelty and brutality are already common, governments are encouraged by a climate of tolerance and acceptance towards such abuses. In other states as well, draconian laws and abusive practices are being regularly introduced.

After Chhattisgarh, Maharashtra and Madhya Pradesh, it is now the state of Uttar Pradesh which has fallen in the same line, by introducing the 'Uttar Pradesh Control of Organised Crime Bill 2007' (UPCOC) in the state Assembly. Its stated aim is 'to eliminate organised crime in UP, so that common people could be saved from the clutches of the mafia and hardened criminals, operating as organised syndicate'. The bill would be passed soon, and will be known as the 'UP Control of Organised Crime Act' (UPCOCA). The rational and defence of this bill, as well as its nature and contents are similar to the 'Maharashtra Control of Organised Crime Act 1999' (MCOCA), the 'Chhattisgarh Special Public Security Act 2006', and the 'Madhya Pradesh Special Areas Security Act 2001'. These Acts provide an effective smokescreen for governments to authorise arbitrary detentions, torture, unfair trials, suppression of political dissent, and selective persecutions, and they know that any questioning, criticism and monitoring will be muted because of these Acts.

MCOCA is actually the model, in letter and spirit, for the bill in Uttar Pradesh. Thus, it is worth remembering that MCOCA came in the state books as a replacement for the infamous 'Terrorist and Disruptive Activities Prevention Act' (TADA) that was allowed to 'lapse' in 1995, in the face of the broad opposition to its draconian provisions and use. Maharashtra government was the only one at that time which had enacted a replacement for TADA, while similar draft legislations had been withdrawn in Tamil Nadu, Andhra Pradesh, Jammu and Kashmir and at the centre, because of popular opposition. MCOCA has been applied to arrest doctors, film personalities, a judge, journalists, workers, youth and people of all backgrounds. While organised crime, contract killings and money laundering continued in Mumbai, this law has emerged as one of the potent tools in the hands of the Maharashtra police to threaten and terrorise people fighting for economic and social justice.

A brief reading of UPCOC is required here: On the first registration of a crime, the criminal would not be able to obtain exparte bail and on the registration of a case for the second time, the offence would be non-bailable. All-powerful state and district-level Organised Crime Control Authorities/Committees will be formed to implement the Act, under the chairmanship of the Principal Secretary of Home and District Magistrates respectively. A state-level Appellate Authority will be created under the chairpersonship of a retired High Court judge, to hear the appeals against the orders passed by the state-level authority within 30 days. However, the Director General of Police and an Officer of the level of Principal Secretary will also be the members of the Appellate Authority. And the punishment proposed, like the MCOCA, is: 'if such an act has resulted in the death of any person, it will be punishable with death or imprisonment for life, and shall also be liable to a minimum fine of Rs.10 lakh' [Sub-section (a) of section 4(1) of the UPCOC]. What does this imply? An eye for an eye, a death for a death! It relies on fear, to achieve its aims. It denies and destroys human dignity. It assumes that the end justifies the means.

Our state governments already have a number of laws. The crimes are registered not only under the Indian Penal Code (IPC), but there are frequent uses of the National Security Act, the Arms and Explosives

Act, the Narcotics Act, the Gangster Act and others. In the specific context of UP, they also have the Uttar Pradesh Control of Goondas Act, 1970. A survey of the crime statistics of the Uttar Pradesh Police Department shows that a total of 118,195 cases were registered under the IPC in 2006, as against 117,748 in 2005. In addition to these, 411 cases were registered under the National Security Act, 2,117 under the Gangster Act, 11,816 under the Goonda Act, and 39,184 under the Arms Act, among others. Yet, we are asked to believe that without new stringent laws and their use, we cannot be safe. The story of Maharashtra and Chhattisgarh is very much applicable to Uttar Pradesh. The police and the administration all over India seem to want Acts that enable them to prevent bails, extract confessions, inflict torture, and yet continue with impunity.

Rule of law is the cornerstone for the protection of peoples' rights and systems of governance, based on the values of our constitution. Yet, domestic institutions at the centre and at the states, which should uphold the rule of law, are often seriously flawed. For example, overall our criminal justice system is undermined by institutionalised discrimination, lack of resources and corruption. In states like Gujarat, administration of justice has been manipulated to perpetuate the domination of political elites or religious groups. The result is continuing widespread violations of peoples' rights. Our history of controlling crime and violence is also a history of failures and shortcomings in the administration of justice.

Unlike the new emphasis on the social sector in our country, there is still a lack of effort and resources in reforming and strengthening the justice sector. Reform of the justice system involves exposing the gaps and loopholes in our legislation that allow people and their entitlements to be abused with impunity, and working for the removal of such legislations and procedures which are a hindrance in the realisation of democracy and justice. It also involves impartial judicial institutions and their accountability, and promoting a vision of policing, which sees the protection of human rights as integral to public security. Fresh opportunities came in the country, with the formation of the UPA government and its common minimum programme. With the repeal of POTA, and a move towards police reforms, some steps were initiated to provide redresses for failures of domestic justice systems. However, these moves remain embryonic and contested. With the introduction of the Human Rights Act to monitor state compliance with human rights standards, the government tried to fill up a serious gap. However, it is too little too late and it also faces a crisis of capacity. A revamped justice system, increased monitoring mechanisms, and accountability platforms would provide safety nets in the fight against criminals and terrorists. Otherwise, we will have shameless defences of encounter killings, disappearances and murders by the states in Delhi, Gujarat and may be next in Uttar Pradesh.

The decade of 2000 has seen many unequivocal signs in our country of an emergence of a country-wide justice movement, responding diversely to injustices related to trade rules, natural resources, women, Dalits, globalisation, liberalisation and many other issues. Those parties and governments particularly, that swear by the *surva jan* and *aam admi* (common man), will need to address the role played by poverty stigma and marginalisation, in denying access to justice to majority sectors of society. None of us can be safe from arbitrary arrests, sexual abuses, violent attacks, farmers' suicides or starvation without all rights and justice. These rights and justice have to come to us undiluted, devoid of any draconian and arbitrary acts, based on a fear psychosis and assertion of power.

(*The Hindu*, 17 December 2007)

Section II

Everyday Life of
Human Rights

9

A World without Torture

26 June 2008 is the International Day in Support of Victims of Torture, marking the 25th anniversary of the adoption of the UN Convention against Torture and Other Cruel, Inhuman or Degrading Treatment or Punishment. Sixty years after it was proclaimed, the words of the Universal Declaration of Human Rights remain as relevant as ever, 'No one shall be subjected to torture or to cruel, inhuman or degrading treatment or punishment.'

Torture dehumanises both the victim and the perpetrator. The pain and terror deliberately inflicted by one human being upon another leaves permanent scars: shattered bones, twisted limbs, recurring nightmares that keep the victims in constant fear. The damage goes beyond the trauma and suffering of the person who is tortured and those around them: each case of torture weakens the values and solidarity that hold a society together. Prohibition of torture is one of the most basic rules of democratic laws. Yet despite all the efforts to stop it, torture remains widespread in India. It is practised systematically and is relatively common. India is one of the few countries in the world that has not ratified the Convention Against Torture, although it has been a signatory since October 1997. Ratification is necessary for appropriate changes to be made in the prevailing laws, and to enable institutions and authorities to be accountable. (The reminders of the National Human Rights Commission to ensure its ratification by the Indian Government has been well documented in all its Annual Reports till the latest in 2004–2005.) Requests to visit the country by the UN Special Rapporteurs on torture and on extrajudicial executions remain pending since decades. Torture has not been specially defined in the Indian Constitution or specifically prohibited in penal laws, even when Right to Life and Personal Liberty of our constitution assures every individual a life of dignity and physical security.

There is a long tradition of judicial activism in India, with courts liberally interpreting the scope of fundamental rights set out in the Indian Constitution. Access by individuals to claim these rights has been assured through the development of Public Interest Litigation: 'in the public interest' on issues of fundamental rights on behalf of those unable to do so themselves. In September 1996, the Supreme Court of India made a landmark judgement in the case of *Basu v. State of West Bengal*, expressing concern that 'torture is more widespread now than ever before ... custodial torture is a naked violation of human dignity and degradation which destroys, to a very large extent, the individual personality. It is a calculated assault on human dignity and whenever human dignity is wounded, civilisation takes a step backward'. The judgement referred to international human rights standards and to the fact that Article 21 of the Constitution of India protects the right to life, a provision that has been held by the Indian courts to include a guarantee against torture. It also made general recommendations relating to amendments to the law on burden of proof and the need for police training, and put forward arguments against the right to sovereign immunity for agents of the state responsible for torture and in favour of compensation. The judgement's most far-reaching legacy is its 11 'requirements' to be followed in all cases of arrest and detention (para. 35). The 'requirements' would, the Court hoped, 'help to curb, if not totally eliminate, the use of questionable methods during interrogation and investigation' (para. 39).

However, this has not deterred officials from inflicting torture on individuals in their custody, nor others in society to discriminate, humiliate and torture people of particular caste, religion, socio-economic, gender, disability and sexual background. Take, for example, the ruling of the National Human Rights Commission (NHRC) on 11 June 2008, asking J&K Government to pay three lakh rupees to the kin of a deceased subjected to torture during unlawful detention. Banarasi Das Sharma was arrested by the police along with his two sons on 2 May 2000 and kept in PS Pasca Danga, North Jammu for his suspected involvement in espionage. His two sons were let off but he was unlawfully detained for a week and flogged to such an extent that he became permanently crippled. He was released on 9 May 2000 and died on 19 October 2000. On NHRC's notice, the state authorities submitted a report saying that Banarasi Das was kept by the verbal orders of senior officers of Army Intelligence.

The Defence Ministry denied its involvement. The Commission after examining the reports from both the J& K Police and the Defence Ministry found that 'though the two authorities have blamed each other yet the fact was that Banarasi Das was kept in detention at Pacca Danga for seven days and the factum of his detention was not entered in the records.'

Campaigns against torture today are more than focusing on stopping the torture of political prisoners by the state. Torture and ill-treatment can also be inflicted in many other settings. Abuses such as 'disappearances', harsh prison conditions, excessive use of force in land acquisition and industrialisation by law enforcement constitute torture or ill-treatment. Violence in the community and the home, such as caste attacks and domestic violence, also violate the prohibition of torture, when states fail to address these acts effectively though protection, prosecution and redress. Despite their many forms, acts of torture share common features. Torture is cruel and inhuman. It should be straightforward. Torture and other cruel, inhuman or degrading treatment are prohibited, full stop. There are no circumstances—war or threat of war, emergency or threat of emergency—that can be used to justify violating this ban. Every human being has the right to be free from torture or other ill-treatment—whether citizen or alien, whether suspected of a crime or not, whether labelled as 'the enemy' or not. Torture is wrong, whatever motivates it and whoever authorises it. The 'ticking bomb' scenario—the hypothesis put forward to seek to justify one-off torture to extract information about an imminent attack—is a crude device improvised to manipulate public fears. There is no such thing as one-off torture; torture all too easily seeps across the moral and legal landscape. If used to obtain information, rather than purely to humiliate the individual or spread fear in the community, that information cannot be trusted, let alone used in a fair trial. Torture is an injustice, not a route to justice. It is a threat to long-term security, not a means to win hearts and minds.

Torture has at least three new developments in contemporary India: In the name of security and fight against terrorism, there is increasing use of torture, arbitrary detention, unfair trial, suppression of political dissent. However, torture does not stop terror. Torture is terror. Second, some of the tools of the torturer's trade seem almost medieval—shackles, leg irons, thumbscrews, handcuffs and whips. However, in recent years there has been a marked expansion in the manufacture, trade and use of other kinds of technology used by security and police forces, especially coercive techniques like narco-analysis, truth serum, brain fingerprinting and others. There is a need to put pressure on governments and on companies to stop this new torture trade. Thirdly, torture is feeding more and more on discrimination and inequality. Discrimination is creating a climate in which torture of the 'other' group subjected to intolerance and discriminatory treatment is taken as accepted. Specific standards and safeguards for the protection against torture of minorities, women, children and others are needed. Ultimately, my security will not be best protected by torturing and ill-treating detainees but by respecting everyone's human rights.

(*The Hindu*, 26 June 2008)

10

Addressing the Issue of Enforced Disappearances

Enforced disappearances, a dominating feature of the second half of the twentieth century as they were committed on a gross scale in Nazi-occupied Europe, are not a thing of past. They are our present, continuing countrywide.

When the Srinagar-based Association of the Parents of Disappeared Persons (APDP), recently released its report *Facts under Ground*, and indicated the existence of multiple graves in localities which, because of their proximity of the Line of Control with Pakistan, are not accessible without the specific permission of the security forces, and the army spokespersons claimed that those found buried were armed rebels and 'foreign militants' killed lawfully in armed encounters with military forces, it opened a lid on many facts. According to the report, more than 8,000 persons have gone missing in Jammu and Kashmir since 1989. The central and state authorities countered that the total amounts to less than 4,000. The government branded them as 'the people who went to Pakistan to join the armed opposition groups'. But the report's detailed testimonies from local villagers states that most of those buried were local residents hailing from the state.

These exchanges also remind us of the intervention of state judiciary in a number of high profile cases, including the Chattisingpura case in which a series of court hearings established that the security services had extra-judicially executed five local residents, while claiming lawful use of force against suspected 'foreign militants'. However, the number of such judicial inquiries into individual complaints has not been much, especially seeing their volume. But it establishes one thing that in the recent years and decades, in the course of our fight against terrorism, the security agencies, sometimes with the complicity of our governments, have carried out enforced disappearances of terror suspects. They have responded to terror with terror. They have lowered the society's standards and undermined the prospects of justice. Those who commit these crimes have done so with almost complete impunity.

To 'disappear' is to vanish, to cease to be, to be lost. But the 'disappeared' have not simply vanished. Someone, somewhere, knows what has happened to them. Someone is responsible. Each enforced disappearance violates a swathe of human rights: the right to security and dignity of a person; the right not to be subjected to torture or other cruel, inhuman or degrading treatment or punishment; the right to humane conditions of detention; the right to a legal personality; as well as rights related to fair trial and family life. Ultimately, it violates the right to life, as victims of enforced disappearance are often killed.

These disappearances and extra-judicial executions are not limited to some specific regions or just terror-specific issues. They are not only happening in Jammu and Kashmir and the northeastern states, but are also being regularly reported from states like Gujarat, Maharashtra, Andhra Pradesh, Uttar Pradesh, Bihar, Rajasthan and Orissa. Those who have disappeared are not only terror suspects. People of all ages, professions and backgrounds have been its victims. These are crimes committed by the order of state organs, and those responsible for them always try to avoid being called to account for the crimes, through lies, cover ups and propagation of misleading explanations and excuses. An institutionalised impunity, which has ensured that almost no one has been brought to justice for human rights violations, is particularly entrenched in the case of forced disappearances. Institutions which should be responsible for ensuring justice, such as courts, prosecution services, investigating police and state human rights commissions, have repeatedly failed in their obligations to investigate crimes of forced disappearances, and have remained subordinate to the interests of state institutions such as the military and the civilian executive authorities, who have sought to prevent access to truth and justice.

Take, for example, Jammu and Kashmir, where the state government pledged that the State Human Rights Commission (SHRC) would investigate all enforced disappearances. However, the SHRC was unable to order any prosecutions against members of the security forces, without prior sanction from the Home Ministry of the Indian Government. In August 2006, outstanding concerns over the existing powers of the SHRC and its ability to effectively investigate enforced disappearances were further heightened when its chairperson resigned over the 'non-serious' attitude of the state government towards addressing human rights violations. Or, see the situation even when India signed the International Convention for the Protection of All Persons from Enforced Disappearances in February 2007. In spite of this, the government does not allow the UN Working Groups on Arbitrary Detention and on Enforced or Involuntary Disappearances to visit the country. India has still not ratified the Convention against Torture, and requests to visit the country by the UN Special Rapporteurs on torture and on extrajudicial executions have remained pending since long.

On 21 December 2006, the UN General Assembly unanimously adopted a major new human rights treaty: the International Convention for the Protection of All Persons from Enforced Disappearance. For over twenty five years, relatives of the disappeared, some governments and non-governmental organisations had worked hard to bring this landmark convention into existence, and it filled a major gap. Before this, the UN Declaration on the Protection of All Persons from Enforced Disappearance was adopted by the General Assembly without a vote in December 1992 'as a body of principles for all States'. The Declaration emphasises the non-derogable right to be free from disappearances, stating in Article 2 that the prohibition of 'disappearance' is absolute, and Article 7 states: 'No circumstances whatsoever, whether a threat of war, a state of war, internal political instability or any other public emergency, may be invoked to justify enforced "disappearance".' This places an obligation on the states to adopt and enforce safeguards against disappearances, and requires states to provide judicial remedy and redressal to victims and their families.

Then why does the Indian State not ensure that their national courts and commissions exercise universal jurisdiction over grave crimes like enforced disappearances? Why do our national legislatures not ensure that their courts and commissions can exercise jurisdiction over anyone suspected or accused of this crime, whatever the official capacity of the suspect or accused at the time of the alleged crime or any time thereafter? Why do we not ensure an investigation and a prosecution, where there is sufficient admissible evidence, without waiting for a complaint by a victim? To ensure that justice is not only done but also seen to be done, should not non-governmental organisations be permitted by competent national authorities to attend and monitor the trials of persons accused of disappearance? Should not the interests of victims, witnesses and their families be taken into account, and courts protect them?

Till such time when broad principles and laws based on them come into being, action is needed on specific issues and incidents that are raised locally by victims' relatives, human rights organisations and many others. We need to ensure the following: that all past and current allegations of enforced disappearances are promptly, thoroughly, independently and impartially investigated, and that, where there is sufficient evidence, anyone suspected of responsibility for such crimes is prosecuted in proceedings, which meet international fair trial standards; that all victims of unlawful killings, enforced disappearance and torture are granted full reparations, including restitution, compensation, rehabilitation, satisfaction and guarantees of non-repetition; assigning the civilian prosecutor's office with the jurisdiction to investigate all cases of suspected enforced disappearances, irrespective of whichever military, security or law enforcement agency is suspected of being involved; and provide the civilian prosecutor's office with the mandate and authority necessary to be able to effectively investigate all such cases. These will give some immediate healing touches to the troubled families and societies. Continuing failure of our states to implement these measures could pave the way for an increase of disappearance in the future. Finally, the crime of disappearance should be introduced into Indian law in accordance with international standards.

(*The Hindu*, 24 June 2008)

11

Persecution and Resistance: Experiences of Rights Defenders

A well-known activist of People's Union for Civil Liberties (PUCL), and a medical doctor Binayak Sen gets arrested in May 2007 in Chhattisgarh state, under the provisions of the controversial black laws, the Chhattisgarh Special Public Security Act 2005 (CSPSA), and the Unlawful Activities (Prevention) Act, 1967 having been amended in 2004 and made more stringent after the collapse of POTA. In August 2007, a woman activist, Roma, working among the women, tribals and Dalits of Mirzapur, Uttar Pradesh, under the aegis of Kaimur Kshetra Mahila Majdoor Kisan Sangharsh Samiti and the National Forum of Forest People and Forest Workers, is arrested and charged under the National Security Act. A young Oriya poet and literary editor, Saroj Mohanty, who is also an activist of the Prakrutik Suraksha Sampada Parishad, an organisation supporting the struggles of the people of Kashipur, who for the past 13 years have successfully opposed the entry of large bauxite mining companies in the region, was picked up by the police in July 2007 at Rayagada, Orissa, on charges of dacoity, house trespass and attempt to murder. Two activists—Shamim and Anurag—of Shramik Adivasi Sanghathana and Samajwadi Jan Parishad, which are working amongst tribals in Betul, Harda and Khandwa districts of Madhya Pradesh, were served externment notices in June by the Harda District Magistrate under the State Security Act.

Dr Binayak, Roma, Saroj, Shamim, Anurag and many like them are crucial actors of our present times. They are individuals, groups of people or organisations who promote and protect human rights in many different ways and in different capacities, through peaceful and non-violent means. They uncover violations, subject them to public scrutiny and press for those responsible to be accountable. They empower individuals and communities to claim their basic entitlements as human beings. They represent some of the most marginalised civil society groups—from tribal people to the landless rural workers and women's groups. However, in India today, because of this work they are facing a range of challenges. They are subjected to death threats and torture, persecuted through the use of the judicial system and silenced through the introduction of security laws. Unfounded investigations and prosecutions, surveillance of offices and homes and the theft of important human rights information and documents are some of the tactics used to intimidate them and prevent them from continuing their work. Many even disappear or are murdered. The pursuit of neo-liberal economic policies, with its emphasis on SEZs, land acquisitions and appropriation of natural resources, is intensifying the attacks on human rights defenders.

This situation reminds us of the 1990s when at the height of the Manmohanomics and its aggressive march, cultural and trade union activists like Safdar Hashmi and Shankar Guha Niyogi were killed. The bankruptcy and increasing isolation of the ruling class provoke its local counterpart and they acquire a new offensive against the human rights activists. Yesterday it was Safdar Hashmi and Shankar Guha Niyogi, today it is Binayak Sen and tomorrow it will be Medha Patkar or Sunilam.

In fact, in spite of Indian democracy and its membership to the Human Rights Council for the second consecutive term, it has made it no different from global trends. In her 2007 report, the Special Representative of the UN Secretary General on the situation of human rights defenders noted that defenders working on land rights, natural resources or environmental issues seem to be particularly at risk of attacks and violations of their rights:

> Defenders working (in the field of economic, social and cultural rights) face violations of their rights by the State and/or face violence and threats from non-state actors because of their work. Violations of their rights seem to take all the forms that violations of the rights of defenders working in the field of civil and political rights take. There are some differences though, perhaps the most important being that defenders working in the field of ESCR often have a harder time having their work accepted as human rights work. This might have several effects, including difficulties attracting funding, a lack of coverage from the media to violations of these defenders' rights,

and a lack of attention paid to these violations and a hesitation in seeking remedial measures at the domestic or international levels. (Hina Jilani, 2007, p. 18)

Over the last 20 years, social justice movements, development practitioners and rights activists have increasingly taken the language and tools of rights into the sphere of economic and social policy. They have faced major challenges along the way. Our governments have remained hostile to the very concept of economic and social rights as enforceable entitlements. At both the domestic and international level, legal mechanisms for claiming redress for economic and social rights violations are severely underdeveloped in comparison to civil and political rights. The challenges involved in identifying violations, attributing responsibility and proposing appropriate measures for redress and prevention have led some to view economic and social rights as inherently less enforceable through legal means. Moreover, the complexity of addressing issues of national resource allocation or national macroeconomic policy through a human rights lens also poses a formidable challenge.

Peoples' rights agenda in India has always been a dynamic and constantly evolving one, with activists applying the principles and tools of human rights to different context and struggles. At different points in history, courageous and visionary people have sought to extend the boundaries of human rights to those outside its boundary, be it those living amidst caste oppression, workers unprotected against social insecurity or women denied any rights against violence. Thus, we see the emergence of new rights on information, food, domestic violence and tribal lands. These achievements have also reflected the work carried out by economic and social rights activists, in cooperation with development experts, social scientists and professionals from such fields as economics, health, education and science, to develop new tools and methodologies for assessing rights violations. These have included identifying indicators and benchmarks for measuring compliance with the obligation to satisfy minimum essential levels of these rights, and budget analysis to gauge whether governments are realizing economic and social rights progressively according to their minimum available resources. Public hearings, social audit and citizens' cards are also developed comprehensively. People forging new frontiers for rights are often the ones most exposed to risk, ridicule and resistance. The contours of human rights shift as patterns of oppression change. Their scope and content will, therefore, always be a matter of contestation. Indeed, the human rights agenda has always been built by its own critique. Those excluded from the way rights are traditionally understood or interpreted—for example, Dalits, tribals, women, labour, lesbian, gay, or the disabled—are fighting for inclusion and are enriching and transforming understandings of human rights as a result.

There have always been challenges for human rights and political activists in our country. Harassment of activists is so often part of their daily life that it goes unreported. Detention or abduction, disappearances and politically motivated imprisonment are used to stop activists. In the recent past, smear campaigns and defamatory tactics are also being used to delegitimise the works of defenders, with the media often colluding in the dissemination of slanderous accusations and attacks on their personal integrity and political independence. However, we are also now living in a new hostile environment. As countless examples are showing, a large area in the country is witnessing armed conflicts, often on a massive scale, where civilian lives and livelihoods are increasingly the principal casualty. It is in such an environment that the work of human rights activists is most needed, yet often least respected. In an atmosphere of tense polarisation, their impartiality is called into question. Further, new security measures introduced have also had a chilling effect on the environment in which human rights activists operate. We have to contend with the governmental discourse that prioritises 'security' (understood as prevention of terrorism) over human rights, and that sees the two as conflicting rather than mutually supporting policy goals. In such circumstances, human rights have come to be equated with 'being soft on terrorism' or concerned only with the rights of suspected terrorists, rather than one with the victims of terrorism. The work of human rights activists has itself to be equated with terrorism or subversion in the eyes of some governments.

However, in the present phase of Indian polity, human rights defenders, social justice movements and development practitioners are more at a receiving end, when they are taking the language and tools of rights into the sphere of economic and social policy. On issues of land, water, forests and mining, our government is hostile to the very concept of economic and social rights as enforceable entitlements. The experiences involved in identifying violations, attributing responsibility and proposing measures for redressal and prevention in these arenas lead us to also view these rights as less enforceable through legal means ('justiciable').

In all the cases of attacks on human rights defenders, there is a broader peoples' resistance, and then activists also fight their cases. However, the main point is that the governments have the obligation to protect human rights defenders as a special category. In 1998 UN adopted the UN Declaration on Human Rights Defenders, which, although not legally binding, draws together provisions from other legally binding conventions and covenants most relevant. The Declaration sets out the prime responsibility of states to take all necessary steps to ensure the protection of everyone who exercises their right to defend human rights. Among other things, the Declaration affirms the rights: to defend human rights, to freedom of association, to document human rights abuses, to seek resources for human rights work, to criticise the functioning of government bodies and agencies and to access international protection bodies. A Special Representative on Human Rights Defenders was also appointed in 2000. Our national human rights institutions, like National Human Rights Commission should take note of this fact for the protection of human rights defenders. True, our human rights activists have many skills and years of honed experience; there is no mystery or mystique to defending human rights. We all hold the potential of becoming human rights defenders.

(*The Hindu*, 29 September 2007)

12

A Trail of Violence:
Rights Activists at Risk

A.D. Babu, Karnataka Convenor of the National Alliance for Peoples' Movement (NAPM) has been killed recently. He was on his way to attend a NAPM-organised meeting of the anti-liquor campaign at Ramnagaram, along with couple of other colleagues when a group of people stopped the vehicle at Mayanagram, some kilometres before the meeting venue, and attacked him with knives and swords. He was killed on the spot. It is believed that the strong liquor mafia in Karnataka is behind this gruesome murder. In mid-May, Lalit Kumar Mehta of Palamau district, Jharkhand, was murdered who had been fearlessly raising the issue of corruption over NREGA. Narayan Hareka, a *naib sarpanch* from Kandha tribal community in the village Kambivalsa, Narayanpatna block, Koraput district, Orissa, who was fighting against liquor brewing, private money lending, land alienation and corruption, was murdered in early May 2008. Credible social activists Leo Saldanha and his wife Dr Lakshmi Nilakantan of Bangalore, are being targeted by the Karnataka police and the Forest Department for sandalwood smuggling, forest encroachment and theft, because of their role in unearthing the land scam in the controversial Bangalore Mysore Infrastructure Corridor Project.

Our monitoring highlights cases of human rights violations, including killings and attacks, threats and intimidation, against rights activists in different parts of the country. They are facing a series of obstacles to their work. They have to stop or radically curtail their activities. Direct attacks or threats to their lives sometimes mean that activists are forced to flee their homes or even areas. However, these violations also have wider repercussions by creating a climate of fear where other human rights activists are only too aware how easily they too could become the targets of direct attack. Harassment comes through a range of means including surveillance. We receive large number of complaints of raids and break-ins at the office of people's organisations or at the homes of rights activists. During these raids and break-ins, crucial human rights information related to their works are seized. The legal system is misused in order to harass and intimidate them. This also has the result of stigmatising the individuals and organisations in question and generating a negative perception of their work. Criminal proceedings that are initiated with unsubstantiated evidence or judicial proceedings that remain unresolved for extended periods of time are also seriously curtailing their ability to carry out their legitimate work. This is especially true of activists working in grassroots organisation at the local level.

The human rights situation in the country has been deteriorating rapidly. The killings of human rights activists are taking place in a context characterised by a fast-growing economy that is being accelerated by government policies. Those policies, particularly on land, agriculture and forced evictions are creating deep tensions. The police and administration are categorising as criminal all legitimate activities of human rights activists. At a time when the patterns of human rights abuses against rights activists are becoming widespread and showing signs of further deterioration, with the governments showing their apathy, we need to draw attention to the situation, point to the concrete failures of the governments to live up to their obligations, and plan on some concrete actions, so that the human rights activists can carry out their important work free from attacks, fear or reprisals.

At the heart of all peoples' rights work is the individual—as the person at risk of human rights abuses, as the survivor, as the partner in the defense of rights, and as the activist speaking out, and working with and for other individuals. Individuals, as part of the political, social and cultural collective and spread over the length and breadth of the country, lie behind much of the activism of Indian socio-political groups, working at local, grassroots and community levels. They try to change lives by acting on their own or with other people and political groups making the same demand—an end to injustice in all its forms. These individuals are always at risk. Despite this, no mechanism exists today at the district, state, regional or national levels, which offers any protection to those working to protect and promote our constitutional rights. The National Human Rights Commission (NHRC) and its state editions, and the Commission established for women, minorities or scheduled castes and tribes, are often addressed by the victim activists for redressal. However, in the absence of a focused system for monitoring, documenting and reporting human rights violations of human rights activists, and the lack of an approach for timely, proactive intervention to provide justice to them, the Commissions more often fail to arrest these continuing violations. Why do the Commissions themselves do not develop a system of taking actions on violations related with the rights activists?

Where are our governments, who are parties to numerous international and regional human rights treaties and, thus, have voluntarily undertaken a legal commitment to protect the rights activists? The Universal Declaration of Human Rights (UDHR) contains important standards relevant for the work of rights activists. In addition to the UDHR, the Declaration on the Right and Responsibility of Individuals, Groups and Organs of Society to Promote and Protect Universally Recognised Human Rights and Fundamental Freedoms (Declaration on Human Rights Defenders), which was adopted by the UN General Assembly in 1998, is a set of safeguards designed to guarantee and ensure the protection of human rights defenders. These include the right to know, seek, obtain and receive information about human rights and fundamental freedoms; the right to participate in peaceful activities against violations of human rights; the right to criticise and complain when governments fail to comply with human rights standards; and the right to make proposals for improvement. In line with the UN Declaration, why cannot the work of rights activists, including those working on economic, social and cultural rights, be recognised and legitimatised? Instead of them being harassed, the governments should take necessary steps to develop a national plan of action that should include multi-disciplinary proposals at the political, legal and practical levels, which aim to improve the environment in which rights activists operate; the measures to ensure their immediate protection and the allocation of appropriate human and financial resources.

In 2000, the UN Secretary General appointed a Special Representative to help implement the Declaration. Hina Jilani, a Pakistani lawyer and human rights activist, was the first Special Representative on Human Rights Defenders. Her mandate included producing reports, monitoring, country visits, individual action on cases of violations and making recommendations to improve protection of human rights defenders. When human rights defenders are at particular risk, the Special Representative can take urgent action on their behalf. In taking such actions, she usually depends on information from local human rights activists or international organisation working on their behalf. Since 2000, the Special Representative has sent over 1500 communications to governments, raising concerns about human rights defenders at risk. The Special Representative also carries out country visits. Unfortunately, not all countries co-operate with this system. Twenty-one countries have failed to issue an invitation allowing a visit, while others have not responded to her communications. (Commission on Human Rights, 2006) The mandate was given a new title of Special Rapporteur on the situation of human rights defenders in April 2008, and a new mandate holder, Margaret Sekaggya, a Ugandan lawyer and academic, was appointed. Why can't this mechanism also be evolved at a national level?

Along with mechanisms and laws, there is a need to call on a wider human rights community for intervention and support. This community must include political activists and leaders, non-governmental organisations, human rights bodies, international organisations and professionals. If the arrest of someone like Dr Binayak Sen is met with a lukewarm response from the established bodies of the medical fraternity and the intergovernmental organisations, if the recent killings of Narayan Hareka and Lalit Mehta do not even arouse an active response of those people and groups who are working on NREGA, it shows the lack of solidarity, networking and common action in the human rights community. Rights are not just concepts and laws. They are not only about project-making, training, advocacy and building capacity. They also mean showing courage and mobilising thousands of activists as fast as possible, when someone is arrested, killed, or facing immediate and often life-threatening human rights violations. If a fragile 'peoples rights concern' is to withstand the vagaries of political ebb and flow, future attacks on activists and practical applicability of rights will need to be anticipated and forestalled. The continuous hardships of rights activists, working in different contexts and cultures, presses the point that they must not remain only our reactive agenda, but should be a progressive proposition for a better future.

The future of rights is inherently connected to the ability of rights activists to operate freely and without fear. The murder of a NAPM or a NREGA activist sent out a clear and chilling message about the dangers faced by all those who speak out against injustice in India. It also sends a message that one of the best ways to attack rights is to attack those who defend them—a message all too frequently felt around the world. Fortunately, there are those brave enough to confront those attacks—among those participating in Lalit Mehta memorial events after his murder, were other rights activists for whom threats and intimidation remain a daily reality.

At a time when we have 'failed states' like Chhattisgarh and Orissa—those without any functioning human rights governance—there is formidable challenge for the work of human rights activists. Where the institutions necessary for the delivery of justice—from law enforcement to health care and education—are either entirely lacking or dependent on weak authority, and the rights are regularly abused by companies, armed groups, security forces and religious leaders, the challenge is how to work creatively with and through political and social structures, in order to prevent and redress immediate abuses, and build a framework of protective safeguards at the local and community levels as well.

(*The Hindu*, 26 July 2008)

13

The Right to a Fair Trial
and Binayak Sen

The right to a fair trial is a cornerstone of democratic societies. How a person is treated, when accused of a crime, provides a concrete demonstration of how far a state respects human rights. Detention is 'arbitrary', where there are often grave violations of the right to a fair trial. Detention and imprisonment, which may be lawful under national standards, are considered 'unlawful' under international standards. A fair trial is indispensable for the protection of other rights, such as the right to freedom from torture, the right to life, and the right to freedom of expression. This right should never be compromised. However, throughout the country, people are being detained and imprisoned without a fair trial. In these circumstances, many face torture and other forms of ill-treatment. The continued detention of Dr Binayak Sen, Vice-President of India's leading human rights organisation, the People's Union for Civil Liberties (PUCL), should trigger a debate, not only in Chhattisgarh, but also around the country, about whether and to what extent the right to a fair trial may be compromised in the name of security.

Dr Sen was detained on 14 May 2007. However, charges were not filed properly for seven months. In the meantime, he was denied bail, and was kept in solitary confinement for three weeks in March–April 2008. Much delayed, his trial commenced on 30 April 2008 and was adjourned till July. Before the trial began, the presiding judge announced that only one human rights activist could attend the hearing at a time, though he later relented, making the trial public. In jail, Dr Sen continued to suffer from severe gout, which posed difficulties for him to take care of his daily needs. He also suffered from frequent micturation, indicative of a prostrate problem. Despite appeals to organise proper medical treatment as per the jail rules, no concrete action came from the trial court. Before and during the trial proceedings, the prosecution and the police were attempting to intimidate the family members and colleagues of Dr Sen. The police so far has not produced any evidence from the materials in its possession, including a computer hard disk that they had seized from Dr Sen's residence and clinic. The police have yet to return the computer disk, ten months after getting it examined from the Hyderabad-based Forensic Science Laboratory, giving rise to doubts that it was being tampered to manufacture evidence. On every occasion that Dr Sen was brought to the court, there was massive police presence, leading to an atmosphere of fear and intimidation. Dr Sen has been charged under several sections of the Chhattisgarh Public Security Act, 2005 (CSPSA), the Unlawful activities (Prevention) Act (UAPA), 1967, and the Indian Penal Code. Both the CSPSA and the UAPA contain vague and sweeping definitions of 'unlawful activities', for which organisations may be rendered 'unlawful', such as 'uttering words...which propound the disobedience of established law and its institutions'. If convicted, Dr Sen could be sentenced to life imprisonment.

Abuse of the criminal process in a trial has a number of different, but related, aspects. Delay in the procedure, loss or destruction of evidence, abuse of power by the executive, use of unlawfully obtained evidence, prosecutor's improper motives, denial of the rights of victims—these are some of the several serious concerns raised, regarding the everyday practices of the criminal justice system in the country. Delay is a cause of serious injustices in India. Lengthy periods of per-trial imprisonment, anxiety, expenses, loss of days and memory—all lead to a situation where the accused cannot get justice. Further, in criminal cases the prosecution has a virtual monopoly on investigation. It is, therefore, axiomatic that the prosecution should not be able to evade their duties of disclosure, by suppressing, loosing, preventing or destroying evidence. Prosecutions in various situations, including in conflict zones, are resulting in an abuse of power by the executive, where unlawfulness or breach of law by the state agents has made it virtually impossible to give the accused a fair trial. So many times the evidences are obtained unlawfully, the admission of which has an adverse effect on the fairness of the proceedings. Not only this, the circumstances in which evidences are obtained are crucial. For example, in any proceedings, international law strictly prohibits the admission of evidence of statements obtained by torture.

Against these methods, there are various kinds of international human rights standards, national laws and court judgements, relevant to fair trials. Impartial, constitutional bodies exist, that give authoritative guidance on how to interpret these standards. Pre-trial rights (the right to liberty, the right of people in custody to information, the right to legal counsel before trial, the right of detainees to have access to the outside world, the right to be brought promptly before a judge or other judicial officer, the right during interrogation, *et cetera*), and rights at trial (the right to trial by a competent, independent and impartial court, the right to a fair hearing, the right to a public hearing, the presumption of innocence, the right to be tried without undue delay, the right to be present at trial and appeal, the right to call and examine witnesses, *et cetera*), are many. Thus, assessing the fairness of a criminal trial, and establishing peoples' rights is complex and multi-faceted. The severe shortcomings in our criminal justice system, and the unaccountability of the police, administration and judiciary, makes it virtually impossible to establish the right to a fair trial in contemporary India.

Derogations are many, and they are now being misused to illegitimately deny people their rights, under the cloak of a threat to national security. The police, army and administration become a law in themselves. However, seeing the various experiences in conflict zones, it must be emphasised that some core fair trial rights, and the right to habeas corpus, should be considered non-derogable. In such cases, the monitoring of trials is an important effort to protect rights. Public or experts' monitoring influences both the judge and the prosecutor to carry out their duties with impartiality and professionalism. The public has a right to know how justice is administered and what decisions are reached by the judicial system.

When an individual stands trial on criminal charges, he or she is confronted by the whole machinery of the state. Every criminal trial tests the state's commitment to respect for human rights. The test is even more severe when the accused is a political prisoner; when the authorities suspect the person of being a threat to those in power. When people are subjected to unfair trials, justice cannot be served. When people are tortured or ill-treated by law enforcement officials, when innocent individuals are convicted, when trials are manifestly unfair, or are perceived to be unfair, the justice system itself loses credibility. Unless human rights are upheld in the police station, the interrogation room, the detention centre, the court and the prison cell, the government has failed in its duties and betrayed its responsibilities. The risk of human rights abuses starts at the very first moment the officials raise suspicions against a person, through the moment of arrest, in pre-trial detention, during the trial, during all appeals, and right to the imposition of any punishment. The human rights community has developed fair trial standards, which are designed to define and protect people's rights through all these stages. They set out the minimum guarantees that all systems should provide. These should be the basis for a collective agreement amongst the community of state actors, for treating people accused of crimes.

Either a fair trial within a reasonable time period, or set the prisoner free without conditions; either an interference by an independent judicial authority to stop prosecutions which result from an abuse of power by the executive, or bail out/release the prisoner immediatelydecisive interventions are the need of the hour.

(*DNA*, 28 August 2008)

Dr Binayak Sen, who was held in Raipur prison in Chhattisgarh state, was released on 25 May 2009 after being granted bail by Supreme Court of India.

14

Wandhama Massacre: Justice Unfinished

I

States have an obligation to respect, protect and fulfill the right of victims of human rights violations to an effective remedy. This obligation includes at least three elements:

Truth: establishing the facts about violations of human rights that occurred in the past;

Justice: investigating past violations and, if enough admissible evidence is gathered, prosecute the suspected perpetrators;

Reparation: providing full and effective reparation to the victims and their families, in its five forms: restitution, compensation, rehabilitation, satisfaction and guarantees of non-repetition.

Basic principles on the right to a remedy and reparation for victims of gross violations of international human rights laws, adopted and proclaimed by UN General Assembly resolution, 16 December 2005, explains: 'Remedies for gross violations of international human rights law and serious violations of international humanitarian law include the victim's right to the following as provided for under international law: *(a)* equal and effective access to justice; *(b)* adequate, effective and prompt reparation for harm suffered; and *(c)* access to relevant information concerning violations and reparation mechanisms.

We can cite numerous international human rights treaties that have been voluntarily accepted by our government and place a legal commitment to protect the human rights of victims and sufferers like of Wandhama Massacre (The massacre refers to the murder of Kashmiri Hindus by unidentified gunmen, in the town of Wandhama near the town of Ganderbal in Kashmir. The victims, all of them Hindus, included four children, nine women and 10 men). Read the Article 2(3) of the International Covenant on Civil and Political Rights (ICCPR). It is also recognised in Article 8 of the Universal Declaration of Human Rights, Article 6 of the International Convention on the Elimination of All Forms of Racial Discrimination, Article 14 of the Convention against Torture and Other Cruel, Inhuman or Degrading Treatment or Punishment, Article 39 of the Convention on the Rights of the Child, Article 3 of the 1907 Hague Convention concerning the Laws and Customs of War on Land, Article 91 of the Protocol I Additional to the Geneva Conventions of 12 August 1949 relating to the Protection of Victims of International Armed Conflicts (Additional Protocol I), Article 75 of the Rome Statute of the International Criminal Court.

States must ensure that the truth is told, that justice is done and that reparation is provided to all the victims. In this context, our state is failed to meet its basic obligations in the context of Wandhama Massacre.

II

The forgotten human tragedy, like Wandhama massacre, is the battle against the impunity which has so far prevailed in all but a handful of cases for the tens of thousands of human rights violations committed by the state security services and armed groups in the past two decades. These violations were exhaustively documented by human rights groups as they occurred and were compiled in great details.

Take, for example, a recent report issued on 29 March 2008 by the Srinagar-based Association of the Parents of Disappeared Persons (APDP), Facts under Ground, that indicate the existence of multiple graves in localities which, because of their proximity of the Line of Control with Pakistan, are not accessible without the specific permission on the security forces. In response to the report army spokespersons again claimed that those found buried were armed rebels and 'foreign militants' killed lawfully in armed encounters with military forces. However the report detailed testimonies from local villagers saying that most of those buried were local residents hailing from the state. These are serious allegations that must be fully investigated. The report alleges that more than 8,000 persons have gone missing in Jammu and Kashmir since 1989, the central and state authorities state that the total amounts to less than 4,000, and that most of these went to Pakistan to join armed opposition groups. In 2006, a state police report confirmed the deaths in custody of 331 persons and also 111 enforced disappearances following detention since 1989. The state has failed to take responsibility to ascertain the fate or the whereabouts of a majority of the disappeared persons, especially in response to habeas corpus petitions filed in the state's courts.

Independent of the colour, creed, caste and religion, the failure of the government to bring the perpetrators of human rights abuses to justice result in a climate in which more and more human rights violations are committed in the state. Thus massacre continues.

III

Wandhama Massacre is not forgotten. *When considering the question 'should we remember?' it is very important to firstly ask, has any victim forgotten? Could they ever forget? Secondly we should ask, who wants to forget? Who benefits when all the atrocities stay silent in the past?*

Our state has a duty to collect evidence, even now, about the massacre. We should ensure a people's knowledge of its history and preserve its collective memory. However, it should not be done in a selective manner.

We must organise activities targeted at the discussion of the state's historical record of human rights violations. We can facilitate a critical debate among Jammu and Kashmir society on past human rights violations, we can establish archives for the preservation of documents and evidence. An important legacy of our work that such archives should be made and remain public. Our remembrance should also contribute to the establishment of an impartial and complete account of the historical past. Although new information will continue to come to light, the efforts would serve as an invaluable source for further and continuing human rights works.

IV

In the light of the above and to provide justice to the victims of Wandhama Massacre and others, we can urge to all, including the Government of India and the state government:

Unequivocally condemn the violence, massacre, enforced disappearances, encounters in Jammu and Kashmir;

Ensure that prompt, thorough, independent and impartial investigations into all sites of massacres, mass graves, encounters in Jammu and Kashmir are immediately carried out.

Ensure that all past and current allegations of massacres, enforced disappearances, encounters are promptly, thoroughly, independently and impartially investigated and that, where there is sufficient evidence, anyone suspected of responsibility for such crimes is prosecuted in proceedings which meet international fair trial standards;

Ensure that all victims of unlawful killings, enforced disappearance and torture are granted full reparations, including restitution, compensation, rehabilitation, satisfaction and guarantees of non-repetition;

Create a single authoritative and comprehensive database of the names and details, including where possible DNA information, of all individuals who have gone missing, who have been subjected to enforced disappearance, or abducted and killed in Jammu and Kashmir since 1989, and create a single official database logging details of all unidentified bodies found in Jammu and Kashmir. Make both databases public and accessible to relatives of these people;

Ratify the Rome Statute of the International Criminal Court;

Facilitate the long-standing requests for visits to India including Jammu and Kashmir, by the UN Special Procedures, in accordance with their long-established terms of reference for missions, in particular the UN Special Rapporteur on torture, the UN Special Rapporteur on extrajudicial, summary or arbitrary executions, and the UN Working Group on Enforced or Involuntary Disappearances by setting dates for them to undertake missions in the near future.

Ensure no one faces reprisals for seeking the truth about the fate of their disappeared relative; establish safeguards against reprisals in order to protect all complainants, victims and witnesses in accordance with international standards.

All of these requires working with a broader human rights community in and outside the state. This requires access to Jammu and Kashmir for human rights monitors. There are times when we are told that justice must be set aside in the interests of peace. It is true that justice can only be dispensed when the peaceful order of society is secure. But we have come to understand that the reverse is also true: without justice, there can be no lasting peace.

15

Death and Democracy

The demand for the execution of terrorists, notably Afzal Guru (convicted by the Supreme Court for attacking Parliament), is being justified now as democracy in action. For example, while alleging that the UPA Government has been pursuing appeasement policies towards the terrorists, Mr L.K. Advani, the leader of the Opposition in Lok Sabha, recently stated at the launch of a *vijay sankalp yatra* in Jabalpur that the issue of hanging of Afzal Guru should be seen as linked to peoples' will and aspirations, and national pride. The people want the death penalty, the argument goes, to eliminate crimes like terrorism. Not surprisingly, death penalty proponents are striking back, resurrecting emotionally-charged and conservative nationalist arguments. Chief among them is the claim that the death penalty deters crimes. When the death penalty is carried out in the name of democracy and nation's population, everyone needs to be aware of what death penalty and deterrence is, what is its actual utility in fight against terrorism, and where do we stand in the contemporary world in our support for executions.

We see a learning curve—downturn in support for the death penalty and time and reason are going against it. In 1970s, only 16 countries had abolished the death penalty. Today there are 90 countries that have total abolition, and 45 others that have abolished capital punishment in practice. In 2007, 89 per cent of all known executions took place in a five countries: China, Iran, Pakistan, Saudi Arabia and the US. Europe is almost a death penalty-free zone—the main exception being Belarus. In Africa, only five of the regions 53 countries carried out executions in 2007 and in the Americas only the USA has used death penalty since 2003. Amnesty International's statistics also showed an overall decline in the number of executions in 2007—a recorded 1,243 executions, compared to 1591 in 2006 and 2,148 in 2005.

Thus, for the first time, the UN's 62nd General Assembly on 18 December 2007 adopted a resolution for a worldwide moratorium on executions by a recorded vote of 104 in favor to 54 against, with 29 abstentions. The General Assembly saw two unsuccessful attempts to address the issue of the death penalty, in 1994 and 1999. In 1971 and 1977 the General Assembly adopted two resolutions on capital punishment, saying that it was 'desirable' for states to abolish the death penalty. Recent resolution goes further, calling on states that still maintain the death penalty 'to establish a moratorium on executions with a view to abolishing the death penalty'. It urges these states 'to respect international standards that provide safeguards guaranteeing the protection of the rights of those facing the death penalty' and 'progressively restrict the use of the death penalty and reduce the number of offences for which it may be imposed'.

Worlds propose, but our political leaders dispose, and continue to argue that executions deter crime. Our elected officials are failing to offer human rights leadership on this issue. However, they have at least the responsibility to show the rest of us that executions provide benefits that cannot be obtained by effective preventive measures, good policing and appropriate prison sentences. At least some standards should apply to questions of life and death. Scientific studies have consistently failed to find convincing evidence that the death penalty deters crime more effectively than other punishments. The most recent survey of research findings on the relation between the death penalty and homicide rates, conducted for the United Nations in 1988 and updated in 1996 and 2002, concluded: '...research has failed to provide scientific proof that executions have a greater deterrent effect than life imprisonment. Such proof is unlikely to be forthcoming. The evidence as a whole still gives no positive support to the deterrent hypotheses.'

Recent crime figures from abolitionist countries fail to show that abolition has harmful effects. In Canada, for example, the homicide rate per 100,000 populations fell from a peak of 3.09 in 1975, the year before the abolition of the death penalty for murder, to 2.41 in 1980, and since then it has declined further. In 2003, 27 years after abolition, the homicide rate was 1.73 per 100,000 populations, 44 per cent lower than in 1975 and the lowest rate in three decades.

Although this increased to 2.0 in 2005, it remains over one-third lower than when the death penalty was abolished.

Further, the situation in Pakistan or Iraq proves that even the executions of hundreds and thousands of their prisoners are not able to counter terror, terrorists and organised crimes. According to the Human Rights Commission of Pakistan, 361 persons were condemned to death in 2005. Thirty people were executed in the country in the months of June and July 2006. Currently, over 7400 prisoners are lingering on death row. Under the government of Saddam Hussain, the death penalty was applicable for a wide range of offences and was used extensively. Following the US-led invasion of Iraq, the death penalty was suspended in June 2003 but reinstated by the Iraqi Interim Government in August 2004. The use of the death penalty has increased rapidly in Iraq since it was reinstated in mid-2004. Since then more than 270 people have been sentenced to death and at least 100 people have reportedly been executed. The Iraqi authorities argued, when reinstating the death penalty that it was necessary as a deterrent in view of the grave security situation prevailing in the country. In the more than three years that have since elapsed, however, the extent of violence in Iraq has increased rather than diminished, clearly indicating that the death penalty has not proved to be an effective deterrent. If anything, it may have contributed to the continuing brutalisation of Iraqi society.

The death penalty has been and continues to be used as a tool of political mobilisation, as a means to silence political opponents or to arouse passion among individuals. Thousands have been put to death under one government only to be recognised as innocent victims when a new government comes to power. As long as the death penalty is accepted as a legitimate form of punishment, the possibility of political misuse will remain. A deficit of human rights and democratic leadership can only believe that urgent social or political problems like terrorism can be solved by executing Afzal Guru or a few or even hundreds of their prisoners. The 'iron fist' proposed by 'iron men' turns out to be discriminatory, unfair, and utterly inefficient. Democracy should not be turned into democratic killings.

Whether or not Afzal Guru's execution will represent Indian democracy in action, the state will carry out a killing far more calculated than the act for which this man is being punished (even presuming he is guilty). Democracy can surely do better than this.

As a Judge on the Constitutional Court of South Africa said more than a decade ago in the decision heralding the end of judicial killing in that country, 'There is ample objective evidence that evolving standards of civilisation demonstrate the unacceptability of the death penalty in countries which are or aspire to be free and democratic societies' (*The State v. T.Makwanyane and M Mchunu*, Constitutional Court of South Africa, 6 June 1995, Ackermann J., concurring). India should join the 135 countries that have abolished the death penalty in law or practice.

16

Land Development and Displacement in Delhi

The resources of lives and livelihoods of poor people in Indian society are being disposed of in innumerable ways. Whether it is land or house, forest or water, common property resources or individual property rights, the poor and powerless are under tremendous pressure in all these spheres to defend or expand their legal and constitutional claims. The land and houses of poor and working class people in urban India, especially in big and industrial cities, are some of the areas where the displacement has been taking place in the crudest and the most naked manner. When such displacement is being done not by any one agency, individual or group but by a close nexus of government and its several agencies, police, politicians, rich and powerful people, the situation is horrendous and sometimes, unbelievable.

On the south-east border of Delhi, about 8 kilometres away from ITO (a centrally located office complex), is situated Ashok Nagar of Chilla. Around 500 families of the area were forcibly displaced from their land and houses some 15 years ago. First, after 1980, the landlords, property dealers and their musclemen, along with the help of police, administration and politicians evicted many families, who had been living there legally. Then a large part of the land, bought legally by lower class families was handed over to a housing society of the rich and influential people of Delhi, breaking all rules and regulations of law and justice. In this case, the directions from the session courts to the Supreme Court were ignored and flouted by the Delhi Administration, Delhi Development Authority (DDA) and other concerned authorities. Not only this, certain facts which have come to light recently reveal that top bureaucrats of various concerned departments, politicians, bussinessmen and others were also involved in this loot of the land/houses of the poor people. And those who are thought to be protectors of the housing rights of poor and displaced have actually become their destructors. In these years, the displaced families have come together under the name of Ashok Nagar Welfare Association and are trying to restore their land and houses.

Situated on the banks of Hindon river, Ashok Nagar touches the border of Uttar Pradesh and is surrounded by Noida in the east, Hindon in the west, Dallupura village in the north and Saraswati Kunj Group Housing Society (SKGHS) in the south. Attached to Ashok Nagar is New Ashok Nagar which has many shops, small factories and houses. It is estimated that Ashok Nagar and New Ashok Nagar are situated in around 920 bighas. The old residents recall that around 1970s, there started a change in the structure and composition of this region. The villagers started selling their land and in this process, colonisers and property dealers also brought huge pieces of land and after cutting them into different sizes of plots, started selling them. Land was cheap and precisely for this reason, it was the relatively weaker sections of the society who bought these plots. The available official documents testify that a coloniser, Jawahar Lal, bought land in 1971–72 from villagers. This land was divided into many khasra numbers, that is, 391/263,393/264, *et cetera*. The land in khasra number 391/263 has about 72 bighas of land, out of which 287 residential plots of 200–200 square yards were made. And in khasra number 393/264, about 76 bighas of land was made into 174 plots of 200, 400 and 500 square yards. Besides that, khasra number 392/264 and 402/268 had 24 bighas of land which was sold by villagers themselves. The residential plots of all these khasra numbers were named as Ashok Nagar and Ashok Market.

It is important to note that Delhi Development Authority gave a No Objection Certificate for the use of this land for residential purposes, which reads thus: 'It is certified that the above-stated land has not been notified for Delhi's planned development' (X.N. Bose, Additional Housing Commissioner, Vikas Bhawan, New Delhi, Utter No F 7(7)72, L and H, 405, dated 11 August 72 and No 7 (58), dated 19 August 72 and No 7 (58), dated 19 August 72). From 1972–73 on, construction of houses began on these plots. Basic necessities like water, electricity, roads, transport, *et cetera*, were not available, yet many families got ordinary rooms made. By 1980, Ashok Nagar was established and more and more families settled there. Those already settled and those who had purchased the land, together formed the Ashok Nagar Welfare Association in 1980, so that various schemes to develop the area could be worked out in a systematic manner. And the Association soon prepared their 'site plan' and submitted it to the government agencies. With time, the importance of this area increased because it was not very far from Delhi's centre and also the areas located near it had developed commercially. The importance and price of Ashok Nagar land increased many-fold. As the region came into limelight, the property dealers, politicians, government agencies and others started getting attracted towards it. The land and houses belonging to poor families became an eyesore for them. Thus came the evil designs to uproot them.

Hundreds of uprooted families of Ashok Nagar are a living testimony of the aggression being continuously unleashed on them for the last 20 years. Most of these families are living in Delhi in rented houses. Mohan Singh, 40 years old, is the president of Ashok Nagar Welfare Association. He says angrily, 'I originally belong to the Hardoie district of U/P. As I got a government job in Delhi in 1971, I rented a house and started living with my family. The house rents were going high and my transfer was also not possible, so I decided to build a small house in Delhi. I took loan from my PF and purchased land in Ashok Nagar in 1978 through court registry. I was desperate, so I immediately built a three-room house and shifted there with my family. From 1978 to 1980, we were living in peace there. In the initial months of 1980, anti-social elements and goondas started harassing us. One night, we were severely attacked by an armed group. Some other families were also attacked. The next day we all went to the local police station and lodged our complaint. Nothing happened. We were being harassed regularly. One night again, the armed people attacked our house and threatened me that if I don't leave the house, they would kill me. Again we went to the police, but they refused to give us any security. Totally shaken, we left our house with all our belongings. After that, we have never been able to go back to our house. Somebody told us that our house is being demolished now by property dealers and they are selling our land to other people.'

Shanker Das, 55 years old, is a fourth-grade employee in a bank. He left Mandi (Himachal Pradesh) in 1952 and finally got a job in

Delhi. In course of time, he sold his house and land in Mandi and took all his family members to Delhi. Shanker Das recalls,

> Some of my office colleagues had purchased land in Ashok Nagar. We were friends. We all wanted to build our house and live together. So I purchased land and even took some loan from my office. At that time, Ashok Nagar was a descried place without any facilities. We all-Gopal Singh, Dhan Singh, Munshi Ram, Bal Kishan, Om Prakash Saini—built our houses in 1972–73 and shifted there with families. Till 1980, everything was normal. After that, we were at the mercy of local goondas. When we formed our Association, goondas got violent. They forcibly took away our hand-pump, bricks and sand. They were throwing stones at our houses in the night. One day when they entered into our house and misbehaved with the family members, we got terribly upset and decided to leave the place. Property dealers and their musclemen have demolished our one room and the other room is lying deserted. But we can't dare to go to our house. We go to Ashok Nagar only in the darkness of a night and come back after taking a glimpse of our land-house. There is no money to buy any other plot. We don't know where will we go after my retirement.

Amar Singh, 65 years, old is a petty shopkeeper. His father and family came to Delhi in 1948 after the partition. He got a small house in Patparganj where his three brothers and their families live till date with a lot of problems. Amar Singh wanted to build a house for his child, as there is no space in Patparganj house. He purchased a 400 square yard plot in 1977. In 1980 he built two rooms along with boundary walls. Amar Singh narrates, 'We actually never got a chance to live in Ashok Nagar. Seeing the situation over there, we decided not to move. But we always thought that this would be a temporary phase and we would be able to claim our house some day. But that day never came.'

Prakash Oari's husband purchased the land in 1971, He died some years ago without any house of his own in Delhi, Oari recalls painfully, 'We shifted in our Ashok Nagar house in 1976. We were living there for seven-eight years. In 1980, all the trouble started and threats, abuse, attacks became regular happenings. Though we remained there till 1984, when all our neighbours moved, we also lost our strength... Many years have passed now. We have no hope. House gives pleasure and peace, but here the house became the root cause of all our problems. My husband died because of this.'

Prabhu Lal, Usha Sahgal, Mulk Raj, Ram Kumar, R.P. Yadav, Prabhu Dayal, Sagarwati, Parasu Ram, Kusum Choudhary, Sharda Mathur, Satpal Uppal, Manju Rani, Som Dutta, Hukumchand—interviews with almost 30 people reveal similar stories. All of them legally purchased land in Ashok Nagar and built their houses. They were also living there for many years. But after 1980, they were being the target of attacks by colonisers, property dealers and their henchmen. Hundreds of them have been displaced in this process. Others are also facing the same threat. And in spite of their repeated appeals to all the government agencies, from the local police station to the prime minister of India, they are being denied the right to reclaim their land and houses.

Role of Delhi Development Authority

It is not only the coloniser, property dealer and their goondas who are the culprits, the DDA too has played a prominent role in the loot of the land and houses of the poor people at Ashok Nagar. A detailed analysis of various facts shows that the DDA has an alliance with colonisers and the co-operative housing societies of powerful people and it has helped in dislodging the residents of Ashok Nagar with a total disregard for laws and court orders.

In 1972, the DDA had issued a certificate for the same land which stated that the land has not been notified for the planned development of Delhi, This certificate was a guarantee that buying land and building houses in this area is legal and safe. That is why, many poor and needy people bought land and built houses. But on 17 November 1980 in the name of public interest, 920 *bigha*s of land of village Chilla Bangar were notified under the Land Acquisition Act 1894 in which the newly emerging Ashok Nagar was also included. Actually the DDA did not care for the proceedings of the act. The residents of Ashok Nagar never came to know when and how, under Section 4 of the Land Acquisition Act, the government expressed its desire to acquire their land. Since the residents did not get any information, they were unable to file in any complaint. Then the Administration declared its intention to acquire the land under Section 6 of the act. In this way, at no stage were the residents of Ashok Nagar given the opportunity to challenge the proceedings of acquisition.

There are many revealing facts in this regard. The DDA conducted the proceedings quickly and quietly. It is learnt from the records of DDA that Land Acquisition Collector declared the award (Award No. 39, 82–83) for the land on 30 September 1982. The next day only, that is, on 1 October 1982, they handed over the land to DDA. That day itself, a list of 103 people was prepared who were to be given compensation for the acquired land. That means, all the proceedings of the award, acquisition and compensation were done within two days, primarily to deprive the residents of their right over land and houses. In fixing the compensation of the awarded land, there are surprising discrepancies. According to the award, a list of 103 people was prepared and Rs 8,183,860 was fixed as its compensation. But out of the list of 103 people, tabulation of land of 88 people is written as 'no evidence' as they have no registered record or any other proof. The remaining 15 people have the registration of land, but all these registries were done in 1980 only. Thus, the list has the names of people who had registrations of as late as 1980 but not of those who had got their land registered in 1970–72 only. Also, as a blatant case of tampering of records, though several claimants have been maintained in the khasra numbers of Chilla Bangar village, in the same document under the title of 'market value', they are being shown to live in some other place/area. Their sale deeds and the areas/places to which they belong do not have any relevance to the area/land of Ashok Nagar or Chilla village. There are a number of such unrelated sale-deeds. Thus it becomes clear that the government officials tampered with the revenue records in which the legal inhabitants have not been included. This fact also establishes the massive corruption in the disbursement of compensation money. It is surprising that not a single person of Ashok Nagar has received any compensation till date. Obviously, the officials, colonisers and their people have together made huge amount of money.

But this whole episode cannot be understood only in terms of the corruption of the officials of the DDA. Many facts reveal that the chief motive of the entire government machinery was to snatch away land from the poor and weak residents of Ashok Nagar and utilise this land for the rich and powerful of the city. Under this motive only, various laws related to land and houses were surpassed. The colonisers and officials were given a free hand. And the land of poor people of Ashok Nagar kept moving into the hands of the others.

Building for the Elite

There are enough facts to suggest that the DDA, even before acquiring the land at Ashok Nagar, had made the plan to use this land for the benefit of rich of the city, The DDA declared the award for the Ashok Nagar land on 30 September 1982 and it usurped it on 1 October 1982. Thus, all the legal proceedings related to the acquisition of Ashok Nagar land were completed on 1 October 1982 itself. But the DDA had already entered into an alliance regarding one part of the Ashok Nagar land even before it declared the award. The DDA had already sold a part of the land of Ashok Nagar residents to Saraswati Kunj Group Housing Society (SKGHS) on 2 February 1982. Five acres of land of Ashok Nagar residents was sold to the society and an advance amount of Rs 2,225,850 was taken (Challan Number 18904, dated 25 February 1982 and 21801, dated 6 May 1982. This process continued and on 15 May 1983, SKGHS was given away 21 acres of land of Ashok Nagar. On 14 August 1986, the DDA even took Rs 9,689,570 from SKGHS as the cost towards the entire land (Perpetual Lease Number 1691 dated 26 August 1986).

SKGHS is a society of the rich and powerful of the city and for the DDA, their interest was uppermost. Though the society was formed and registered in February 1980, soon it was allotted land at two sites, Patparganj and Ashok Nagar. Plots were allotted measuring 5 acres and 21 acres at each of these locations. Some of the prominent persons who have flats in the housing complex of the SKGHS include Sheila Kaul ex-central minister, Rajesh, son of Gundu Rao, ex-chief minister, Karnataka, Mubeena, Sabnam and Naveed, children of central minister A.R. Antulay, Zamila Kidwai, daughter of A.R. Kidwai, ex-governor, S.R.M. Burney, son of S.M.H. Burney, ex-governor, Haryana, Lily George, wife of V. George, private secretary to Sonia Gandhi, Priyadarshini, wife of S. Narendra, ex-principal information officer, government of India, A.N. Verma, principal secretary to the ex-prime minister. Ramu Damodaran, former PS to the prime minister, Bharat Kaushal, son of former Delhi police commissioner, M.B. Kaushal. K.J. Alphonse, commissioner (Land), DDA, Natasha Gill, daughter of M.S. Gill, ex-election commissioner, Aditya Arya, Deputy commissioner of police, Neera Jakhanwal, wile of former DDA vice-chairman, Sudipto Roy, commissioner (land), DDA, Kewal Sharma, commissioner (housing), DDA. This is a long list which also includes some prominent judges, journalists, artists and corporate executives. The presence and power of these people made it possible for SKGHS to acquire full control over the land and houses of Ashok Nagar residents and even the various court orders did not dither them.

The displaced families have taken recourse to-various agitational and legal methods in these years. From individual applications to collective memorandums, delegations, dharnas, demonstrations, they are struggling endlessly. In a desperate search for justice, they have also moved different courts at different times. They were able to get some favourable judgements, though there are still a large number of cases pending in the courts for the last several years. But all these judgements and the cases have, for all practical purposes, no bearing on the Delhi Administration, the DDA, the Delhi Police or the SKGHS.

When the DDA was handing over the land to SKGHS, Ashok Nagar Welfare Association sought the help of the courts. A stay order was passed by the High Court of Delhi against the housing ministry, Delhi Administration, Land Acquisition and Delhi Development Authority (CMP Number 2040/84 in CWP Number 1507/84, dated 1 June 1984). The same order was confirmed on 18 July 1985. Besides this, on the plea of one villager, the high court (CWP Number 3796 of 1982) and ultimately Supreme Court gave a stay order against any kind of use of this land (SLPNo 9381 and 31221 of 1985), But in spite of this order, the land went to SKGHS. When SKGHS started construction on the land, the Association submitted an application to the court and then they also filed a contempt of court petition (vide number 144/91). The high court appointed a local commissioner to look into this issue and the commissioner in his report blamed the society's administrator and the DDA officials for contempt of court. But even then the construction continued. In an extremely depressing situation, the association filed a special leave petition in the Supreme Court (SLP No 16852-53/1992). The Supreme Court ordered on 15 February 1992 that 'within three months this case must be resolved in the high court'. But to no avail.

There are several stay Orders in favour of the displaced families of Ashok Nagar. The high court stayed the proceedings of land acquisition on 18 July 1985 against the government of India, Delhi Administration, DDA and Land Acquisition Collector and confirmed the same order on 18 July 1985. The court ordered for the regularisation of the colony (CMP Number 1507/87 in CWP Number 1507/84 dated 8 September 1989). The high court passed two orders against unsocial elements and trespassers (Suit Number 273/86, dated 6 February 1986 and Suit Number 1704/90, dated 5 February 1992). Apart from this, there are six cases pending in the high court against the DDA and the police officials and the trespassers. There are seven cases pending in the district court against the trespassers. There are three cases pending against the trespassers in the SDM and metropolitan magistrate court since 1982. And above all, there are three cases pending in the Supreme Court. As the displaced families and their association have been getting more and more involved in the long legal battles, the government and the rich societies have found ways either to ignore the court orders or to make them totally ineffective.

It is really amazing to know how the state and its various organs worked vociferously in all directions against the poor people of Ashok Nagar. Though their colony is in existence since the 1970s and the association had filed its claim for its regularisation in the 1980s, they have never been included in the list of regularised colonies. During these years whenever the government has passed an order regarding regularisation of some colonies, Ashok Nagar has always been left out. For example, the government of Delhi passed an order regarding the water and electricity policy in the left out pockets of the regularised unauthorised colonies and other unauthorised colonies which were existing as on 31 March 1993, However, Ashok Nagar was left out. They are also not being included in the new list of colonies to be regularised in the future in spite of fulfilling all the conditions and filing all the documents to the concerned departments.

The poor and weak families of Ashok Nagar have countless experiences of attacks and repression by colonisers and goondas: the loot and plunder by a housing society: the conspiracy and connivance of the state; and the indifference of socio-political organisations. It took several years to complete the process of displacement of Ashok Nagar's families and to this date, illegal sale and occupation of their land and houses is continuing. But the way the various powerful interests are united today in the big cities against the land and housing rights of the poor is really revealing. That is why, the cry for justice, raised many a times by the families of Ashok Nagar and supported sometimes by the judiciary, has been suppressed. For the last 15–16 years, these families have been lacing repression, failure and uncertainty, which is back-breaking. But amidst all this, they are also trying to look for ways to survive as well as to strengthen their efforts. As Mohan Singh, president of the association says, 'Since the 1980s we have had to pass through extremely difficult situations at several stages, so many times entirely alone. But the fact that we are still there and are determined to be there, in our struggle for justice, proves that sheer force and brutality is not going to finish us'.

Section III

Business and Human Rights

17

Conscience of the Company

Jagatsinghpur, Orissa

Tension was high in Jagatsinghpur district in January–February 2008 after the state government, amidst the presence of heavy police force, resumed socio-economic survey for the POSCO steel project in four villages of Gadakujang gram panchayat in Jagatsinghpur district. Since June 2005, Jagatsinghpur district has witnessed frequent protests against possible displacement following the Government of Orissa's decision to enter into an agreement with POSCO to enable the latter to set up its integrated steel plant. Since February 2006, protestors have erected barricades in the area where the plant is to come up and prevented officials from entering several villages. The area witnessed violence in February, April and September 2007.

As recent as in November 2007, reports say that in Jagatsinghpur district, a 500-strong armed militia encircled the villages of Dhinkia, Nuagaon and Gadakujang and started attacking farmers. More than 20 protestors have been injured in attacks by militias using country-made weapons including crude bombs. At least one protestor has been taken hostage by the militias. Reports also indicated that despite the fact that around 1,000 police officers have mobilised in the area, they have not acted to protect the communities.

Instead of forcing and pushing ahead with the project, should POSCO not be thinking of the ways of avoiding forced evictions? Should they not be announcing and implementing a prior and consistent policy of full consultation with local populations before putting in place any measures which could affect their human rights and livelihood opportunities? Should they not be concerned about the use and misuse of force and firearms by the state in favour of the business interests?

Bhopal, Madhya Pradesh

A gas leak in 1984 took the lives of more than 7,000 people in Bhopal over a three-day span, and a further 15,000 in the years that followed. The leak came from a pesticide plant owned by Union Carbide Corporation (UCC), now owned by Dow Chemical (DOW). The company is still denying its responsibility, and refuses to reveal the toxicological information of the gas, thwarting medical efforts to deliver appropriate treatment to more than 100,000 surviving victims. Should not there be a conscience of the company, which ensures that the Bhopal factory site and its surroundings are promptly and effectively decontaminated, that the groundwater is cleaned up, that the stockpiles of toxic and hazardous substances left at the site are removed, and that full reparation, restitution, compensation and rehabilitation are promptly provided for the continuing damage done to people's health and environment by the ongoing contamination of the site? Should they not be ashamed of the lack of effective regulation and accountability systems, which have meant that court cases are dragging on, and corporations and their leaders continuing to evade accountability for thousands of deaths, widespread ill-health and ongoing damage to livelihoods?

Of course, our government has the primary obligation to secure universal enjoyment of human rights, and this includes an obligation to protect all individuals from the harmful actions of others, including companies. However, while the government has been frequently failing in regulating the human rights impact of business or ensuring access to justice for victims of human rights abuses involving business, the companies too have been complicit in their human rights abuses. In a democracy, a government will be taken to task for its failure. At the same time, there has also to be a call for the companies to be conscience and accountable for their activities related to human rights. A few of them claim to engage with human rights responsibilities through voluntary consultations, relief and rehabilitation initiatives. While these have a role to play, such voluntarism can never be a substitute for concrete standards on businesses' mandatory compliance with human rights. In India, as a minimum requirement, all companies should respect the right to information; free, prior, informed consent; and no displacement without rehabilitation, regardless of the sector, state or context in which they operate.

We all know that India today is marked by a rapid increase in business, trade and investment, facilitated by the government and its institutions, the World Trade Organization, and regional and bilateral trade agreements. The role of national and international companies as major investors in Special Economic Zones (SEZ) and beyond has created a new dynamic, where they have no qualms about moving fast and operating in contexts where contests over human rights issues are intense, and where conflicts over violations form the backdrop to the companies' activities. Our foray into the field of investment and people's rights should reflect a wider critical focus on the human rights implications of investment and industrialisation from a broad spectrum of bodies, ranging from national–international laws, UN basic principles and conventions, to peoples' organisations and pressure groups. Of particular concern is the ad hoc nature in which investment rules are framed, often without reference to other laws (for example, SEZs do not take note of the Panchayat Act or the Forest Rights Act), as well as the lack of transparency on application of these rules, and on mechanisms for resolving disputes. At the heart of our concern is an individual, a village, a community, whose rights are adversely affected by the investment, and who lacks access to justice, and effective remedies for damage caused.

A Right-to-Information Loophole

Ironically, domestic right-to-information laws drafted partly in response to corruption and peoples' demands do nothing to reveal on information outside the government domain. The Indian and foreign companies operating in the country are not required to disclose any information. The lack of disclosure has resulted in environmental, labour, and human rights abuses, which have given rise to public distrust and unrest among communities around the country.

In a country that has become pro-active in new industrial projects, this disclosure gap is a dangerous imbalance that challenges economic and political stability and contributes to a growing number of people who have limited means of protecting and empowering themselves. Because of the lack of disclosure, we have several documented cases where reputed foreign companies have engaged in irresponsible and destructive practices in India. When companies act irresponsibly, they are on the fire. At the time of integrated markets, peoples' networks and political consciousness, campanies cannot afford to close themselves or to relate only with the government. It is also in their own self-interest, to promote more transparency and accountability around their work so that communities are empowered and civil society has the chance to flourish. This could start with establishing Right to Information disclosure standards based at least on the principles of existing domestic disclosure standards that protect people in the government sphere.

What is the Right to Information in this context? Put simply, by requiring companies based in India or trading in Indian stock exchanges, their foreign subsidiaries and major contractors, to disclose information on industrial operations, including the Memorandum of Understanding (MoU) with the governments, land requirements, potential employment generation and rehabilitation. This goes beyond environmental disclosures and public hearings, and includes information relating to labour and human rights practices. This is because there are too many cases where companies are complicit in forced relocations, forced labour, child labour and a wide range of other unsafe operating practices. There are practical and ethical reasons for empowering communities around the world through right to information disclosure standards. These include standing up for our natural resources, defending people's health and safety, promoting labour rights, and championing community rights.

Information disclosure standards for industries should must include informations on *(a)* **Environmental impacts**—data on production, process and toxic releases and health risks to the local community *(b)* **Labour standards**—information on worker exposure to chemicals and basic labour practices including child labour *(c)* **Human rights practices**—terms of agreements between companies, government and local authorities including security agencies and *(d)* **Community relocation**—information on whether and how many people are going to be relocated from their homes or lands to accommodate business interests.

Legally binding disclosure requirements must be an important part of the Right to Information. Unfortunately, voluntary right-to-information initiatives have always failed to produce uniform and complete information. For example, when non-governmental organisations and governments alike have sought unilateral disclosure of pollutant releases through voluntary reporting initiatives, most companies have refused to provide data. In Mexico, where reporting of toxic emissions has been voluntary, only about five per cent of companies release data.

Disclosures have worked in many countries. For example, in the United States, the Toxic Release Inventory (TRI) has been hailed as a model by both citizens and businesses. TRI requires companies in a wide range of industries to publicly disclose their annual emissions of toxic chemicals into land, air and water. The TRI program provides communities and workers essential information about the conditions they face, information that has often been used to take action. For example, TRI has been used to convince IBM to phase-out ozone depleting CFCs, and helped a local community obtain a commitment from BF Goodrich to reduce its toxic airborne emissions by 70 per cent. Many other businesses have improved their practices in response to the toxics right-to-know law, following the dictum that 'what gets measured gets managed'. According to Environment Protection Agency data, industries reduced releases by almost 50 per cent in just the first decade of TRI. In 1995, the Chemical Manufacturers Association lauded TRI as a 'very successful venture'. Investors in the stock market have also benefited. Statistical analyses show that valuations of companies have been affected by TRI data —with the benefits going to more responsible companies.

This standard is not onerous. The argument one can make against right to information is that the disclosure requirements would be too onerous and costly and would put an unfair burden on companies. However, this is contradicted by the fact that some of this reporting is already taking place at some development projects. ExxonMobil's Chad-Cameroon oil development pipeline project is one example. ExxonMobil began construction on the World Bank sponsored project in 2000. One of the terms of the World Bank agreement required ExxonMobil's subsidiary, Esso Chad, to produce a progress report four times a year. The report documented many aspects of construction, including environmental, labour, community consultation and human rights issues. Many supporters of the Chad-Cameroon pipeline, including officials in the US government and at the World Bank, tout the project as a 'model for development'. While we can disagree with this assessment and can stand with local communities organising to improve conditions, Esso Chad's disclosure requirements proved two things. First, that such reporting is not too onerous, and second that reporting standards are generally recognised as important aspects of successful projects.

Free and Prior Informed Consent

The key principle for safeguarding people's rights in industrial development is the establishment of mechanisms that ensure a full and effective participation, and a 'free and prior informed consent' (FPIC) of the communities concerned. The companies and the government together must realise that the principle of FPIC is increasingly emerging as a methodology for designing programmes and projects, which either directly or indirectly affect people. 'Free' should imply no coercion, intimidation or manipulation. 'Prior' should imply consent has been sought sufficiently in advance of any authorisation or commencement of activities, and respect time requirements of indigenous consultation/consensus processes. 'Informed' should imply that information is provided that covers (at least) the nature, size, pace, reversibility and scope of any proposed project or activity; the reason/s or purpose of the project and/or activity; the duration of the above; the locality of areas that will be affected; a preliminary assessment of the likely economic, social, cultural and environmental impact, including potential risks; and fair and equitable benefit sharing in a context that respects the precautionary principle. For 'Consent', consultation should be undertaken in good faith. The parties should establish a dialogue, allowing them to find appropriate solutions in an atmosphere of mutual respect, and full and equitable participation. Consultation requires time, and an effective system of communication among interest holders. Indigenous people should be able to participate through their own freely chosen representatives and customary or other institutions. This process must include the option of withholding consent.

The notion of FPIC is a much more recent expression. It is only since the mid-1980s that indigenous peoples have made their demand for recognition of their right 'to give or withhold their free, prior and informed consent to actions that affect their lands, territories and natural resource' a central part of their struggle for self determination. Governments and private companies have made very varied responses to the demands of indigenous peoples for respect for their rights, both to their lands and to have control over what happens on them. We have positive example from countries like the Philippines, where the law provides recognition of indigenous peoples' rights to their ancestral domains and explicitly requires Free, Prior and

Informed Consent, and where detailed procedures have been developed to guide the application of FPIC. The right of indigenous peoples to FPIC is now increasingly recognised in the jurisprudence of international human rights treaty bodies. Observation of this right has now been recognised as 'best practice' or as required policy in a number of standards including in development projects, resettlement schemes, environmental and social impact assessments, dam construction, extractive industries, logging and plantation schemes, palm oil estates, the use of indigenous peoples' intellectual property or cultural heritage, micro-finance and the establishment of protected areas. In other sectors—such as for soya, eco-tourism, biofuels—discussions about the principle are underway.

A report, 'Making FPIC – Free, Prior and Informed Consent – Work: Challenges and Prospects for Indigenous Peoples' by Forest Peoples Programme, summarises some indigenous peoples' experiences with applying the principle of FPIC in Suriname, Guyana, Peninsular Malaysia, Peru, Indonesia, Papua New Guinea and the Philippines. National laws vary widely in the extent to which indigenous peoples' rights to their lands and to FPIC are recognised. Even where these rights are recognised, there are notable deficiencies in implementation. In the same way, even where corporations profess to respect indigenous rights and international law, they may not adhere to their own standards in their actual dealings with communities. Corruption, manipulation and other malpractices are all too common but these are problems confronted by indigenous peoples everywhere and are not specific to FPIC. The report also explores the options of who should verify that the right to FPIC has indeed been respected and how this should be done. It summarises some experiences with third-party audits for the FSC in Indonesia and suggests that verifiers are unduly lenient about what constitutes adequate compliance, thereby weakening any leverage that communities may gain from companies' obligations to respect their rights and priorities in accordance with FSC voluntary standards. However, verification of FPIC procedures by government as in the Philippines has also proven problematic.

Company's conscience can be driven by different references. In the 60th anniversary year of the Universal Declaration of Human Rights (UDHR), we should remind ourselves that every individual and every organ of society, which includes companies and business operations in general, has a duty to protect the interests, health and safety, and human rights of employees and their dependents, of business partners, associates and sub-contractors, and of the communities in which they operate. The eight Fundamental Conventions of the International Labour Organization, the Declaration on Fundamental Principles and Rights at Work, the Basic Principles on the Use of Force and Firearms by Law Enforcement Officials, the Human Rights Principles and Responsibilities for Transnational Corporations and Other Business Enterprises, the Global Compact, and many such principles must be translated into operating policies. Taking massive advantage of the growth in foreign direct investments, and the globalisation–liberalisation of international trade in goods and services, companies cannot only restrict themselves to the imperfect national laws and practices, for their advantage. As the company integrates into the global economy, it must play by global rules. A POSCO-India or Vedanta needs to realise that their plants should come up without the use of state security, force and firearms. Otherwise the results can be fatal. Lessons should be learnt by the companies from the unfortunate episodes of violence which took place in Kalingar Nagar in 2006 (also in Orissa) and Nandigram (in neighbouring West Bengal) in 2007, where local communities were protesting possible displacement due to the planned construction of an industrial project. The use of disproportionate violence by the police resulted in 13 deaths in Kalinga Nagar in January 2006. In Nandigram, over the last year, at least 50 people, mostly local farmers, were killed. And in both the cases, the companies couldn't commence their projects. Today, the companies, including Dow, who are lobbying with the Indian government to allow and guarantee them trouble-free investment in the country, should understand that without a conscience of the company, such conflicts will abound in future. The only effective remedy for these companies is to make respect for people's rights an integral component of their business, and adopt an explicit company policy based on the principles stated above. Company's problems today in Jagatsinghpur, Kalinga Nagar or Singur are closely intertwined with the way the companies operate, and that unless important changes are made to enhance respect for rights and the rule of law, the business environment will not improve in a sustainable manner. Common minimum standards which aim to protect people from unfair treatment and abuse from companies should be the basis of the rule of law.

Global steel company POSCO and Orissa Government signed a Memorandum of Understanding (MoU) in June 2005 for the construction of a steel plant as well as development of iron ore mines in the state. According to the MoU, POSCO will build a 3 million tonne capacity steel plant during the first phase in Paradeep, Orissa between 2007 and 2010 and expand the final production volume to 12 million tonnes. The investment proposed is to the tune of US$12 billion, including an initial investment of US$ 3 billion during the first phase. The Government of Orissa will grant POSCO mining lease rights for 30 years that will ensure an adequate supply of 600 million tonnes of iron ore to POSCO. The government will also promote the construction plan for railways, roads, industrial water and electricity keeping up with the steelwork construction plan of POSCO. According to POSCO India, Indian subsidiary of POSCO, the key factors that have been taken into account by POSCO for entering Orissa included the highest projected growth rates over 2006–2020, the skilled workforce and abundant natural resources, especially of iron ore, coal and chrome.

18

Corporate Complicity and Gujarat

The fourth 'Vibrant Gujarat Global Investors' Summit, organised by the Gujarat government on 12–13 January 2009 in Ahmedabad, and the statements by some prominent Indian corporate leaders, have spawned protests, analysis, debates and questions about corporate accountability, complicity, responsibility and rights in Indian democracy. At this biennial event, 'Jai Jai Garvi Gujarat' has been showcased as an 'ideal investment destination, both for Indian and foreign investors', where prospective investors have 'only Red Carpet and no Red Tape and it is where investors can sow a rupee and reap a dollar as returns' (see Official portal of Gujarat Government).

Bringing together business leaders, investors, corporations and policy makers by a democratically-elected government, exploring business opportunities and signing memorandum of understandings are legitimate economic activities. However, the projection of the chief minister of the state, Narendra Modi, as the next prime minister of India by corporate cheerleaders is much more than mere economic activity. It is turning a blind eye to gross abuses of rule of law, and knowingly assisting a political leader and his government to continue committing them. It is becoming party to a specific political vision in a manner that incurs responsibility and blame. Corporate leaders are 'complicit' with a government and its leader in serious human rights abuses. It is negative and unacceptable. Our understanding is continuously emerging and developing about where to draw the line between corporate conduct that should be stopped, and conduct that reflects a legitimate business choice or at most could be criticised in policy or ethical terms. Even if we do not offer companies the certainty about their legal liability for such complicity, we can certainly point broadly to thresholds of action and behaviour beyond which the businesses will be at least in a zone of potential public liability and legal scrutiny. On this basis, we can suggest that the corporate must, at a minimum, avoid this sort of conduct.

Six decades ago senior company officials were convicted for actively helping the Nazi regime to commit some of the worst war crimes imaginable. These business leaders, often working through their companies, supplied poisonous gas to concentration camps, knowing that it would be used to exterminate human beings; actively sought slave labour to work in their factories; acquiesced or helped in the deportation, murder and ill-treatment of slave workers; donated money to support the criminal, and enriched their companies by plundering property in occupied Europe. Reports of business participation in regressive political regimes did not stop with the end of World War II. The proposition that thriving trade and business investment can help to raise people's standard of living has not allayed concerns that businesses can also do considerable harm. With this development, there should also be a spotlight on corporate conduct across the state—some of which stretches back over the last six years—and calls for accountability.

Gujarat today is also the place of some of the worst human rights abuses, which often have devastating effects, not only on individual victims and their families, but also on the communities and societies in which they are taking place. Abuses that are an infringement of a flagrant nature amount to a direct and outright assault on universally recognised rights. These abuses include, for example, killings of minorities, enforced disappearances, encounters, extrajudicial executions, prolonged arbitrary detentions, and torture. Remember the communal violence in March 2002, in which 2,000 people, mostly Muslims, lost their lives and an armed attack on Akshardham temple in September 2002, in which 37 Hindu devotees and three security personnel were killed. Police and other security personnel, believed to be responsible for widespread violations of human rights against the Muslim minority, especially the youth, in Ahmedabad and elsewhere in Gujarat, continue to operate without fear of investigation or prosecution. Remember the case of Sohrabuddin Shaikh, where the Gujarat state government admitted in the Supreme Court of India that senior state police officers, who were part of an Anti-Terrorist Squad (ATS), were directly involved in the killings of a 38-year-old man, Sohrabuddin Shaikh, and his wife, Kausar Bi, in 2005.

After his killing in 2005, the ATS branded him as a terrorist member of Lashkar-e-Toiba (LET), an armed organisation in Kashmir, and accused him of conspiring to kill senior leaders of the Bharatiya Janata Party, including the Chief Minister Narendra Modi.

The Government of Gujarat remains unrepentant for its failings to protect the Muslim minority, and to ensure that victims obtain justice, truth and reparations. Several credible organisations have reported that a climate of alienation and fear has been deliberately fostered among the Muslim minority in Gujarat since the violence in 2002. These reports have also been corroborated by the findings of a central government-appointed high level committee led by a former Supreme Court judge, Rajinder Sacchar (the Sacchar Committee), and mandated to look into the 'social, economic and education status of the Muslim community in the country'. Commenting on the committee's findings, which had been tabled before the Indian parliament in November 2006, one of the committee members, Prof. T.K. Oommen, stated that Gujarat continues to reel under a state of 'economic apartheid and ghettoization' of Hindus and Muslims and that 'ever since the 2002 riots, the polarisation of communities in Gujarat has acquired a physical dimension'.

In the specific context of Gujarat, and otherwise as well, business is a major actor, and is gaining greater than ever reach and power. Complex relationships between businesses and individuals, communities and governments mean that business operations do impact immeasurably on human beings. Some businesses now wield considerable political influence and possess more economic power than government officials. Many have developed close business and political relationships with those in power. Thus, corporate and company have to face questions of complicity, as they have business operations in regions where gross human rights abuses are occurring, and they fail to intervene with the authorities to try and stop, or prevent, such abuses. They are silent onlookers. How could corporate be silent when abuses occur in or around its business operations, such as when its workers from a particular religious group are arbitrarily detained or killed, or an armed group kills civilians in an area where the company is operating? Their silent presence is proudly portrayed by the perpetrator to communicate approval, and encouragement, of their model. Greater the economic and commercial influence wielded by a company, more is the likeliness of corporate finding themselves in such situations. Presence and silence might be neutral in law, but it has great political, moral and ethical values.

Closely related to the question of silent presence is the concern that companies are considered complicit because they are benefiting commercially from a business relationship with those who commit gross abuses. The so-called 'red carpet' business environment—infrastructure, access to resources, absence of trade unions—are often a result of a rights-free setting. Even though corporate today may not in general incur legal responsibility solely for making profit in a business environment built on abuses, in reality and practicality, seeing their enthusiasm and pro-activeness to appease certain political regimes, the passive economic benefit quickly slides into a more active contribution that enables, exacerbates or facilitates gross abuses.

Our companies can open their eyes to other experiences. The different degrees to which businesses contributed to the perpetuation of apartheid in South Africa and the associated gross human rights abuses illustrate the complexities of analysing whether company conduct is sufficiently close to human rights abuses to be said to have enabled, exacerbated or facilitated the abuses. The South African Truth and Reconciliation Commission (TRC) concluded that business was central to the economy that sustained the apartheid state. It distinguished three levels of moral responsibility. Companies that actively helped to design and implement apartheid policies were found to have had 'first-order involvement'. This included, for example, the mining industry which worked with the government to shape discriminatory policies, such as the migrant labour system, to their own advantage. Companies which knew that the state would use their products or services for repression were considered as having 'second-order involvement'. This included more indirect assistance, such as banks' provision to covert credit cards for repressive security operations, or the armaments industry's provision for equipment used to abuse human rights. This contrasted with more indirect transactions that could not have been reasonably expected to contribute directly or subsequently to repression, such as building houses for state employees. Finally, the Commission identified 'third-order involvement', that is, ordinary business activities that benefited indirectly by virtue of operating within the racially structured context of an apartheid society.

Corporate have common defences and excuses: we are carrying out a legitimate business activity; if we did not go there, another company would have done; we are nowhere near the place where the abuses occurred; we had no control or influence over the actions of the government, so why should we be blamed; we are just abiding by laws; we are a socially responsible company and have spent a lot of money to improve the humanitarian and developmental well-being of the community. However, with the emergence of a broadening concept of corporate responsibility in our interconnected world, these defences are weak and outdated. We are all seen in some way to be implicated in the harm being inflicted in often distant lands, whether it is fuelling the loss of rainforests by buying furniture made of tropical wood, or encouraging child labour by buying footballs made in child sweatshops. With this heightened sense of moral responsibility for the fate of others, even the distant, indirect and most complex actions of businesses have to be closely scrutinised. Mary Robinson, former United Nation's High Commissioner for Human Rights, asserts that 'business decisions can profoundly affect the dignity and rights of individuals and communities'.

While there are many situations in which businesses and their officials are the direct and immediate perpetrators of human rights abuses, allegations are frequently made that businesses have become implicated with another actor in the perpetration of human rights abuses. In such circumstances, human rights organisations and activists, international policy makers, government experts, and businesses themselves, now continuously use the phrase 'business complicity in human rights abuses' to describe what they view as undesirable business involvement in such abuses. Just as the concept of impunity in the sphere of human rights has taken on a multi-faceted meaning, much more sophisticated and colourful than its strict historical–legal connotation, in the context of business and human rights, the concept of complicity is now used in a much richer, deeper and broader fashion than before. It is critical to develop such tools of accountability, which can have a significant impact in terms of improving business practises. The work of the corporate should not be to only nullify or limit the concept of complicity to situations in which legal liability may arise or be alleged. The law too is changing and evolving rapidly, and complicit conduct, for which businesses may not face legal responsibility today, may well attract legal liability in the future, as the law responds to developing concepts of moral responsibility. Businesses should, therefore, be guided as much by the Indian constitution, public policy and ethical considerations as by marketplace realities, and beyond a technical appreciation of whether they currently could face allegations of legal liability or legal sanctions.

What does it mean for a business to be 'complicit'? What are the consequences of such complicity? How can businesses avoid becoming complicit? How should they be held to account for their complicity? In many respects, although the use of the term is widespread, there continues to be considerable confusion and uncertainty about the boundaries of this concept and in particular when legal liability, both civil and criminal, could arise. In order to address some of these questions, the International Commission of Jurists asked eight expert jurists to form the Expert Legal Panel on Corporate Complicity in International Crimes in March 2006. The Panel was created to explore when companies and their officials could be held legally responsible under criminal and/or civil law when they are involved with other actors in gross human rights abuses. The Panel members were leading lawyers in different fields of expertise, from five continents, and representing both common law and civil law legal traditions. The focus of the Panel's analysis has not been the legal accountability of businesses and their officials when they are the direct and immediate perpetrators of gross human rights abuses. Rather it has addressed avenues to legal accountability when businesses are allegedly involved with other actors in gross human rights abuses. The Panel asked in what circumstances international criminal law, and to some extent domestic criminal law, could hold companies and their officials criminally responsible when they participate with others in gross human rights abuses that amount to crimes under international law. They also looked briefly at the important role that criminal law plays in ensuring the accountability, and preventing the impunity, of actors involved in such abuses and considered the ways in which international criminal law has developed over time.

Notwithstanding these positive initiatives, the prospects for human rights-based approaches to corporate complicity remain elusive. Gujarat shows that business is not ready to accept an analogy between private corporations and the state in terms of human rights responsibilities. The legal issues rose by such situations need to be properly developed. We need to set some precedent whereby it is possible to show that the corporate directly violated fundamental rights or aided and abetted the host state in such a violation, including 'turning a blind eye' to state violations from which the corporation profited.

Section IV

Asia/Africa

19

Bangladesh: Faces of Emergency and Human Rights Issues

Cholesh Richil had no charges of corruption or criminal activity in Bangladesh, which is ruled under emergency and a civilian caretaker government, backed by the army. An outspoken leader of the Garo indigenous community, who live in the Modhupur area north of Dhaka, Cholesh had been campaigning against the construction of a so-called 'eco (ecology) park' on their ancestral land, on the grounds that it would deprive them of their land and means of livelihood. He was arrested by the Joint Forces (army and police) personnel on 18 March 2007 and taken to Modhupur Kakraidh temporary army camp. Tortured for several hours before being taken to Madhupur Thane Health Complex, he was declared dead the same evening.

After Choesh Richil's body was handed over to the Garo community church on 19 March, his family observed multiple bruises, nails missing from his fingers and toes, and cuts and scratches consistent with blade wounds. His testicles had been removed. Local government officials have stated that an 'administrative inquiry' into the case has been initiated, but none are aware of the terms of reference or the progress of the inquiry.

A country where more than 100,000 people have been detained, often in mass arrests, since early January, and no way to establish the total number of those who remain in detention, abuses against human rights defenders, social activists, journalists and NGOs in Bangladesh are occurring frequently during the emergency. According to a Dhaka-based human rights organisation Odhikar's report, prepared on the basis of 11 national dailies and its own fact-findings, during the first 130 days of emergency in Bangladesh, from 12 January to 21 May 2007, a total of 96 persons were reportedly killed during different operations by the law-enforcement personnel. In addition, 193,329 were reported arrested, inclusive of general arrests for violations of law. Of the 96 reported killed, 54 were killed by the paramilitary Rapid Action Battalion (RAB), 25 by the police, 7 by the joint forces, 6 by the army and 3 by the navy. One person was reported killed by officers of the Department of Narcotics Control.

Of course all the successive governments in Bangladesh have shown a disregard for human rights, but with the emergency, along with political rallies and other political activities banned, and restrictions imposed on the right to freedom of expression, the excesses are neither exposed nor protested against. What is further disturbing is that in the name of cleaning up of corruption or criminal activity, emergency and subsequent measures are being used to institutionalise a cycle of cumulative disregard for human rights in general, and for abuses against human rights defenders in particular. A cycle of impunity for human rights violations, which has prevailed in the country over its decades-long existence, is becoming a daily affair today.

In this environment, a larger social constituency is at severe risk. Take another recent case of Shahidul Islam, the founding director of Uttaran, a NGO working for the social and economic empowerment of the poor and the disadvantaged communities in the western districts of Khulna, Satkhira and Jessore, who was arrested and taken into Joint Forces' custody on 27 January 2007. Following the arrest, he was served with a Detention Order under the Special Powers Act (SPA) on the unspecific grounds that he had 'engaged in acts of terrorism and had harboured terrorists'. The police subsequently filed several criminal charges against him, apparently as additional means of securing his continued detention. Several days later when Shahidul Islam was allowed to have visitors, it was discovered that he had been severely beaten on his legs and his back, as the Joint Forces personnel accused him of possessing illegal weapons. He had to be sent to the Satkhira Sadar Hospital for treatment, and was later returned to the Satkhira District Jail, where he remains till today.

Agents of the state, including the police, the army and the other law enforcement personnel, for whom successive governments in Bangladesh have been directly accountable, have perpetrated several human rights violations in the past. Other perpetrators of human rights abuses are individuals or groups linked to armed criminal gangs, parties of the ruling coalition or the opposition, or mercenary gangs allegedly hired by the local politicians to suppress revelations about their unlawful activity. Hundreds of social and human rights activists have received death threats. Scores of them have been attacked. Several journalists have had their fingers or hands deliberately damaged so as not to be able to hold a pen. Many have had to leave their homes and localities in the face of continued threats. An Amnesty International report documents that from 2000–05, at least eight human rights defenders have been assassinated by assailants who are believed to be linked to armed criminal gangs or armed factions of political parties.

A detailed analysis reveals that people and groups working in areas of search for truth and justice, strengthening of the rule of law, increasing government accountability, struggle for gender, sexual and racial equality, children's rights, rights of refugees, struggle against corruption, environmental degradation, hunger, disease and poverty, have particularly been the targets of attacks. With the emergency, arbitrary arrests and detentions of a wide spectrum of social activists have taken place. Such detainees are also reported to be tortured or ill-treated, while in custody. Special Powers Act, Code of Criminal Procedure, Dhaka Metropolitan Police Ordinance 1986, and other similar acts are being excessively used. Special Powers Act overrides the safeguards in Bangladesh law against arbitrary detention, and allows the government to hold a detainee for up to four months without charge or trial. The Dhaka Metropolitan Police Ordinance empowers the police to detain anyone 'found under suspicious circumstance between sunset and sunrise'.

The liberal space for expression of opinion has been progressively shrinking under successive governments in Bangladesh. However, under the emergency and army rule, it is becoming much worse, chiefly due to three reasons: fundamental rights to freedom of expression, and to equality before the law have been curtailed by individuals or groups connected to the army or the ruling coterie; the continued prevalence of corruption in the police force; and the abuse of institutions of the state by caretaker government authorities for their undemocratic agendas, which further strengthens a cycle of impunity for human rights abuses.

We know for sure that in South Asia, including India, administrative detention procedures during a state of emergency result in torture, and at such times there are no established clear and enforceable safeguards against such abuses. Proclaiming emergency is a non-desirable, anti-people act, and it plays no part in the sustainable combating of crime or corruption, or the maintenance of public order. Bangladesh has performed badly in the areas of law reforms and institution building from a human rights perspective. One of the few countries in the region, governments in Bangladesh have failed to set up a National Human Rights Commission, and the office of the Ombudsman—which is a constitutional requirement—has never been established. Frequent concerns have been raised about a number of legal practices which allow the executive to improperly influence the judiciary.

Failing to address such many serious issues, the caretaker government is suppressing the voices that are raising these concerns. The stories of Cholesh Richil and Shahidul Islam are illustrative of broader patterns of killing, torture, violence and impunity that are happening within the country. The power seized by the president or the army has not at all meant action against shielded politicians, military, police and other officials responsible for grave human rights violations; rather just the reverse is happening. Seeing the repressive regime within, it is important to raise concerns outside about the human rights situation in Bangladesh, so that the government can be taken to task in bilateral or multilateral forums.

(*Economic and Political Weekly*, Volume 42, No. 32, 11 April 2007)

Bangladesh emergency was lifted on 17 December 2008. The country went through the general elections on 29 December 2008.

20

The Road to Al-Qa'ida
Starts in Pakistan

Serial killings of human rights activists, lawyers, journalists and political party activists, and assault on key institutions of accountability, combined with sweeping powers to the army, have exacerbated patterns of human rights abuses, including torture and other ill-treatment, arbitrary detention, enforced disappearances and use of excessive and blind force, to suppress dissent in Pakistan. In the name of 'war on terror', the country is destroying the very guarantors of stability that it claims to be defending. Without an immediate end to the outrageous assault on Pakistan's vibrant human rights community, institutions of justice and independent media, the climate of fear and suspicion, threat and harassment, murder and killings, will further aggravate. Yesterday it was Hayatullah Khan, today it is Benazir Bhutto, and tomorrow it will be Asma Jehangir.

Remember the killing of journalist Hayatullah Khan, who was working for an English language daily, *The Nation*, and an Urdu language newspaper *Ausaf*, and was also the Secretary General of the Tribal Union of Journalists. A 32-year-old father of four, his body was found on 16 June 2006, near Mirali, North Waziristan, after more than six months of enforced disappearance. His body was reportedly emaciated; he was hand-cuffed and had apparently been shot five times in the back of his head. He had been abducted by armed men in civilian clothing on 5 December 2005, while on his way to cover a rally in Mirali Bazaar, protesting against a missile attack four days earlier. Hayatullah Khan was the first journalist to photograph pieces of shrapnel that the local villagers said they had found in the rubble of a house in Haisori, North Waziristan, which was destroyed in a missile attack. The shrapnel found at the site was reportedly stamped with the words 'AGM-114', 'guided missile' and the initials 'US', and apparently belonged to a Hellfire missile. These missiles are usually used by the US Air Force's remote controlled Predator drones. After countrywide protests by journalists and tribal groups, the federal government on 19 June 2006 announced a judicial inquiry under a Peshawar High Court judge, and the provincial government set up a departmental inquiry. However, nothing came out in the public.

We also know how Dilawar Khan Wazir, *Dawn* and *BBC Urdu Service* correspondent from South Waziristan, was abducted by men in plain clothes from Islamabad on 20 November 2006. He was released on the evening of the following day, after over 24 hours in detention. In a statement, fellow journalists said that they had reasons to believe that 'Dilawar's abductors...wanted to silence one of the few remaining journalists who have been reporting independently from the tribal areas'. No investigation was carried out, and no steps taken.

President Musharraf's autobiography, *In the Line of Fire*, published in September 2006, claimed:

> We have done more than any other country to capture and kill members of Al-Qa'ida and to destroy its infrastructure in our cities and mountains.... We have captured 689 (suspected Al-Qa'ida members) and handed over 369 to the United States. We have earned bounties totalling millions of dollars. Those who habitually accuse us of 'not doing enough' in the war on terror should simply ask the CIA how much prize money it has paid to the government of Pakistan.

However, this statement also sheds significant light on Pakistan's illegal conduct in the name of 'war on terror'. The descriptions of raids, arrests and transfers to US custody contained in the book, corroborate several of the other findings—that arrests were carried out in breach of custodial safeguards under either the regular criminal law or the Anti-Terrorism Act; that no criminal charges were brought against terror suspects; and that detainees were denied the rights guaranteed by the Constitution of Pakistan, including to engage a lawyer of their choice and to contact their families. Hundreds of Pakistani and foreign nationals have been picked up in mass arrests in Pakistan since 2001; many have been 'sold' to the USA as 'terrorists', simply on the word of their captors; and hundreds have been transferred to Guantánamo Bay, Bagram Airbase or secret detention centres, run by the USA. It is also to be noted that enforced disappearances rarely occurred in Pakistan before 2001, but since then the practice has been used frequently against perceived political opponents, including Baloch and Sindh nationalists.

In this scenario, Pakistan has now the largest number of disappeared people in this region, regarding which the Human Rights Commission of Pakistan notes in its report of 2004: 'A relatively new form of violation of citizens' most fundamental rights...was the phenomenon of disappearance, something that was not witnessed before or at least not to the extent now recorded.' Similarly, the Pakistani Senate's Functional Committee on Human Rights in July 2006 expressed concern about rising enforced disappearance in the country. The precise number of those subjected to enforced disappearance is difficult to ascertain. The Human Rights Commission of Pakistan estimates there are at least 600 cases in Balochistan alone, Baloch groups put the number in the thousands.

After the court cases, several people subjected to disappearances have reappeared after being arbitrarily detained in secret locations for over two years on average. Each was warned not to speak publicly about their experiences and detention. For example, Ali Sher (28), a mechanic, was released late on 20 November 2006 after over 18 months of enforced disappearance. Ali Sher was arrested by an intelligence agency on 3 May 2005 in Mardan for alleged links to al-Qa'ida. According to the petition filed by his father and elder brother, Mohammad Israr, Sher Ali had been dropped off by his brother at around 9 am at Mardan Bazaar. When he failed to return home, his family searched for him, without success. On the following day the *Daily Mashriq* reported that two suspicious (unnamed) people had been arrested. The *Daily Express* on 25 May 2005 reported that Sher Ali had been arrested by an intelligence agency.

Any hopes were further dashed after the proclamation of a state of emergency in Pakistan on 3 November, and the disarray in the Supreme Court. On 13 November 2007, Pakistan's Supreme Court was due to hear the cases of 485 individuals, all victims of enforced disappearance over the past six years. The dismissed Chief Justice Iftitkar Choudhry was instrumental in ensuring that previous cases of disappeared persons were heard in the Supreme Court. And the Supreme Court had been taking a tough stance on alleged disappearances, calling on the government and state security services to bring detainees to court.

The proactive role of the Supreme Court in seeking to provide redress to victims of enforced disappearance helped to trace several individuals subjected to enforced disappearance who were released either on the orders of the Supreme Court or were simply released by the detaining authorities once the Supreme Court had begun hearing such cases. The higher judiciary may have anticipated that this process would be halted if it held those responsible for enforced disappearances to account. On several occasions, the Supreme Court emphasised that its primary task was to trace people and that it would address questions of accountability later. This in itself is an indictment of the executive which made it impossible for the higher judiciary to ensure full redress of enforced disappearances by ensuring accountability and ending impunity for this grave human rights violation. Provincial high courts have routinely dismissed habeas corpus petitions when state representatives denied detention of the persons concerned or knowledge of the whereabouts of detainees without questioning these statements further. Similarly the Supreme Court did not question in whose custody persons subjected to enforced disappearance had been once they were released.

There are dozens of cases on record where no attention was paid to the identity of the detaining authority and consequently no one was held to account for enforced disappearances. The father of Ansar Ali, Aziz Akbar Kiyani, stated before the Supreme Court on 11 October 2007 that his son had been picked up in his presence on 7 January 2004 by a team of ISI personnel, comprising three persons in plain clothes. Ansar Ali was taken away on the pretext of questioning him but his whereabouts remained unknown until, on 10 October 2007, his father was contacted by phone and asked to go to a particular location on Talagang Road, Chakwal, Punjab province, where his son would be brought from Lahore. Intelligence agents arrived in two cars and released his son. His son later told him that a colonel and two majors of the Federal Investigation Unit (FIU) had brought him from Rawalpindi to Chakwal. Despite clear evidence that he had been subjected to enforced disappearance for three years and 10 months in the illegal custody, the Supreme Court did not initiate any inquiry in this regard and did not hold anyone to account.

Despite the urgency of habeas corpus matters, courts have permitted long adjournment of hearings and failed to respond to Human Rights Commission calls to set up a separate bench to hold daily hearings of cases of enforced disappearance. Faced with defiance by state officials when the latter refused to adequately respond to judicial directives, courts did not always exhaust all means at their disposal to enforce their directions. Judges did not take any judicial action, such as recourse for contempt of court legislation, when after the state's denial of detention, the person concerned was found to be in state detention. Judges, while threatening criminal prosecution for enforced disappearance, did not initiate any action.

Even worst, several children of various ages have been detained in Pakistan in the pursuit of 'war on terror'. Some were arrested alongside their adult relatives; some were alleged to be terror suspects; and some were held as hostages to make relatives give themselves up or confess. Some of the juveniles were arbitrarily and unlawfully transferred to the US custody, and later shifted to Guantánamo Bay. Clive Stafford Smith, lawyer for some 40 Guantánamo detainees, confirmed the presence of Pakistani juvenile detainees at Guantánamo.

Pakistani nationals, handed over to US custody in war of terror, have suffered immensely. Amongst them is a famous case of Majid Khan. He migrated to the US with his family in 1996, was granted asylum in 1998 and subsequently worked for the state of Maryland. In 2002, he returned to Pakistan to get married. On 5 March 2003, Pakistan security officials raided his brother's house in Karachi and arrested Majid Khan, his brother Muhammad Khan, sister-in-law and their month-old baby. They were bound and blind-folded taken to an unknown location. His wife was at the time with her family in Hyderabad. Majid Khan's sister-in-law and her baby were released one week later, his brother about a month later, after warnings not to publicise the arrest and whereabouts of Majid Khan. In the US, Majid Khan's family members were repeatedly interrogated by the FBI. They heard nothing from Majid Khan until President Bush's announcement on 6 September 2006 about the transfer of the 14 men, including Majid Khan, to Guantánamo Bay. Majid Khan has been held incommunicado for three and a half years in secret custody. He may have been subjected to torture or other ill-treatment. He has not been charged with a crime or brought before any court. The US authorities have said that he will receive a hearing by Combatant Status Review Tribunal (CSRT) to review his status as an 'enemy combatant'. The US government also indicated that it may bring to trial some or all of the 14 transferred detainees before military commissions, which would have the power to admit coerced evidence and hand down death sentences. On 28 September 2006, the New York-based Center for Constitutional Rights (CCR) filed a habeas corpus petition on behalf of Majid Khan in the District of Columbia (DC) District Court, challenging the lawfulness and conditions of his detention, and his designation as an 'enemy combatant'. On 8 October 2006, CCR followed this with a request for emergency access for legal counsel to Majid Khan, including to be able to assess his mental and physical health in the light of his time in secret CIA custody and the use against him of any of the 'alternative' interrogation techniques authorised for use in that programme. The US government responded by arguing that under the Military Commissions Act (MCA), signed into law by President Bush on 17 October 2006, the District Court did not have jurisdiction to consider Majid Khan's petition. The government also filed its opposition to access to legal counsel, arguing that the 14 detainees transferred from CIA custody might be in possession of information about the CIA programme—including location of facilities, conditions of detention and specific interrogation techniques—which could cause 'exceptionally grave damage' to US national security were it to be revealed. On 17 November 2006, the DC District Court denied the lawyers access to Majid Khan. In a footnote, the judge urged the government to address Majid Khan's medical and psychological state but stated that he could not order the government to do this. On 20 November 2006, Rabia Yaqoob filed a constitutional petition in the Sindh High Court requesting to be informed of the grounds for her husband Majid Khan's arrest and detention, of the grounds for not producing him in any court in Pakistan, of the legal basis of his transfer as a Pakistani citizen to US custody and of any government efforts to ensure his return to Pakistan. Till end-2008, there was no relief/release for Majid Khan.

The Government of Pakistan appeases Taleban. Take the case of the designated tribal areas of the country, particularly those bordering North Wazirstan, where Taleban fighters appear to enjoy a safe haven. Taleban control over the area has consolidated as a result, with quasi-governmental structures—administrative bodies, tax collection, judicial structures and a 'penal code'—being established by them. An indication of the government's lack of control in the region is the impunity with which a growing number of people have been killed for their alleged sympathy with the government, the army or the US. Some 160 tribal elders are believed to have been killed over the last two years in these tribal areas, with no one being held accountable for their deaths.

In September 2006, a document prepared by an official of the Defence Academy, a think-tank linked to the UK Ministry, which was leaked to the press, alleged that the Inter Service Intelligence (ISI) was supporting the Taleban. Seth Jones of the Rand Corporation, a think-tank which works closely with the US military, stated in November 2006 that his government believed the ISI to be involved in providing training, money and sensitive information to the Taleban, especially 'information…about movement of US and NATO forces, in some cases very strategic information'. During his visit to the US and UK in September 2006, President Musharraf admitted the possibility of 'some dissidents, some retired people' in the ISI supporting the Taleban. He told the BBC on 30 September that 'if the ISI is not with you and Pakistan is not with you, you will lose in Afghanistan'.

The killing of Benazir is, of course. a high point of the destruction of democracy and dissent in Pakistan. However, in the everyday life of Pakistani society, the clandestine nature of the 'war on terror' and the dismantling of democratic institutions, make it impossible to ascertain exactly how many people have been killed, forcibly disappeared, or extra-judicially executed. Terrorism is an assault on Pakistan people's fundamental rights. However, a narrow focus on 'terror' by the Pakistan government and its allies has led to a scandalous neglect of Pakistan's poor. Violence and terror is only breeding more violence and terror. Pakistan is miserably failing to meet the Millennium Development Goals. Disparity, discrimination and alienation continue to fester in the hearts of majority citizens of the country. The only way to fight the menace and to go forward is for the people to stand up and for others within political wings to recognise that protecting peoples' rights is an essential component for protecting democracy.

After general elections on 18 February 2008, a coalition government comprising the Pakistan People's Party (PPP) headed by Benazir Bhutto's widower Asif Ali Zardari, the Pakistan Muslim League-N (PML-N) led by former Prime Minister Nawaz Sharif, the Pashtun nationalist Awami National Party (ANP) and the Jamiat Ulema-i-Islam (JUI) was sworn in on 31 March 2008. On 9 March 2008,

PPP and PML-N leaders issued the 'Murree Declaration' in which they committed their parties to jointly take measures to reinstate the unlawfully deposed judges within 30 days of assuming office. On being elected by the National Assembly as new prime minister on 23 March 2008, Yusuf Raza Gilani's first act was to order the release of all Superior Judiciary judges who were still under unlawful house arrest after their dismissal on 3 November 2007. However, the deadline set in the Murree Declaration and a further deadline on 12 May passed without the parties reaching agreement on the modalities of reinstatement. PML members of the cabinet resigned in protest on 13 May but Nawaz Sharif pledged his party's continued support for the PPP-led coalition government. In late May 2008, the PPP presented a comprehensive set of constitutional amendments that include ensuring the independence of the judiciary and providing steps for the judges' reinstatement. Differences over how the independence of the judiciary can be ensured and the judges reinstated have persisted and continued to weaken the coalition government. The lawyers' movement, consisting of members of the country's Bar associations, began a new phase of agitation for the reinstatement of judges in mid-June 2008. Pervez Musharraf resigned on 18 August as the new elected government in Pakistan threatened him with impeachment proceedings. Asif Ali Zardari was elected as the new president on 6 September 2008 by the members of the national parliament and four provincial assemblies who formed the electoral college for the election of the president.

21

Legacy of the Beijing Olympics: China's Choice

As the Olympic torch approaches China for its momentous entry into the Olympic stadium, the stage is overshadowed by grave human rights concerns in Tibet. Olympics are certainly a collective celebration of sports. However, according to the International Olympic Committee (IOC), the goal of the modern Olympic movement is also 'to contribute to building a peaceful and better world by educating youth through sport practised without discrimination of any kind and in the Olympic spirit'. And remember, when Beijing was chosen to host the Games, the Chinese authorities themselves repeatedly drew a link between the Olympic Games and human rights during the selection process itself and further made assurances that human rights situation in China would improve in the run-up to the event.

Beijing Olympics and Human Rights

Read Liu Jingmin, Vice President of the Beijing 2008 Olympics Games Bid Committee, stating in April 2001, 'By allowing Beijing to host the games, you will help the development of human rights'. Or hear Liu Qi, Mayor, Beijing on 14 June 2001, '[The Games] will help promote all economic and social projects and will also benefit the further development of our human rights causes.' The IOC has echoed these statements: 'We are convinced that the Olympic Games will improve [China's] human rights record' (Jacques Rogge, president of the IOC, 24 April 2002). It has also claimed that it is the role of human rights organisations to monitor and report on the state of human rights in China before the Olympics. And that if the human rights situation in China was not acted upon to its satisfaction, thus undermining the Games, the IOC would step in. Thus, there is no wrong in holding the Chinese authorities and the IOC to their statements. In this context, the Games are indeed a milestone by which to measure the Chinese government's resolve to improve the situation in Tibet and elsewhere in the country. Human rights issues should be presented as a decider between a positive or a negative legacy for the Games—the opportunity is there, and it is for the Chinese authorities to take it.

Crackdown on Tibetan Protestors

Events in Tibet and neighbouring provinces since 10 March 2008 speak a volume about the violation of protesters' right to freedom of expression, association and assembly, including through excessive use of force. Estimates by overseas Tibetan organisations of those having died in the crackdown across Tibet and neighbouring Tibetan areas range from 79 to 140, with estimates of those detained ranging from 1200 to over 2000, and with at least 100 having disappeared. The government claims 19 people have died in Lhasa, including 18 civilians and 1 policeman, and that one police officer has been killed and more than 600 people wounded in the unrest throughout the area. On 26 March the official Xinhua news agency said that 661 people had so far 'surrendered' to the authorities, 280 in Lhasa, and 381 in Sichuan province, with over 1000 detained. Violations share common characteristics with broader patterns of human rights violations in China. For example, measures taken by the authorities to seal off the area from foreign journalists follow a more individualised pattern of obstruction and harassment of foreign journalists who try to cover stories deemed politically sensitive in China. The incomplete picture of the protests transmitted to the Chinese public—focusing largely on violence perpetrated by Tibetans—is a further indication of both official government control over the domestic media and its intermittent censorship of broadcasts by the international media. The crackdown on the protests has been severe. The Chinese authorities have announced that anyone detained for taking part in the violence faces charges of 'endangering national security' under provisions of the Criminal Law which have long been used to convict and imprison peaceful Tibetan activists. Excessively broad and vague definitions of 'national security' and acts which endanger 'national security' have characterised China's treatment of human rights defenders more generally.

Undermining Freedoms

Detention without trial, repression of human rights defenders, internet censorship, and repression of spiritual and religious groups, death penalty, China has huge human rights deficits. Many activists are held as prisoners of conscience after politically motivated trials. Growing numbers are kept under house arrest. Broad and vaguely defined crimes against national security, such as 'separatism', 'subversion' and 'stealing state secrets', are used to prosecute those engaged in legitimate and peaceful human rights activities. Land rights activist Yang Chunlin was sentenced to five years in prison on 25 March for 'inciting subversion' after he spearheaded a petition campaign under the banner 'We don't want the Olympics, we want human rights'. Housing rights activist Ye Guozhu is serving a four-year prison sentence after he applied for permission to hold a demonstration against forced evictions in Beijing. He was convicted in December 2004 of 'picking quarrels and stirring up trouble' because of his opposition to the seizure and demolition of property to make way for new construction projects for this year's Olympic games.

In May 2006, Beijing extended use of a form of detention without trial called Re-education Through Labor (RTL), to 'clean up' the city's image before the Olympics. The system targets those who have committed minor offences but are not legally considered criminals. They are forced to work for long hours, and can be detained for up to four years. RTL is much criticised within the country Beijing housing rights activist Wang Ling was reported to have been sentenced to 15 months RTL in October 2007 for signing petitions and making banners in protest against the demolition of her property to make way for Olympic construction.

The internet is being heavily censored too. Cartoon police icons now warn many of China's 210 million internet users to stay away from 'illegal' websites. These virtual police appear to encourage self-censorship by reminding users that the authorities closely monitor web activity. China is also believed to operate the most extensive, technologically sophisticated and broad-reaching system of internet censorship and filtering in the world. Text messaging is also being monitored. In December 2007, the Beijing city authorities issued a notice stating that those who use text messages to 'endanger public security' or 'spread rumors' will be investigated. China is the world leader in the use of the death penalty.

China's Choice

The majority of Chinese citizens feel enormous pride in Beijing hosting the 2008 Olympic Games. It is seen as a sign of China's growing stature in the world. The urgency for the Chinese authorities is to push forward with political reforms so that when August 2008 arrives the China could be proud in every respect of what their country has to offer the world. It is China's choice. But the responsibility is shared by the Olympic movement that stresses the importance of 'universal fundamental ethical principles' and 'the preservation of human dignity' to the Olympic spirit.

22

Myanmar Diary: Rhetoric and Reality of Indian Democracy

I

Union of Myanmar (Burma). Head of State: General Than Shwe. Head of Government: General Soe Win. A military rule in your neighbourhood for over three decades, which has become a part of your routine. You see them now entering your homes, at Rajghat in Delhi on 25 October 2004, when Than Shwe pays homage to Mahatma Gandhi; at National Defence Academy in Khadakvasla; at Tata Motors Plant in Pune; and many other places. You find your ministers, like Pranab Mukherjee, defence secretaries and army chiefs visiting them, with friendly hands and full kitties. Remembering, recognising and legitimising a brutal military rule is becoming a natural, practical, economical act in India today, either in the name of an official 'look east' policy and flush out northeast armed groups, or to tap the natural gas reserves and develop bilateral trade relations.

These myriad social practices of acknowledgement to the Myanmar military rule are leading to a new formation, or rather malformation, of the Indian state and its diplomacy. A global India, with high growth and regional–international ambitions, has to move away from Daw Aung San Suu Kyi, the leader of Myanmar's political opposition, who has been under arrest for more than 15 years intermittently since 1989. It has to forget about U Win Tin, a journalist, who is serving a 20-year sentence for writing and publishing 'magazines, news bulletins and papers that were all against the government'. It has to leave San San New in the lurch, who is serving a 10-year prison term on the basis that she allegedly gave information to foreign journalists/diplomats 'against or critical of the government'.

Truth has not changed with time and calendar. In fact, across the political spectrum, civil society and media, there is support for the Burmese democratic movement. People sympathise with Daw Aung San Suu Kyi, who lived and studied here when her mother was the first Burmese ambassador to New Delhi in the 1960s. However, our government today is preferring convenience to conviction, and is valuing privileges over principles. Everyday our new country emerges on the pages of newspapers and in the statements of our political, economic and military leaders, with its changing appearance and appeasement, with its new opportunism, driving over various deals, of course without its people.

Indian Express reported on 22 November 2006 that the Air Chief Marshal S.P. Tyagi made a three-day visit to Myanmar to discuss several arms offers made almost two years ago by his predecessor, Air Chief Marshal S. Krishnaswamy, including a comprehensive fighter aircraft upgrade programme and the sale of Hindustan Aeronautics Limited (HAL) built advanced light helicopters, Bharat Electronics (BEL) radars, airborne radio equipment and surveillance electronics(*Indian Express*, 2006). On 11 October 2006, *Jane's Defence Weekly* reported that negotiations for the proposed 'arms for military co-operation swap' were conducted during a 21 September 2006 visit to Myanmar by India's Defence Secretary Shekhar Dutt. During his two-day trip, he held discussions with the Vice Senior General Maung Aye, alongside with other senior Myanmar military officers, focusing on New Delhi providing Yangon with T-55 main battle tanks, which the Indian Army was retiring, armoured personal carriers, 105 mm light artillery guns, mortars and the locally designed advanced light helicopter at a 'special' price. *Himal South Asia* wrote in February 2007 that since 1998, India has extended more than US$ 100 million in credit to the Burmese regime, including for upgrading the Rangoon-Mandalay railway line. In addition, it has contributed US$ 27 million to the building of the 160-kilometre Tamu-Kalewa highway in Burma's Sagaing Division. India has also emerged as Burma's second largest market after Thailand, absorbing 25 percent of the country's total exports, and it hopes to double bilateral trade to a billion US dollars per annum in the next few years. India is also providing training to Burmese armed forces personnel and helping it build border infrastructure. As a part of its energy strategy, it also plans to buy natural gas from Burma's reserves. This would benefit the military regime millions of dollars annually (http://www.himalmag.com/2007/february/cover2.htm).

On 16 July 2007, Amnesty International and Saferworld released its report titled 'Indian helicopters for Myanmar: making a mockery of the EU arms embargo?' saying that Government of India may transfer military helicopters, including the Advanced Light Helicopter (ALH), to the government of Myanmar as part of the two countries' increasing military co-operation. Such transfers risk undermining existing EU and US sanctions and arms embargoes on Myanmar (Amnesty International, 2007).

These umpteen examples of the recent past exemplify how the same thing is being repeated over and over again, creating a 'neat' cushioned regime. However, our government continues to practise the virtues of denial, and keeps reiterating lies in these years. When did you last hear our Indian government making a strong case against Myanmar's military rulers? Have you heard of cancelling of any trip by the Indian dignitaries to Myanmar, for example, against the arrest of U Aung Thein, a 77-year-old very respectable member of the National League for Democracy's central committee, who was arrested with three others in April 2006, and all four were sentenced in July to 20 years imprisonment? U Aung Thein was said to have 'confessed' to possessing a satellite telephone used to speak to NLD leaders outside the country. When were our leaders in SAARC (South Asian Association for Regional Cooperation) or ASEAN (Association of South East Asian Nations) seen trying to push for some democratic agenda on Myanmar? When was the last time you took a stand?

If you live in Myanmar, you can be forced into unpaid labour. Many people are subjected to it, mainly by the army, to build roads, military camps and other infrastructural projects. You can be forced to leave your home. Hundreds of thousands of civilians have been compelled to leave their villages, as part of a strategy to cut off support to armed opposition groups. Whole villages have been razed, obliterating people's homes and possessions. You can be denied citizenship, even if your family has lived there for generations. You can be locked for years for writing a poem or acting on behalf of political prisoners. Thousands of government critics have been imprisoned for peaceful activities, like writing histories or poems, or taking other steps to defend human rights. You can be locked up for years without knowing why, with no right to go to court. You can be tortured, even to death, by the police and the army. And, you cannot complain. If you do, you may be further tortured and imprisoned. Myanmar authorities consistently reject reports of human rights violations, whether from Myanmar citizens or by international officials like the UN Special Rapporteur on Myanmar, as politically motivated propaganda. The Indian authorities speak in a similar, twisted tongue about the defence deals as 'completely baseless'; asking not to attach 'much credence to reports'; stating that 'India does give defence support but the equipment is not offensive'; or that 'the matter is delicate... We have to keep Myanmar in good humour' (*The Guardian* and AFP, 2007; EUbusiness, 2007).

However, the facts cannot be muted, as lines between rhetoric and reality are clearly visible. Standing neither here nor there, sometimes in the middle of the road is dangerous. You can be knocked down by traffic from both sides—this is a threat imminent to our government. The Indian government has to state on whose side it is, and take clear-cut positions. Truth shall prevail, says our motto *satyameva jayathe*. The important question is, how? The coalition Indian government, bound by a common minimum programme, must stop their vacillation and join the campaign to end repression and dictatorship in Myanmar.

II

Myanmar: India Backtracking

India did it again: it voted against the UN resolution condemning the recent crackdown on anti-government protests by Myanmar's ruling generals. The UN resolution, adopted on 20 November by UN General Assembly committee by 88-24 vote with 66 abstentions, 'strongly condemns the use of violence against peaceful demonstrators who were exercising their rights to freedom of opinion and expression and to peaceful assembly and association'. India's negative vote, in the words of the Indian delegation to the UN, says: 'by adopting a condemnatory, intrusive and unhelpful tone, this draft resolution will not contribute or strengthen the initiatives being taken (in Myanmar) by the UN and may, in fact, prove to be counter-productive'.

India is in news frequently: Prime Minister Manmohan Singh's meeting with Myanmar Head of State General Than Shew after arriving in Singapore to participate in ASEAN-India Summit and the East Asia Summit; India backing UN role in Myanmar; India's

External Affairs Minister's meeting with the UN envoy and giving UN the centrality to deal directly with the Junta. However, India's diplomatic moves are devoid of expressing solidarity with the struggling and suffering population of Myanmar, inside or outside the country. This is at a time when there are new evidences coming of mass detentions, hostage taking, death in custody and disappearances in Myanmar which disprove claims of returning normality. The continued detention of some 700 political prisoners including at least 15 individuals sentenced to prison terms of up to nine and a half years, the continuing, official policy of taking family members and friends as 'hostages' to force others to turn themselves in, deaths in detention due to severe beatings and others forms of torture, appalling detention conditions including the denial of adequate food, water and sanitary facilities as well as the keeping of detainees in 'dog cells', enforced disappearances since the crackdown, including at least 72 individuals whose whereabouts the authorities have failed to account for, failure by the Myanmar authorities to account for the number of people killed during the crackdown, evidence of marksmen atop military trucks and bridges using live ammunition to target individual demonstrators during the crackdown resulting in the death of at least two students and the serious wounding of others; and many more like this should also prompt India democracy to go beyond the UN and military junta. The government, now almost unconnected to the democratic and peaceful movements of the Myanmar people, continues to compromise at the level of discourse and direct action.

See the actions of our government along the Indo-Myanmar border in Manipur and in other north-eastern states, to prevent the influx of individuals who are fleeing the ongoing crackdown in Myanmar. Take the cases of several other Myanmar nationals who are now at risk of being forcibly returned to Myanmar. After the crackdown on peaceful protests, along with searches, surveillance and harassment of individuals who took part in these protests, numerous Myanmar people have had to go in hiding. They are also fleeing to neighbouring India and Thailand. The state-run *New Light of Myanmar* newspaper warned that 'anyone who is detained for his violation of law must be charged and serve prison terms if he is found guilty'.

However, instead of allowing the individuals fleeing human rights violations in Myanmar access to its territory, and giving them full rights to refugee status determination procedures and to seek political asylum as well as access to the internationally accepted rights and practices, including access to the UN High Commissioner for Refugees (UNHCR), the Indian government decided to close the Indo-Myanmar border and intensified security checks to prevent their entry in our borders.

Those who could enter met with hostility and aggression. The cases of Habibulde, Haroon and Rashid, all Myanmar nationals from the city of Yangon, are some such examples. The three men were arrested by the troops of the 24 Assam Rifles, a paramilitary force, during a security check of vehicles on 2 October 2007 at Khudenthabi, near the border town of Moreh in Manipur. They were handed over to the custody of police from the state capital of Manipur, Imphal. The Imphal police charged them with illegal entry into the country and later transferred them to the Moreh police station. On 9 October, they were produced in court and were remanded to judicial custody. Like them, others may have been detained in the escalating Indian security response at the Indo-Myanmar border, and more individuals are likely to be detained, and at risk of being forcibly returned. The government plans are not to support the struggling population and save their lives, but to increase security arrangements, along the Indo-Myanmar border in Manipur and in other northeastern states, to prevent their influx.

The Indian government's dubious dealings with the struggling Myanmar people have had other manifestations as well in the recent past. We have 34 Rakhine (Arakan) and Kayin (Karen) Myanmar nationals, who have spent years, detained without charge in India and are now being tried in Kolkata (West Bengal). They are at risk of being denied their right to a fair trial and then forcibly returned to Myanmar. The 34 men are reportedly members of the National United Party of Arakan (NUPA) and the Karen National Union (KNU) and were detained in India in February 1998. Both organisations are involved in armed conflicts against the ruling military authorities in Myanmar. India's Central Bureau of Investigation (CBI) is prosecuting the men on charges of illegal possession of weapons. The accused reportedly contend that they were arrested during a meeting with the Indian intelligence officials, who had allegedly promised them assistance, and that six others were detained at the time, reported to be their leaders, and were then handed over to Myanmar officials. The Indian defense ministry denies both these allegations.

Following a campaign by the local human rights organisations, the government of West Bengal withdrew an earlier decision that the trial be held in secret within prison premises. The trial is now being heard in a Kolkata High Court. However, the media and the public were reportedly barred, when the Indian intelligence officials presented their evidence, in accordance with a CBI petition. Whether convicted or not, the 34 persons could be forcibly deported to Myanmar, where they are likely to face torture and other ill-treatment, as well as arbitrary detention, unfair trials and forced labour. These concerns have been underlined by the recent violent suppression of protests by the military government in Myanmar. As a democratic country, supporting a democratic movement, should we not be under an absolute and unconditional obligation not to forcibly return any person to a militaristic, dictatorial regime, where they risk torture or other serious human rights violations? Should we not be refraining from forcibly returning them to Myanmar after the completion of their trial and jail terms, if any, as a mark of solidarity towards the democratic struggle in Myanmar?

We may also remind ourselves that according to the Amnesty International Report 2007, military operations against the Karen National Union in eastern Karen state and neighbouring districts increased tremendously during 2006. More than 16,000 people were displaced by the conflict. Destruction of houses and crops, enforced disappearances, forced labour, torture and extrajudicial killings of Karen civilians increased. Many villages faced food shortages after the authorities banned them from leaving their villages to farm or buy food. The widespread practice of forced labour was reported throughout the year in Karen.

Foreign policy is about political and social accomplishment, and not just economic achievement. The foreign policy of a democratic government has many dimensions. It relates to government, people, economy, society and culture. All these aspects are interconnected and influence one another. Weakness in any area can very well damage the fairness and justice, respect and credibility of the government in domestic and international arenas. Therefore, the need at present of the Indian government expressing its concrete solidarity to the suffering people of Myanmar is just as important to them, as it is to us. Democracy should not put a price tag on humanity. Fairness is definitely more important than some immediate financial gains.

III

Myanmar: India Must Suspend All Military Support

The military cracking down on protestors and taking an increasingly prominent position on the streets of Yangon. Hundreds of arrests and worrying reports of a rising death toll. Thousands of protesters continuing to organise marches. Protests around the world. In this critical situation, the world expects a more meaningful reaction from the Indian government. The government must increase the pressure on the Myanmar government if the mounting human rights crisis in the country is to be reversed and further bloodshed averted. The Indian government should immediately suspend the supply to Myanmar of all direct and indirect transfers of military and security equipment, munitions and expertise, including transfers claimed to be 'non-lethal'. They should maintain these cessations until the Government of Myanmar takes concrete independently verified steps to improve the democratic situation, including the release of all prisoners of conscience. India has many-a-times visited other countries of concern, most recently Nepal, in the similar manner. Why should it not do the same for people in Myanmar whose rights have been trampled upon so long?

Myanmar needs a comprehensive arms embargo. Since 25 September 2007, Myanmar security forces have raided monasteries, beaten and arrested hundreds of protesters including monks and other public figures, used tear gas, baton charges and warning shots to disperse protestors and fired at fleeing protestors and journalists. At least nine people have been killed. Monks were injured in the beatings and one monk suffered a gunshot wound to his head. There is a grave risk that the military and security forces will react with escalating violence to continued mass protests by those calling for democratic reforms.

The government of Myanmar and its military, security and police forces of around 400,000 personnel have a well documented record of serious human rights violations. China has been the principal source of arms supplies to the Myanmar security forces, followed by India, Serbia, Russia, Ukraine and other countries. Indian government should come clean at this moment as they have a very dubious track record on arms transfer in the recent past.

In January 2007, the Indian Foreign Minister Pranab Mukherjee promised to give a 'favourable response' to the Myanmar Government's request for military equipment (Bruce Loudon, 'India to snub US on Burma arms embargo', *The Australian*, 23 January 2007; 'India to supply military equipment to Myanmar', *The Hindu*, 22 January 2007) and in April 2007 it was reported that Indian and Myanmar security forces were 'conducting joint military operations along the 1,643-km Indo-Myanmar border to neutralise insurgent groups' (India Defence, 2007). India has not reported on any arms transfers to Myanmar to the UN.

The European Union (EU) and the US imposed arms embargoes on Myanmar in 1988 and 1993 respectively. In 1996, the EU strengthened its arms embargo on Myanmar to become an EU Common Position, and noted with concern 'the absence of progress towards democratization and at the continuing violation of human rights in Burma/Myanmar'. The embargo was renewed in 2002 and again in 2006. The EU arms embargo is legally-binding and requires all EU member states to implement and enforce its provisions at the national level. The EU embargo also bans the direct and indirect provision of technical or financial assistance, brokering and other services related to military activities and military and related material. Indirect transfers of military components are covered within the scope of the EU embargo, yet there is no comprehensive EU-wide control system in place to ensure that governments can effectively implement and enforce their embargo commitments.

The current situation demands resolute interventions to prevent the massive repression. Stopping all Indian military support and the involvement of their agencies, companies and nationals in the direct or indirect supply to Myanmar of any military, police or security equipment will be a first concrete step in support of the democratic movement of Myanmar.

IV

India and Human Rights Emergency in Myanmar

There is again a need for urgency by the Indian government, to use its influence with the Myanmar government, and put pressure on them to end all human rights violations in their country. A lesser known human rights emergency is ravaging eastern Myanmar—the ongoing military offensive against ethnic Karen civilians in the eastern parts of the country. Little known to the world outside, the Myanmar army (*tatmadaw*) is waging an offensive against ethnic Karen civilians in Kayin State and Bago Division, involving widespread and systematic violations of human rights and humanitarian law. These violations amount to crimes against humanity. The Karen civilian populations are subjected to killings; torture and other ill-treatment; enforced disappearances and arbitrary arrests; forced labour, including portering; and the destruction of villages, crops and homes. Nearly 150,000 people are internally displaced as a result of the military offensive.

A 2008 UN General Assembly, resolution on Myanmar is expected during the middle of November. 14th ASEAN summit is expected in mid-December. India is hosting the BIMSTEC Summit (Bangladesh, India, Myanmar, Sri Lanka and Thailand Economic Cooperation Economic Cooperation, a regional Body comprising Bay of Bengal nations) in New Delhi in mid-November and Myanmar Prime Minister General Thein Sein will be attending the Summit. Thus, India has many opportunities to play a crucial role at the regional and international levels, and to help end the forgotten human rights emergency in eastern Myanmar, with a view towards increased regional stability.

In the past fourteen months, Myanmar has witnessed pivotal moments in the country's turbulent recent history: the brutal crackdown, following mass demonstrations in September 2007; the adoption of a deeply flawed constitution after a highly problematic referendum; and a humanitarian and human rights disaster in the wake of Cyclone Nargis.

Karen villagers are targeted simply on account of their Karen ethnicity or their location in Karen majority areas, or in retribution for activities by armed opposition groups. Some villages have been totally or partially destroyed. In other villages the *tatmadaw* prevented farmers from cultivating their land or purchasing food supplies, announcing a shoot-to-kill policy for those found outside their villages. Tatmadaw demands for forced labour, destruction of crops and extensive food requisitioning have made it extremely hard for civilian villagers to survive.

Unlike previous counter-insurgency campaigns against the Karen National Union (KNU) and its armed wing (the Karen National Liberation Army, KNLA) for nearly 60 years, the current offensive has civilians as the primary targets. The current operation is the largest in a decade and is unique in that, unlike previous seasonal operations that have generally ended at the start of the yearly rains between May and October, this offensive has continued through two consecutive rainy seasons, and shows no signs of stopping as a third season is underway.

India's positive role has been sought after in all these months by Indian citizens, wide range of civil society organisations, including Amnesty International, and political parties. The UN secretary general Ban Ki-moon recently urged India to play some role to promote democracy, the rule of law and good government in Myanmar.

However, what we continue to witness is contrary to our expectations. Myanmar has become the gateway to India's 'Look East' policy, and Indian government is going all out to develop its economic and trade relationship with Myanmar. In October itself, India's Minister of State for Commerce and Power, Jairam Ramesh inaugurated a new Indian-backed IT training centre in Rangoon and discussed various measures, including the offer to give duty free tariff preference scheme meant for Least Developed Countries. This is the same minister who 'saluted the people and the Government of Myanmar for their resilience and fortitude in facing the devastation caused by Cyclone Nargis' in May 2008. India has recently signed three important agreements with Myanmar: exploration of natural gas, satellite-based remote sensing, and promotion of Buddhist studies. India has got involved in several river and land-based projects in Myanmar. Thus, India today stands Myanmar's 4th largest trading partner after Thailand, China and Singapore. India has become Myanmar's second largest export market after Thailand, absorbing 25 percent of its total exports. So much so that Indian and Myanmar governments had set a target of achieving $1 billion trade in the fiscal year 2006–07.

Indian government had been so enthusiastic, almost blind, in its pursuit that at the height of the citizens' unrest in September 2007, our Petroleum Minister Murli Deora went to Myanmar and finalised contracts on deep water gas exploration projects. With the active support of the Indian government, the Indo-Myanmar Chamber of

Commerce and Industries organised Small and Medium enterprises exhibition at Yangoon in November 2007. And many more things like this have happened. Not only this, during the same time, the Indian government voted against the UN resolution condemning the crackdown on anti-government protests by Myanmar's ruling generals.

This is a critical time to reflect whether the Indian government's policy of economic and political engagement with the Myanmar government, known as the State Peace and Development Council (SDPC) is having any result in changing human rights situation in Myanmar. Daw Aung San Suu Kyi, icon of the Burmese human rights movement, is under detention. There are at present more than 2000 political prisoners, more than a third of whom the government detained during its violent crackdown on the protests last year. Nothing speaks louder of the Myanmar government's poor record than the fact that there are more long-standing political prisoners in Myanmar today than at any other time since the beginning of pro-democracy struggles twenty years ago, popularly known as 8.8.88. UN Secretary General's Special Advisor, Ibrahim Gambari, and the UN Special Rapporteur on the situation of human rights in Myanmar, Thomas Ojea Quintana are making a visit to Mynamar and other countries, including India, but without any results. In this context, the Indian government should persuade the Myanmar government to cooperate with the UN, including by implementing the recommendations of the Special Rapporteur on the situation of human rights in Myanmar, the (former) Commission on Human Rights, the Human Rights Council, the General Assembly, and the Security Council, and to ensure full and unhindered access for UN officials, in conformity with the Terms of Reference for Fact-finding Missions by Special Procedures.

V

Sixty Four for Aung San Suu Kyi

Burma's imprisoned democracy leader Aung San Suu Kyi will mark her 64th birthday on 19 June 2009, her 14th year in detention. An iconic symbol of Myanmar's political resistance, she is the world's only imprisoned Nobel Peace Prize winner. She has committed no crime, she is the victim of crime, yet her detention can continue for many more years. The United Nations has ruled that Aung San Suu Kyi's detention is illegal under international law, and also under Burmese law. The United Nations Security Council has also told the dictatorship that they must release her. Comparable to the personal, moral and democratic power of Mahatma Gandhi and Nelson Mandela, her continued detention is a powerful reminder of the unrelenting repression in Myanmar, and what must be done to make democracy and human rights a reality.

Detentions and repression, widespread reports of ill-treatment and torture, and sentencing in closed and grossly unfair trials behind prison walls, make a mockery of commitments made by the Myanmar authorities to cooperate with the United Nations. Will her 64th birth year be free from prison and detention greatly depends on the UN Security Council, notably China and Japan, ASEAN countries and India, who all are best placed to bring the necessary pressure to bear on the Myanmar government. The release of Aung San Suu Kyi must not wait for the conclusion of any political or diplomatic process.

Military dictatorship is now using a new trail to keep Aung San in prison: Her current house detention order was set to expire on 27 May 2009. However, on 18 May, she was put on another trial, charged with breaching the terms of her house arrest after an American man, John Yettaw, swam to her house and refused to leave. The dictatorship is using the visit as an opportunity to extend her detention. Her trial is ongoing and she could face a further five years in detention. Nothing has changed for Aung San Suu Kyi and the other more than 2200 political prisoners. Remember October 2008, when the government began sentencing *en masse* those who had peacefully taken part in the August/September 2007 anti-government protests and more than 350 political activists were jailed. Some of these political activists have been given lengthy jail terms—some as long as 65 years. The severity of these sentences flies in the face of the government's claims that its new constitution and plans for elections in 2010 are genuine efforts towards increasing political participation. They also serve as a powerful reminder that the government is still ignoring calls from the international community to improve the country's democratic rights record.

Co-founder of Myanmar's main opposition party, the National League for Democracy (NLD), Aung San Suu Kyi is also one of the world's best-known political figures and campaigners for human rights. Aung San Suu Kyi has endured unofficial detention, house arrest and restrictions on her movement since July 1989, all aimed at preventing her from becoming the national leader of Myanmar. Her sufferings and struggles have been immense. A few references will give us a glimpse of the injustice and violence meted to her for so long.

Aung San Suu Kyi's party won the general elections in Myanmar in 1990. However, instead of taking her position as a national leader, she was kept under house arrest by the military authorities and remains so today. The process began, following the brutal crackdown of the 1988 pro-democracy protests. A year later, her party won the elections by an overwhelming majority. But the military rulers declared the results null and void and continued to deny Aung San Suu Kyi her freedom. She is generally not allowed any visitors, is held in increasing isolation, and permitted only infrequent visits by her doctor. She has most recently been detained since 30 May 2003, after a violent attack on her and other party members during a trip through upper Myanmar. The attack is believed to have been carried out with the involvement of the state and state sponsored civil organisations, and still has not been independently investigated.

Aung San Suu Kyi and her entourage were stopped on the road at night between villages near Depeyin in a remote part of Sagaing Division. They were set upon in a violent coordinated attack. Men with sharpened bamboo sticks, iron rods and stones, attacked vehicles, pulling individuals out of cars and beating them repeatedly on the head and body. NLD Youth members and others attempted to protect the leaders, including Aung San Suu Kyi and her deputy U Tin Oo. At least four persons were killed, and scores more seriously injured. Aung San Suu Kyi and her security detail escaped, but they were soon taken into detention and held incommunicado.

After the attack, the authorities stated that Aung San Suu Kyi was being held in protective custody and that measures against the detained leaders would be lifted as the situation normalised. They promised in July 2003 that she would be released 'when the time comes' and that they were waiting for a 'cool down'. In August 2003, they urged, 'Let us not call it a detention... We don't have any kind of intention of animosity against Aung San Suu Kyi. That is why we have not taken any legal action against her and her party'.

After being held incommunicado in a military camp, Aung San Suu Kyi was transferred to her house in September 2003 and held under de facto house arrest. In November 2003, the authorities handed down a one-year detention order under an administrative detention law that has been regularly extended since. Aung San Suu Kyi was previously held under house arrest on account of her prominent role in opposition politics between 1989 and 1995, and 2000 to 2002. During her time in house arrest, the authorities twice amended the legislation under which she is held to allow for a longer period of detention without charge or trial. Even when she was not under official house arrest, Aung San Suu Kyi had her freedom of movement heavily restricted: the authorities blockaded roads, often arrested those seeking to meet her and denied family members, including her critically ill husband, permission to visit the country to see her.

Major celebrities, including George Clooney, Brad Pitt, Archbishop Desmond Tutu, Vaclav Havel, David Beckham, Daniel Craig, Stephen Fry, Eddie Izzard, Kevin Spacey and the British Prime Minister, Gordon Brown are asking for one thing today. Major organisations like Burma Campaign UK, Amnesty International, Trades Union Congress, Not On Our Watch, Human Rights Watch, Christian Solidarity Worldwide, Open Society Institute, Avaaz, English Pen and US Campaign For Burma are campaigning for one issue: write a 64 word message for Aung San Suu Kyi's 64th birthday for a free birth year. Will we all be a part of this?

(Sections of this essay have been published in various newspapers, *The Hindu*, *DNA*, and *The Hindustan Times*. This is an expanded and revised version.)

23

Nepal: How To Seek 'Truth' in Truth Commissions?

When considering the question 'should we remember?' it is very important to firstly ask, has any victim forgotten? Could they ever forget? Secondly we should ask, who wants to forget? Who benefits when all the atrocities stay silent in the past?

—Roberto Cabrera, 'Should We Remember?
Recovering Historical Memory in Guatemala', 1998.

Societies emerging from a history of crimes and other human rights violations ought to create a long-term strategic action plan to ensure that the truth is told, that justice is done and that reparation is provided to all the victims. Judicial measures here need to combine with non-judicial measures, like truth commissions, effective procedures for granting reparation, and mechanisms for vetting armed and security forces. Such an action plan can develop through a coordinated process of national consultation, tailored to the situation of a particular country, but in compliance with the international law. In South Asia, India-Pakistan at the time of partition, Bangladesh during the liberation war, Sri Lanka under civil war and Nepal during the armed conflicts has witnessed unprecedented human rights violations. However, at present it is Nepal, going through the unique democratic experiments of nation building, which has shown the courage to initiate the establishment of a Truth and Reconciliation Commission (TRC) to 'investigate truth about those who have seriously violated human rights and those who were involved in crimes against humanity in course of the war and to create an environment for reconciliations in the society'. It is further worth noting that the TRC has been agreed upon through a Comprehensive Peace Accord, signed by the Government of Nepal and the Communist Party of Nepal (Maoist) in November 2006.

Truth Commissions are a worldwide phenomenon, with Asia too beginning to establish them in countries like Indonesia (Truth and Reconciliation Commission, 2004), Indonesia and Timor Leste (Truth and Friendship Commission, 2005, bi-national), Philippines (Presidential Committee on Human Rights, 1986) and South Korea (Presidential Truth Commission on Suspicious Deaths, 2000). Sri Lanka also tried something similar to the truth commission in cases of disappeared persons. Between 1974 and 2007, at least 34 truth commissions have been established in 28 countries. More than half of these have come up in the past ten years.

At a time when Nepal is boldly debating the TRC Bill, proposed by its Ministry of Peace and Reconstruction, it is timely for us to understand the role of truth commissions. How do they protect, promote and respect human rights? How do they represent the right to truth, justice and reparation? How are they established and what are their functions and powers to build their future in the region? Truth Commissions are an effective tool and an important first step for ensuring that countries, territories and populations living through the memories of severe injustices in their region have access towards some accountability under the international law for crimes committed during armed conflicts. They are a means for guaranteeing that victims of these crimes have the benefit of their rights to truth, justice and reparation. In the context of political transitions, either to peace or to a democratic regime, truth commissions can play a significant role in providing an account of past human rights violations. They can contribute in the investigation and the eventual prosecution of the perpetuators of these crimes. They can prevent their repetition and ensure that victims and their relatives are provided with full reparation, including restitution, compensation, satisfaction, rehabilitation and guarantees of non-repetition.

As far as the specific case of Nepal is concerned, continuing discussions by the government officials, parliamentarians and other interested parties, as well as by the international community, reveal that the Nepalese civil society has not been sufficiently involved from the early stages in the discussions regarding the establishment, mandate and powers of the Commission. The process of nominations of the TRC members is led by a body open to political influence and does not offer sufficient guarantees of independence from the government. The commission's subject matter mandate is limited. For example, cases of enforced disappearances are excluded from the mandate of the commission if family members filed writs of habeas corpus, whether or not they received from the courts a full and accurate account of the fate and whereabouts of their 'disappeared' relative.

Prosecutions are often the logical outcome of a truth commission and an obligation upon states under international law—whether explicitly spelt out in the peace accord or not. No part of the TRC Bill explains that the work of the TRC should be followed by prosecutions, and that evidence collected by the commission should be handed over to judicial authorities, with the aim of bringing perpetrators to justice. At present, if the Commission's investigations result in the establishment of a *prima facie* case of individual criminal responsibility, the Commission has the power to choose one of three possible actions: *(a)* if the suspected perpetrator is found to have committed gross violations of human rights or crimes against humanity while 'abiding his/her duties or with the objective of fulfilling political motives', the Commission has the power to re-commend amnesty (section 25, with the only exception of perpetrators involved in any kind of murder committed after taking under con-trol or carried out in a inhuman manner, inhumane and cruel torture, and rape); *(b)* whatever the crime allegedly committed by the suspected perpetrator, the Commission has the power to initiate procedures for 'reconciliation' between the suspected perpetrator and the victim/s (section 23); and *(c)* the Commission can recommend 'necessary action' against the suspected perpetrator (section 24)— but not in cases where 'reconciliation' has been reached. These provisions are said to be violating of Nepal's obligations under international laws. Amnesties for serious crimes under international law are prohibited, as they deny the right of victims to justice.

It is also being said that no attention has been paid to the rights and protection of victims and witnesses, and they have been ensured no support for participating in the TRC process. Grave concerns have further been raised about its power to organise 'reconciliation' processes and ceremonies, by which a suspected perpetrator meets with the victim, makes an apology and provides reparation for the loss and damage caused. The 'reconciliation' process leads to a *de facto* amnesty, because 'necessary action' cannot be recommended by the Commission if the perpetrator and the victim have been involved in a 'reconciliation' procedure. At present, nothing in the TRC Bill guarantees that victims will not be coerced into 'reconciliation' procedures, including by believing to be under a legal requirement to be involved in such practices.

Under the Bill, the Commission will submit its final report to the government of Nepal, which will then present it to parliament. The responsibility for the implementation of the report will lie with the Ministry of Peace and Reconstruction. The National Human Rights Commission will have the task of monitoring the implementation of the recommendations made in the report. Serious concerns have been raised that the TRC Bill does not include any guarantee that the report be made public, nor it determines any deadline for its submission to parliament. As the report may not be released to the public, civil society and the Nepalese society as a whole have no means either to know the findings of the Commission's inquiry, or to monitor the implementation of its recommendations.

Truth Commissions are defined as 'official, temporary, non-judicial fact-finding bodies that investigate a pattern of abuses of human rights or humanitarian law, usually committed over a number of years'. The object of their inquiry (a pattern of human rights violations, rather than a specific event) distinguishes them from other commissions of inquiry. Their temporary character separates them from many national human rights commissions and other national institutions for the promotion and protection of human rights, which are permanent monitoring and enforcement bodies. They are required to take a victim-centered approach and conclude their work with a final report containing findings of facts and recommendations. However, the success of any truth commission lies in its clarity of principles and practices, and there should be sufficient understanding in the region about it, including Nepal.

The value of truth commissions is that they are created, not with the presumption that there will be no trials, but to constitute a step towards knowing the truth and, ultimately, ensuring that justice prevails. Victims of gross human rights violations and their families, as well as other members of society, have the right to know the truth about past abuses. The right to truth, both in its individual and collective dimensions, is an inalienable right, which stands alone. It should be considered as a non-negotiable right and should not be subject to any limitations. With respect to the individual dimension of the right to truth, international humanitarian law expressly guarantees the right of family members to know the fate of their missing relatives. The right to know the fate and whereabouts of 'disappeared' relatives, both in times of peace and in times of armed conflict, has been confirmed in the jurisprudence of international and regional human rights bodies, as well as of national courts.

Further, while the respective functions of truth commissions and courts are complementary, they are different in nature and should not be confused. Truth commissions are not intended to act as substitutes for the civil, administrative or criminal courts. In particular, truth commissions cannot be a substitute for the judicial process, to establish individual criminal responsibility. For example, take the case of Chile, where the Inter-American Commission on Human Rights noted that

> [The National Commission for Truth and Reconciliation] was not a judicial body and its work was limited to establishing the identity of the victims whose right to life had been violated. Under the terms of its mandate, the Commission was not empowered to publish the names of those who had committed the crimes, or to impose any type of sanction on them. For this reason, despite its important role in establishing the facts and granting compensation, the Truth Commission cannot be regarded as an adequate substitute for the judicial process.

Similar is the case with El Salvador.

Reparation is a right and should be proportional to the gravity of the violations and the harm suffered. It should be provided even if the perpetrator has not been identified, and must include measures to prevent further abuses from happening in the future. In the realm of establishment, functions and powers of the truth commission, the drafting of statute, mandate (both subject-matter and temporal mandate), and period of operation become crucial. Issues like competence, impartiality and independence of the commission, public information, a victim-centered approach, a fair procedure, ensuring that victims are provided with effective support and security to participate in the commission's process, and special measures for child victims and victims of sexual violence have to be thought of and cared for in detail.

As in the case of Nepal, since the Commission is usually established during a period of transition, they rarely coexist with a fully functioning national justice system. The national justice system may have been seriously deprived of human and material resources during an armed conflict, to the point that it is unable to function effectively. Alternatively, it may have a record of collusion with those in power who were responsible for committing human rights violations in the past. In many cases, a truth commission is called to cover, at least in part, the vacuum left by an ineffective national justice system. Its work should assist and should not prejudice current or future criminal proceedings.

The Truth and Reconciliation Commission of Peru noted that 'Neither reconciliation nor forgiveness equate to impunity. Impunity is another name for injustice. That's why the TRC understands justice as the foundation of reconciliation, its precondition and effect, its point of departure and arrival. The exercise of justice guarantees the realization of reconciliation.' Some truth commissions, most notably the Truth and Reconciliation Commission in South Africa and the Commission for Reception, Truth and Reconciliation in Timor-Leste, have designed their activities, in particular public hearings, to provide victims and perpetrators with a forum for public and private acts of reconciliation. Individual reconciliation between victims and perpetrators was seen as conducive to collective, political reconciliation. Undoubtedly, the establishment of the facts is a pre-condition for, and can help to promote, individual and collective reconciliation. However, reconciliation, both at the individual and at the collective level, cannot be imposed by either a truth commission or any other official body or procedure. If a truth commission decides to adopt specific procedures to promote individual reconciliation, such as traditional mechanisms of conflict-resolution or religious practices, they must fully respect the rights and dignity of both victims and alleged perpetrators. In particular, victims and their families should not be forced to meet alleged perpetrators or to engage in any act of reconciliation. On the other hand, reconciliation procedures should not be at the expenses of fair procedure.

Ensuring accountability for human rights violations is of funda-mental importance to us. There are times when we are told that justice must be set aside in the interest of peace. It is true that justice can only be dispensed when the peaceful order of society is secure. But the reverse is also true: without justice there can be no lasting peace. Truth Commissions should unearth and reveal the whole truth, or as much as is possible to find. They are a critical means for laying a sound foundation and building a strong and lasting reconciliation in countries that have been in turmoil or are undergoing transition.

(*Economic and Political Weekly*, Volume 42, No. 51, 22 December 2007)

24

Use and Abuse of Africa in India

In 2007–08, Africa finds itself at the centre of attention in India. A convergence of social forums and summits, research reports and civil society mobilisations have hoisted the needs and challenges of African countries visible on the political agenda, both at the national level and within different constituencies. Three initiatives are pivotal in this plethora of African activities: the recently-concluded India-Africa Forum Summit, the World Social Forum-India's events in 2006–07, and the 'Focus Africa' along with the Team Nine activities, in the early years of the decade. An impression of Africa is entering the Indian people's imagination, in a way that has not happened before. The focus is on trade and investment, state cooperation and peoples' solidarity. Attention is not directed towards any specific famine or war, and the appeal is not for money but for equality and justice. The task of mainstreaming Africa in India presents both a challenge and a risk: not only are the means to achieve it contested, the very nature of justice is a subject of fierce debate, which poses fundamental questions about the relationship between the powerful, rich, industrialised world and the poor, developing countries.

'Africa' has been endlessly recreated and deconstructed, used and abused by the state and the market, by popular and elite discourses on the nation and the people that were to be created and moulded in the New World and, last but not the least, by progressive and conservative politics. For analytical purposes, three periods can be identified in India–Africa relations in modern times, each corresponding to different levels of political and economic developments in India, and integration of the Indian population into the African economy and politics. The first period began in the era of imperialism during the 1900s, when Indians got deeply involved in Africa: from Indian capitalists, especially from Gujarat who traded with the continent, to the Indian troops, who were part of the British colonial ventures. Other than Mahatma Gandhi's long sojourn in Africa, and some other Indians' contribution in the political awakening of the region, the Indian–African relations were shaped by an economy and society which was highly exploitative, unequal and hierarchical. The second period started with the politics of decolonisation, followed by the newly independent Indian and African nations, often displaying an emphasis on modernisation, technological cooperation and scientific progress. Jawaharlal Nehru's speech, delivered at the concluding session of the Asian–African Conference (Bandung, Indonesia, 24 April 1955), richly captures this aspect of decolonisation and development between Asia and Africa. The third period spans the corporate globalisation from the eighties to the present day, when Indian big companies and private capital, their trade and investment in Africa, has became the prime engine to drive the India–Africa relations.

This historical journey has had many deficits. For example, people-to-people contacts between India and Africa have hardly increased. Even though the cultural exchange between people in India and Africa in some ways involves groups that are discriminated against in both contexts, it still contains many characteristics of an unbalanced North-South exchange. No period is characterised by the incorporation of any aspects of black culture into the making of our national self-image, for example in the way US and Europe are reference points for the new middle-class intellectuals and activists in India, who often refer to them for their politics of human rights and identity. Corporate globalisation hardly encourages any horizontal exchanges of capital, goods and services between India and Africa. Many 'Indian' and 'African' people and commodities that reach each other's shores, do so through a complex and far-reaching triangulation, starting their journeys in the South to reach the North and, from there, often with an increased status that a passage to the North implies, moving on again to the South.

In these contexts, the Summit's Delhi Declaration and the Africa-India Framework for Cooperation, India's decision to expand unilateral duty free and preferential market access for exports from all 50 Least Developed Countries, 34 of which are in Africa, an offer of lines of credit amounting to US$ 5.4 billion to African states, coupled with several events before or concurrent with the Summit, like India–Africa Editors Conference, joint performances by Indian and African cultural troupes, business conclave and others, should act like sparks in the on-going debate about how to engage with Africa today. It should also be a critical exercise in the context of the Chinese controversial expeditions in Africa, the almost fiasco of the G8 commitments towards Africa in 2005, the forgotten Report of the Commission for Africa set up by the British prime minister, and the dismal performance of the high profile Make Poverty History campaign.

While Indian and African states explore new opportunities for trade market and prosperity, the globalisation of ideas and practices commensurate with further democratisation of politics in India and Africa since the 1980s. Hitherto marginalised populations and groups in both the continents have sought more voice and par-ticipation in the affairs of the states. The 'developmentalist' side of decolonisation at the time of Bandung, and the clear and conscious desire of Indian–African states to 'catch up' with the west is highly contested today through different means and contexts. Further, the 'south-south solidarity', as being called in the Delhi Declaration, cannot afford to miss contemporary burning issues in Africa like the MNCs or corporate accountability, or focusing India–Africa partnership in specific areas of struggles against poverty; debt relief, aid and policy conditionality; HIV/AIDS, intellectual property rights and WTO, privatisation of natural resources, and war, conflict and hegemony.

India and Africa reach to each other through a variety of vehicles and agents, which have changed, especially over the last few decades. Both the state and the social scientists contributed immensely in the first and second periods to the discourse making and agenda setting. However, today there is less state and more market than a generation ago, more commerce and cacophony. There are more novelties. Also, the networks formed by some universities, academic institutions and NGOs have contributed to the import and distribution throughout India-Africa of a number of expressions of India–Africa solidarity, such as 'empowerment' and more recently, 'black is beautiful'. As a concrete follow up to the recent state confluence, the question is how do we develop diverse agents, vehicles and circuits within the political and civil society?

Ironically, African-born population and products are almost negligible in India today. You might have heard of, probably even cavorted to salsa, hip-hop and rap, but you have no chance of discovering the black dance, like the Dogon or the Manjini, in this country. We see TV channels broadcasting some 'black' series, but almost all of them are US-produced and sometimes we get only a limited number of 'black-exploitation movies'. People and objects, lexicon and music beats are defined as African by superficial association and similarity rather than through respectful inter-action, careful research and regular exposure, which is quite scarce. Amidst this, India–Africa Summit and other initiatives signify major shifts in the use of 'Africa' in India. The 'poverty' and 'primitiveness' of Africa have given way to 'partnership' and cooperation' with Africa. This shift should be banked upon not only the market, but also on peoples' aspirations and needs in an emerging new Africa, which is more varied and democratically vibrant than ever.

(*The Hindu*, 18 April 2008)

25

Naagbanton, Binayak Sen and Kampala Declaration

Patrick Barigbalo Naagbanton is a well-known human rights activist. Born in Rivers State, Nigeria, he trained as a journalist before working as a trade unionist at the Port Harcourt factory of the Union Dicon Salt PLC, where he was elected chairman of the workers union, Maritime Workers Union of Nigeria (MWUN). He was eventually fired for campaigning for improvement in working conditions. Naagbanton recruited many workers to join human rights/pro-democracy groups like the Civil Liberties Organisation (CLO), Campaign for Democracy (CD), and Committee for the Defence of Human Rights (CDHR). Naagbanton served as a board member of Civil Liberties Organisation (CLO), representing the Niger Delta region of Nigeria. He also worked with the Environmental Rights Action (ERA) and Friends of the Earth Nigeria (FOEN), documenting, researching and campaigning against human rights and environmental degradation in Nigeria. In recognition of his role in promoting and defending victims of rights abuse in Nigeria, Naagbanton received the Indianapolis University Human Rights Award in 2001; and in 2002, the Rivers State branch of the CLO conferred on him the Saro-Wiwa Award for human and environmental rights defender.

Under military rule in Nigeria, Naagbanton was arrested and held in solitary confinement. However he had to be freed, because there are some networks, institutional mechanisms and accountability of the state towards human rights activists in Africa. Naagbanton remains consistently vocal on issues of human rights and environment and has continued to contribute opinion articles, along with writing news and features for several newspapers. He remains free, in spite of raising his voice against the misuses of government security forces and militia and their consequences on people, especially women and children.

Compare him with Dr Binayak Sen, an equally well-known human rights activist, Vice President of the People's Union For Civil Liberties (PUCL), and General Secretary of the Chhattisgarh unit of PUCL, and also a paediatrician, who will complete two years in a Raipur prison on 14 May 2009, on false charges of abetting Maoist activity in Chhattisgarh, sedition, waging war against state under various sections of the draconian Chhattisgarh Special Public Security Act, 2005, the Unlawful Activities Prevention Act, 2004 (amended) and the IPC. Dr Sen raised his voice against Salwa Judum, and disappearances and encounters in the state of Chhattisgarh. Though in the past two years, there have been several calls and actions within and outside India by Nobel laureates, medical professionals, academicians, journalists, human rights and health activists, students, workers and rural folk for the release of Dr Sen, he continues to be in jail. Human rights and social movements have been protesting against the Chhattisgarh Special Public Security Act 2005 and the UAPA (amended) 2004, demanding for their repeal, and release of those arrested under it. Some 178 people have been detained under these draconian laws in Chhattisgarh. These include traders/businessmen, tailor, journalists, doctors, NGO workers, media persons, filmmakers, farmers, landless agricultural workers and cultural activists. There is no institutional mechanism to address the harassment and prosecution of human rights activists in India.

Thus, when 85 human rights defenders (HRDs) from 45 African States, and 33 partners from across the world, gathered at the All-Africa Human Rights Defenders Conference held in Kampala, Uganda from 20 to 23 April 2009, which was hosted by the East and Horn of Africa Human Rights Defenders Network (EHAHRD-Net) in close collaboration with all other sub-regional networks, and came out with a Kampala Declaration on human rights defenders, it should ring a bell in India as well. Kampala meeting was a follow up of the Johannesburg meeting, where the All Africa Human Rights Defenders Conference took place in November 1998. This meeting had agreed to identify challenges facing HRDs in Africa; train them in all existing local, regional and international mechanisms, identify advocacy measures for their freedom of action, look into measures for their security, ask States to adopt legislation to protect HRDs, in particular women, ask all intergovernmental bodies to protect HRDs and organise themselves in networks to respond urgently to human rights. And there are several milestones achieved since 1998 in the Africa region: appointment of a United Nations Special Rapporteur on HRDs, adoption of a UN Declaration on HRDs, appointment of a Special Rapporteur on HRDs at the African Commission on Human and People's Rights (ACHPR), adoption of several intergovernmental international and regional legal instruments, including the EU Guidelines on HRDs, and non-governmental action on protecting HRDs, establishment of HRD regional networks in Africa, notably in the East and Horn of Africa, Southern Africa, Central Africa and West Africa.

Human rights defenders from across Africa say that they remain deeply concerned regarding the threats, harassment, intimidation and physical violence they face in carrying out their work. However, they have also resolved to build on existing sub-regional networks and create new ones where needed, based on the lessons learned from existing ones. They will be undertaking an updated assessment of HRDs' needs in Africa. They will design a national, regional, and international strategy for their protection, and strengthen national HRD coalitions and sub-regional networks, to render them more dynamic and effective. They will work on the African Union to draft, under the auspices of the Special Rapporteur on HRDs of the ACHPR, and pass an additional protocol to the African Charter, which will protect and promote the rights of HRD. They will pay particular attention to vulnerable HRD groups, including women HRDs, and those working in conflict situations or oppressive regimes, as well as lesbian, gay, bisexual, transgender and intersex (LGBTI), and minority rights activists. They will pressurise all the African States to ratify and domesticate international and regional Human Rights instruments without reservations. There will be a comprehensive Kampala plan of action in future.

Of course, 14 May 2009 will be marked by several activities in India and internationally, to demand the immediate and uncon-ditional release of Dr Binayak Sen. However, unless we begin our work specifically in terms of a clear recognition of the status and role of human rights defenders, have a better organisation and com-munication regarding the activists at risk, and evolve and strengthen protection mechanisms at the national and regional levels, these human rights defenders will always remain at the receiving end. Amongst the well known cases of vicitimisation recently, we can remember Ms Shamim Modi, a leading activist of Shramik Adivasi Sanghathana and the office bearer of Samajwadi Jan Parishad in Madhya Pradesh state, who was arrested by Harda police on 10 February and remanded to 14-days judicial custody by the Harda CJM court. Shamin, educated from Lady SriRam College, Delhi University and Tata Institute of Social Sciences, Mumbai, has been instrumental in organising labour of 60 saw mills and plywood factories of the city. She had also taken up the causes of more than 1000 load workers of several Krishi Upaj Mandis in Harda district. Sanghathana and Shamim, along with her husband Anurag Modi, are raising the burning issues of tribal in the region, like minimum wages, bonded labour, ownership of forest land, illegal mining, atrocities, corruption and many more. Another burning example is of Abhay Sahu, president of the POSCO Pratirodh Sangram Samiti (PPSS), who is in jail since 12 October 2008. He was picked up by the Orissa police near Pattamundai in Jagtsingpur district while returning from a medical check-up. The police have registered as many as 25 criminal cases against him. For the past more than three years, the people of Dhinkia, Gobindpur and Nuagaon panchayats in Kujang tehsil of Jagatsinghpur district, under the banner of PPSS, have been agitating against the establishment of a 12-million ton mega steel plant by POSCO. The area has witnessed repeated episodes of intense violence.

Seeing the experience of Binayak Sen, it must also be said that the justice system needs to find new and concrete ways to protect rights activists, by giving teeth to the international and regional declarations that exist, and legislating and implementing them at the national level.

(*The Hindu*, 22 May 2009)

Section V

Challenges of Human Rights

26

Dalit Rights: Social Inclusion or Social Justice?

Inclusion and inclusive society is a widely-shared concern in contemporary times. However, what exactly is inclusion and how can we achieve it against the prevalent exclusion is a seriously-debated issue. What objectives and values should guide us in this journey towards an inclusive society? Is it social cohesion or social justice that is the over-arching principle? Is the aim of equality of opportunity enough in an unequal labour market? What are the models of citizenship and rights required to construct an inclusive society? How does equality and universality go, along with respect for diversity and people's aspirations for their respective identities? More broadly, how should we position the model of social justice and citizenship, in the local as well as the global context, amidst the entrenched/old and emerging/new inequalities, and new initiatives/ movements of discriminated people and their organisations?

What is Exclusion/Inclusion?

Social exclusion has different faces in diverse national situations and therefore there are different paradigms and policy measures needed to address it. 'Poverty' has usually been the expression traditionally used in lieu of 'exclusion' in many countries like UK and France, as well as in the European Commission well till the early 1990s. But the experiences of Dalits and Blacks have clearly revealed that exclusion has a much deeper implication, with poverty just an aspect of it. Rights and citizenships are denied to them in myriad ways in civil, economic, political and social spheres. One denial dates and develops with others. Indian Dalits or Black Americans have demonstrated that it is not only poverty that makes them more vulnerable than others; their exclusion is expounded by casteism and racism. Casteism, racism and other forms of discriminatory and oppressive practices can operate as mechanisms of exclusion, even in the case of those who have adequate material resources.

Social exclusion is also being seen as a combination of horizontal—in or out, and vertical—up or down characteristics. While poverty is about the unequal distribution of material resources, it is also understood that social exclusion is about the social relations of power, participation and integration. The concept of social exclusion has not only to do with products and their final outcomes; it is also about processes. These processes also involve the agency of the excluded, who encounter the structures of exclusion. If exclusion is someone or something being excluded by the other, then the role of the agency and the mechanisms involved in exclusion have to be looked into, to break this cycle of exclusion. Our notion of exclusion will also be very much determined by our understanding of whether the primary objective is social cohesion and inclusion or social justice.

The objective of social inclusion and cohesion is a limited one, which internationally has been deployed by the states to integrate the socially deprived population through employment and paid work. Essentially rooted in the concept of reservation and positive intervention in the public sectors, it sees the availability of work as the prime means of countering exclusion. Social inclusion and cohesion often also have a moralistic discourse, which highlight the 'underclass' and the 'poor', their distinct culture and language, their individual behaviour and values. Many of the programmatic works of NGOs and private agencies have this underlying understanding behind their work. However, the concept of social justice refers to a radical, redistributive and an egalitarian discourse that embraces notions of citizenship and social rights. Social justice associates itself with social activism and social movements, and goes beyond the state and the governments, and envisions itself ahead of even policies and programme formulations. While the importance of employment and work can be recognised in varying degrees within all the discourses, what distinguishes one from the other is the relationship of the work sphere with wider inequalities and disempowerment in the society.

Employment and Jobs for Inclusion

The creation of employment and jobs is central to the activities of the government, to build an inclusive society. Governments across countries and continents—India, South Asia, and Europe—have time and again reiterated the centrality of employment as their prime vision for an inclusive society. The politics of reservation in the Indian political arena since its independence has all along been dominated by the number of jobs the Dalits have and the avenues it opens for the enlistment of the community. The social and political discourses of Dalits themselves have also been echoing this throughout. European Commission's Social Action Programme 1998–2000 says that employment is the central means to achieve 'an active, inclusive and healthy society... because it is a Europe at work that will sustain the core values of the European social order'. In the UK, the Green Paper, *A New Contract for Welfare*, 1998 outlines that 'the government's aim is to rebuild the welfare state around work'.

It is true that employment and work play an important role in countering social exclusion. Unemployment and worklessness have a devastating impact on the lives of millions of people. Jobs and work fulfil certain basic needs, and thus play a very positive role in building a sense of confidence and inclusiveness in society. However, the assumption that jobs and employment necessarily spell social inclusion, and that they are the foundation on which an inclusive society can be built, needs to be substantially questioned.

Jobs cannot ensure social inclusion unless they not related with the quality and the position of work. If employment is expanded, and at the same time the gap between the higher and the lower ranks is expanding, then it is not an inclusive policy. Low-ranking jobs and jobs that are traditionally seen as only meant for the Dalits, create their own set of problems. Similarly, low pay has been a growing problem in the developed countries. It is not only the low-paid, low-ranking jobs, but the growing informalisation and contractisation of the job market has created a large number of temporary, part-time, contractual, self-employed or lower skill level jobs. Several studies have also found that the people affected by the closure of factories and privatisation are getting into the job market at a considerable low level than their previous work and earnings. 'Marginal jobs' by 'marginal people' is the scenario that we also face today. Thus, by the definition of inclusion and exclusion, the holder of marginal jobs is not excluded from the labour market. But by the definition of the quality of job and by the real meaning of social inclusion, certain sections of the employed will continue to be marginal and stigmatised, in spite of their jobs.

The lack of employment and worklessness are like chronic diseases for the excluded and the discriminated. The unemployed cannot even meet the basic necessities of their life and are forced to live an undignified life. Long-term unemployment leads to hunger, starvation, ill-health, and also to the loss of self-esteem and pride in oneself. Unemployment, of course, means exclusion from the labour market, but it does not necessarily mean social exclusion in all ways. The discriminated, the excluded have many other ways to relate with each other and with the broader society. Their everyday lives and survival strategies often also lead them to find ways of social bonding with surroundings and people who are like them. The more that we continue to define social inclusion in terms of only jobs and reservations, employment and work, the more we are caught in a small circle of interventions, the more we are ready to be exploited by the narrow range of politics and political parties, the more excluded people see their exclusion only in terms of jobs and the more the possibilities of a radical and comprehensive agenda of social inclusion are not met. Further, in such a scenario, the agency of the discriminated and the excluded people will remain be limited.

The discriminated have also their agencies other than jobs, to counter social exclusion. Their organisations, networks, enterprises, community-based and voluntary activities can be seen as strengthening their cause of social inclusion. Thus, the politics of social inclusion is defined in terms of the active citizenship of the discriminated, where jobs and employment go hand-in-hand with organisational, community and social work. Thus, the way we question the centrality of work in the overall strategy of inclusion, we also question the definition of work, which only includes jobs and services, and the limited security they provide. Other than the quality of work, the definition of work in case of the discriminated people should also include those elements which are not measured in currency and coins. The social and political empowerment and the broader issues of inequality and polarisation, both inside and outside of the labour market, need to be taken into account in our conceptualisation of inclusion, and the strategies to counter exclusion.

Justice and Inclusion

The politics of inclusion has seen many twists and turns in the last two decades. The new labours and the new democrats have shifted the meanings of social inclusion from the notion of equality to the equality of opportunities. The equality of opportunities has been defined in attractive terms like 'life-long opportunity', 'realising the potential to the fullest', 'comprehensive'. At a time, when the need to counter the inequalities of various kind is much higher than any other times in our history, and the concentration of wealth and power is unparallel, the proponents of 'equality of opportunities' are not being able to define as to how to locate themselves in the context of profoundly unequal economic and social structures and power relationships, and as to how to deal with the massively un-equal starting points that seriously determine the ability to grasp the opportunities opened up.

The social justice approach that roots itself in the Left notion of equality has to equally comprehend the diversity of the social classes that goes beyond the inequalities of wealth. Caste, race, gender, religion, disability or sexuality could be the other dimensions of in-equality and may or may not interact with the material inequalities. Thus, the democratic polity demands that first we recognise the diverse categories of exclusion, which are not only socio-economic in nature, but also to comprehend them in such a manner that a broader map of excluded people and their inclusionary politics and programmes can emerge. The interrelationship between different forms of discriminations and their politics requires both redistribution and recognition. There is always a positive tension to balance the two: the recognition drives one to accept the differences, whereas redistribution claims tend to do the opposite. If the recognition is a medium to, or an element in, socio-economic equality and justice, and the denigration of discriminated groups, breaks up the cultural and economic hegemony of globalisation and raises questions of structural economic oppression, the tensions and the two struggles can live together.

The struggles of Indian Dalits are a good example of this com-bination of recognition and redistribution. Dalits assert their right to speak as Dalits. They demand equal citizenship rights and eco-nomic justice through the assertion of Dalit as a different social and political category, rather than through its negation in the name of equality. In democracy, they continue to work for redistribution, and to gloss over their conflict of interests, for broader social–political interests.

Assertion and not assimilation is the core of inclusion from the perspective of social justice. Rights and not benefits are the nerve of a just society. From the core values of equality and justice, there also comes the need to challenge some of the traditional notions of inclusion. The guarantee of citizenship rights has been a main plank of struggles of the discriminated people across countries, and it is also true that citizenship works as a force for inclusion in any society. However, within nations, women and other minority groups never come fully into the citizenship fold, and many a times they have to enter at levels lower than others. Internationally, in a world getting hostile and closed to immigrants and asylum seekers, the issue of citizenship has gone against them. The borders of nation states are getting more rigid in the light of contemporary interpretations of citizenship, defined and delegated by the nation states. Thus, a just model of inclusive society has to be both local and global, with a multilayered and internationalist perspective, where the social and economic policy issues of justice and redistribution take the centre stage at the national and transnational political stage.

Social Justice for an Inclusive Society

The social justice policy in an inclusive society has to be defined in a broader way, and not only in the realm and language of the discriminated and the excluded. The social justice policy has also to be integrated with the overall economic policy. If economy is not driven by the principles of inclusion, then it is self-defeating in many ways. If the policy of reservation for Dalits is not combined with the overall employment, labour and industrial policy as a whole, it will not take us very far. Economic policies that generate employment have to promote social justice policies, designed to promote employability.

Education is the key to the social justice policy. Social exclusion thrives on the lack of education for the discriminated people. A good education is the most effective way to overcome inequalities of birth and status, to enable people to create and seize new opportunities, and to promote social improvement and mobility. Universalisation of education and equality in imparting education to all are the two key indicators to measure the commitment of a society towards the excluded.

Social security for the excluded is part and parcel of the social justice policy. The umbrella of social security involves the basic health and medical facilities, sufficient and nutritious food, right to work and right to information. The basic health care and medical facilities include the availability of clean drinking water and sanitation, because health is not only restricted to hospitals, medicines and doctors. The issue of food rights and food sovereignty has emerged as a focal point in our contemporary socio-economic and political discourse. The food rights under the social security system should be visualised as a way that meet the basic food required by every individual, family, and local community on a self-dependent basis. They should take into account not only the food distribution but also the distribution system, so that the excluded people have the capacity and the power to feed themselves.

It is not only social inclusion in terms of reservation of jobs, employment and work, but the social justice plank also voices for the right to work. The right to work is closely related with the right to life, food and education. In fact, the lack of quality and decent employment cause at times hunger and poverty, and through the opportunities of work, the excluded will get the avenues to fulfil their basic needs with dignity. At a time when the number of marginal and informal workers is increasing, this right could only bring a much-required security and confidence among the excluded.

Right to education, health and food have to combine themselves with right to information. An inclusive society should guarantee its population the information that is basic for the discriminated, to realise their rights in a democracy. Right to information is a basic right of the citizens, and it is the government's responsibility to defend and implement this right. In the struggles of the discriminated and the excluded across the world, the right to information and its democratic dissemination have acquired an expanding space as one of the chief democratic rights. Information is essential to live and to live with dignity.

The social justice framework of inclusion also puts emphasis on the rights of the discriminated and the excluded on the productive forces and their usage for a sustainable future. Who owns? Who commands?

The question of ownership of natural resources becomes prime and thus, the struggles on the ground for land, water, forest or coastal reforms against the interests of corporations and industries opens up a radical agenda for socio-economic transformation.

The journey towards a socially inclusive society has to be diverse and dynamic enough to capture the different facets of exclusion. Exclusion has material, cultural, historical and symbolic connotations and covers multiple dimensions of inequalities. Jobs, employment, reservations—all have important roles to play in strategies for social inclusion. However, if they are taken as our sole strategies, they would ultimately exclude more that they would include. Social inclusion, cohesion and social justice are necessarily not mutually exclusive, but the narrow model of inclusion that is being promoted by the exclusivist, identity-based, corrupt political forces does not comprehend the social justice aspects of power, resources and economy. The issue of jobs and employment has also to be questioned by the quality and positioning of these jobs and opportunities. We are not for the new *avatar*s of caste and race.

27

Forest Rights: Cost of Action and Inaction

The process towards the implementation of 'The Scheduled Tribes and Other Traditional Forest Dwellers (Recognition of Forest Rights) Act, 2006' is entering its crucial stage. In the present political environment, charged with an electoral context, the government is bound to notify the draft rules. The original co-sponsors—majority of tribal organisations and rights groups, and left and progressive political parties—are in agreement to mobilise support for its implementation. However, similar to the time of declaration and implementation of the National Rural Employment Guarantee Act (NREGA), the apathy and the opposition towards these rights and entitlements of the poor, is becoming shrill and shady. Special Economic Zones (SEZs) can be notified in no time in this country, but the millions of tribals and forest dwellers have to wait endlessly for anything that goes in their favour. There is a cost of action and there is a cost of inaction. The coalition government has to decide which is more expensive!

It is ironical that since the time of the discussion and the passing of the Forest Rights Act, conflicts in the forest areas have not subsided, and forced evictions and displacements continue to be a regular occurring. And this is unfolding at a time when after more than two decades of work within the UN system, the United Nations Declaration on the Rights of Indigenous Peoples was adopted in September 2007, with India speaking in favour of it. The declaration was adopted by a vote of 143 to 4 with 11 abstentions. The vote was called by Australia, New Zealand and the US. Only Canada joined these three states in voting against it. The declaration recognises the rights of indigenous people to the land, territories and natural resources that are critical to their way of life. It affirms that the rights of indigenous people are not separate from, or less than, the rights of others; they are an integral and indispensable part of a human rights system, dedicated to the rights of all. The declaration presents the Indian central and state governments a historic opportunity, which they must seize by adopting it, and entering into a new relationship with the tribal people, based on a principled commitment to the protection of their human rights. Through the Forest Rights Act, the government can work in good faith to implement their domestic law, and practice this vitally important, and long overdue, human rights instrument.

There was a positive thinking behind bringing this Act: to 'undo the historical injustice towards the forest dwelling scheduled tribes and other traditional forest dwellers'. It was passed in the winter session of 2006 in the Lok Sabha. Though the Act is a diluted version of the recommended draft proposed by the Joint Parliamentary Committee (JPC), it still has various positive features like individual and community rights to tenure, right to access, right to ownership over forests, right to in situ rehabilitation, including alternative land in cases of illegal eviction or displacement. However, positive thinking without affirmative action ends in zero results. It is imperative that the actual implementation of the Act be as constructive in tone as possible, so as to facilitate future work of holding the states to a commitment to implement the Act in letter and spirit.

In the immediate context of the Act as well, there are many concerns: First, the draft rule circulated by the government should end its discrimination towards non-ST populations, who are mainly tribals (non-scheduled in many states) and pastoral communities (OBCs and Muslims) living in forest areas, who are being asked to submit 75 years of proof of residence. Second, the powers of Gram Sabhas should not be diluted in the rules, which at present privilege the Forest Department over them. Further, there are no mechanisms at present to protect the tribals from the Forest Department utilising the situation to create divisions among the communities. Third, the government's ceaseless sanctions of SEZs and other industrial projects in the tribal heartland are bound to conflict with the bundle of rights conferred by the Act. This will force the tribals into confrontation with the state, the companies, or any other force that the government may deem to use. Additionally, in most of the tribal areas, free and prior consent of the people has not been sought for various projects. Compensations have not been fair; nor has rehabilitation by the state been legally assured in a comprehensive and substantive manner. Fourth, tribal leaders are constantly being beaten, detained and rearrested. Their organisations and activists are under tremendous pressure under the so-called security and anti-terror laws that will come in conflict with the implementation of the Forest Rights Act.

It appears that resembling each of the policy arenas in India today, two nations are at war in the forest areas as well, marking the space of people and profit. The fight is on between forest dwellers and private–public companies, between land acquisitions and land struggles, between displacement and development. Governments' policies on forests and tribals are a bunch of contradictions. For example, the situation in around 95 national parks and 500 wildlife sanctuaries, covering a little more than 22 per cent of the total forest cover in the country, reveals that the forest dwellers have no rights here whatsoever, be it grazing, cultivation, non timber forest produce (NTFP) collection or homestead. And the forest department has proposed 74 and 217 more national parks and wildlife sanctuaries respectively. The World Bank supported 'Public Private Partnership' in our forests is promoting industrial wood for pulp and paper industry, in the name of conservation of old growth forests and regeneration of new growth forests. The government and its wings, for example the Ministry of Environment and Forests, are also working as collaborators in promoting plantations for the pulp and paper industry. In this war of the two nations, people must win over profit. However, the power lies in the hands of our government to choose—what do they want most to be: facilitators of people's interests or corporate ones?

Forests face new threats in the name of 'global resources' and 'ecosystem services'. These cover an entire range of services offered by any natural ecosystem, including non-tangible and abstract values such as carbon-absorption potential and aesthetic values. Forests have become marketable products in entirety. Though the policy talks about community benefits and safeguarding community interests, this new environment can make way for legislative and policy changes at the national level that can irreparably damage the shared resource base of indigenous communities.

If tribals in India have suffered from historic injustices as a result of their colonisation and dispossession of their lands, territories and resources, thus preventing them from exercising, in particular, their right to development in accordance with their own needs and interests, then there should be no delay in establishing their rights, affirmed in the present Act. There is an urgent need in the country to respect and promote the inherent rights of indigenous people, especially over their lands, territories and resources, which derive from their political, economic and social structures and from their cultures, histories, philosophies and spiritual traditions. An honest implementation of the Act will contribute towards demilitarisation of lands and territories of tribal people, towards peace, development and economic and social progress, and a deeper understanding and friendly relations within the nation. Instead of finding impediments in implementing the Act or being unnecessarily fearful of it, we must welcome the fact that the tribals are organising themselves for political, economic, social and cultural enhancement. The Act is a step in the right direction to end various forms of discrimination and oppression, in whatever form or wherever they occur.

The Scheduled Tribes and Other Traditional Forest Dwellers (Recognition of Forest Rights) Act, 2006 was passed on 18 December 2006. The Act was notified into force on 31 December 2007. On 1 January 2008, this was followed by the notification of the Rules framed by the Ministry of Tribal Affairs to supplement the procedural aspects of the Act.

28

Minority Rights: Freedom of Conscience and Religion

The idea that fundamental rights are enjoyed by all, without any distinction of race, sex, language, ethnic origin, nationality and religion, is a basic principle of democracy and international human rights law. Violent attacks on the Christian minorities in different parts of the country are an assault on the very notion of democracy and universal human rights. Despite the country's obligation to respect and protect the right to freedom of conscience and religion, the wave of killings, beatings, sexual assaults, looting, destruction of property and displacement have created a climate of fear and insecurity, particularly among the Christians. Representatives of Christians and minorities are exposed to the grave risk of communally motivated verbal abuse and physical attacks. Worst, the governments of Orissa and Karnataka continued to deny the extent of violence prevalent, and failed to face up to their minimum responsibility of securing the life of their people. If India has to live up to any human rights standards, it must show a clear political will to combat attacks on Christians: speaking out strongly, and at all levels of governance; publicly acknowledging the seriousness of the issue; and the need to take concerted action. This is not 'hooliganism' or 'anti-social' activity, motivated by some hooligans and anti-social elements. It is a violent, and apparently a communal attack, carried out by organised groups. Crimes which are communally motivated must be effectively and thoroughly investigated and prosecuted as such. Treating communally induced violence and brutality on an equal footing with cases that have no communal overtones would be to turn a blind eye to the specific nature of the acts that are particularly destructive of fundamental rights.

Religious conversion is not the issue. The important matter at stake is the right to freedom of thought, conscience and religion that is guaranteed by our constitution, and a wide array of instruments of national and international laws. The right to freedom of religion declares that 'everyone shall have the right to freedom of thought, conscience and religion' and the freedom 'either individually or in community with others and in public or private, to manifest his religion or belief in worship, observance, practice and teaching'. The principle of non-discrimination is inherent in the enjoyment of the right to religion. Targeting Christians, Churches, campuses, and communities is clearly striping away these rights. Committed within the society generally, and at the hands of official omission and commission, as amply demonstrated in Kandhamal and Mangalore, are serious abuses of civil and political laws. Equally worrisome is the immunity continued to be enjoyed by those responsible for such heinous acts.

The large-scale violence against Christians in Orissa, Karnataka, Madhya Pradesh, Kerala, Chhattisgarh and Jharkhand is indicative of several developments in our country. It reflects the rise of communalism and conservatism. It reveals believes and practices of some organised groups, who openly justify contempt for other groups of people based on their religion. They want to carry out notions of superiority against any rule of law. Within this broad canvass, hate crimes are becoming one of the most brutal manifestations of intolerance and discrimination in our country today. Hate crimes have a more devastating effect on us than ordinary crimes. As various reports and testimonies suggest, they are reviving old, and creating new, biases, prejudices, and negative imaging of the 'other', and are also generating cycles of mistrust and tension within the affected states. Hate crimes have been allowed to recuperate themselves through crude and simple hate speeches—through word of mouth, graffiti, posters, newspapers, meetings, yatras, rumours, gossip, and internet. Speeches at rallies have been used to instigate attacks in Orissa and Karnataka, in fully view of official eyes.

It also needs to be noted that violence by the non-state actors on religious minorities is on an increase. It is indeed a sorry state of affairs that state authorities do not provide any official statistics on the number of reported incidents of violence against Christians. However, monitoring carried out by the press, human rights groups and NGOs working in these states indicates that there has been an alarming rise on violent attacks against the Christians over the last two years particularly. Many of them have been carried out by well-known groups like the Bajrang Dal and the Vishwa Hindu Parishad. The state has an obligation to prohibit, and bring to an end by all appropriate means, including immediate ordinance or legislation as required by pressing circumstances, attacks on minorities by any leader, group and organisation. Violence inflicted by government forces and by communal and terrorist groups—both should be our concern. We should also try to establish systems for recording and monitoring communal incidents, and also see how these incidents are prosecuted.

It is quite noticeable that the state authorities of Orissa, Karnataka, Madhya Pradesh and others have failed to protect the rights and freedom of Christians. They have failed to ensure a prompt, thorough, impartial and an independent investigation of reported assaults on minorities. They have thus also been unsuccessful in preventing the emergence of a climate of impunity with regard to such assaults. Immediately acknowledging the communal aspect of these assaults, which is to say that they are directed against the freedom and rights of members of a particular minority community, would have been a necessary step towards countering violence, discrimination and impunity. Instead, however, the state and its vital agencies restrained in applying even the existing legislation. The failure of the local administration and police in Kandhamal, Phulbani and Gajapati districts of Orissa, and in Mangalore and Udupi in Karnataka, to acknowledge the gravity of these communally motivated crimes and respond adequately, has led to virtual impunity for the perpetrators.

Sadly, it is also true that in many cases the victims did not report the crimes, as they had no confidence that they would get justice. Even if the victims do complain, the authorities are reluctant to take action. If the case manages to reach the court, the perpetrators will usually be prosecuted for 'law and order' problems, while the communal nature of the crime will go unacknowledged and unrecorded. This has led us to a situation in Indian polity, also realised in the past, where religious and ethnic minorities are exposed to a continuous risk of communally motivated abuses and violence from members of the public and officials. The present political dispensations cannot be relied upon to stop religious discrimination and fundamentalism, unless we have binding obligations under the national and international human rights laws to eliminate religious discrimination from state policies and practices, to completely protect minorities from violence by non-state groups and public officials, and to ensure constitutionally that the right to live freely from communal violence is enjoyed by all who live in India.

We all hold that communal violence is a particular affront to human dignity. In view of its perilous consequences, a special vigilance and vigorous reaction is required from the state and society. It is for this reason that we ask that the authorities must use all available means to combat communalism and communal violence, thereby reinforcing democracy's vision of a society in which diversity is not perceived as a threat but as a source of enrichment. However, our state and society has so far failed to evolve a strategy to protect the potential victims, before the violence escalated further.

The language of communalism is often violent. Violence can come from different quarters. However, it is equally true that the language of communalism is often silent: hostile comments and suspicious glances, threatening letters, stone throwing, and abuses. It is also embedded in the official practices that do not care for the everyday practices of communal organisations. It is worth recalling hear a comment of the Delhi Catholic Archdiocese Director, Dominic Emmanuel:

> The biggest worry of the Christian community is not that the Sangh Parivar is coming down heavily on the peace-loving community. What is shocking to the Christian community is that millions of Hindus who study in their institutions and hold great posts or businesses or in government today and who never even got so much as an indirect indication of the missionaries so called nefarious plans to convert them to Christianity are all quiet. We ask them to stand up and speak up.

29

Right to Work and Rights at Work

The 42nd Indian Labour Conference's (New Delhi, 20–21 February 2009) discussion on the global financial crisis and revelation of its effects, viz., large scale downsizing, layoffs, wage cuts and job losses, should be a wake up call for all those who care about the economic, social and cultural rights of majority of the Indian population. The right to work and rights at work have been heavily curtailed in India in the recent past. And the responsibility for denial of these rights frequently lies not only on governments but also on individuals, groups and enterprises. Defending and promoting job, employment and work should be an urgent priority, not only for the government, but also for the national community, the peoples' movement and civil society as a whole. There can be no higher precedence than the right to work, and live with dignity.

Let us see the government's own revelation in the Indian Labour Conference: A sample study conducted by the Department of Commerce for 121 export related companies showed loss in export orders to the tune of Rs 1792 crore, and loss of about 65,500 jobs. The Ministry of Labour and Employment had got a quick survey conducted by the Labour Bureau to assess the extent of job loss in the industries/sectors affected during the quarter October to December 2008, due to the economic slowdown. A sample of about 3000 units from organised and unorganised sectors, viz. Mining, Textiles, Metals, Gems, Automobiles, Construction, Transport and IT/BPO, was covered in Delhi (Delhi and NCR towns), Punjab (Jalandhar and Ludhiana), Tamil Nadu (Chennai and Tirupur), Karnataka (Bangalore and Bellary), West Bengal (Kolkata and Howrah), Jharkhand (Ranchi and Jamshedpur), Gujarat (Ahmedabad and Surat), and Maharashtra (Mumbai and Pune). The total employment in all the sectors covered by the survey went down from 16.2 million during September 2008 to 15.7 million during December 2008, thus resulting in job loss of about half a million people. The exporting units were observed to have had a higher decline in employment, for example in Gems and Jewellery (8.43 per cent), followed by Metals (2.6 per cent), Textiles (1.29 per cent), Automobiles (1.26 per cent) and Mining (0.32 per cent). The overall decline in contract workers was observed to be higher. The average earnings declined at the rate of 3.45 per cent per month during October–December 2008. This is when the smaller units were not covered in the survey, and tourism, financial and construction sectors were not included, which have also been severely affected by the financial crisis.

This situation is further compounded due to the prevailing global and national trends on employment. In 2008, roughly three billion people around the world were employed. As regards the three Asian regions, comprising South Asia, South-East Asia and the Pacific and East Asia, these accounted for about 57 per cent share in global employment. The global employment-to-population ratio decreased by 0.2 per cent during 2008 in comparison to the previous year, which was a result of rising unemployment in 2008 and labour force participation rate in the world remaining constant at around 65.1 per cent in recent years. The global number of unemployed in 2008 is estimated to be 190.2 million, indicating an increase of 10.7 million people, over 179.5 million during 2007. The global unemployment rate also increased from 5.7 per cent observed in 2007 to 6.0 per cent during 2008.

Going by various credible projections, labour misery will continue further. According to the Global Wage Report 2008–09, published by the International Labour Office (ILO), the global economic crisis is expected to lead to painful cuts in the wages of millions of workers worldwide in the coming year. It predicts that the slow or negative economic growth, combined with highly volatile food and energy prices, will erode the real wages of the world's 1.5 billion wage-earners, particularly low-wage and poorer households. Between the years 1995 and 2007, for each one per cent decline in GDP per capita, average wages fell even further by 1.55 percentage point, a result that points to the possible effects on wages in the current crisis.

The Indian government's response to the impact of global economic slowdown on the economy mainly comprises additional spending, interest subvention and excise duty cuts, which would prevent large scale job losses through the growth in industry and production. However, there is no guarantee that enterprise owners will use these benefits to save labour and employment, and will not continue to pass their burden on employees. In fact, this is precisely what we are witnessing now. It is also not clear how the government's flagship schemes like the Rajiv Gandhi Shramik Kalyan Yojna, the National Rural Employment Guarantee Act, and the Unorganised Workers Social Security Act will be reoriented to meet this serious crisis. As usual, since it is not a priority, we are nowhere near finalising the National Employment Policy and the National Skill Development Policy, which would have helped in promoting employment and employability in the country. The duty to 'take steps' towards employment is an immediate obligation: deliberate, concrete and targeted steps, as 'expeditiously and as effectively as possible, in similar ways as are being taken to support the economy and industry. Such steps might include adopting legislation or administrative machinery, or establishing action programmes and appropriate oversight bodies to stop retrenchment and lay offs. An understanding of a progressive upliftment of economy does not justify government's inaction on the immediate and massive suffering of labour.

The right to work and rights at work are perhaps the least prioritised in our country today. The concerns for workers' rights these days include worries in the international community over processes of globalisation and social consequences of trade liberalisation. Nowhere more than in the workplace do we see, in practice, an absolute indivisibility of rights. Examples of labour violations coming from throughout the country prove how abuses of civil and political rights compound an already grave situation, where breaches of economic, social and cultural rights previously exist. Basic fundamental rights at work—elimination of forced and compulsory labour in all its forms, equal pay for women and men for work of equal value, freedom of association, and ban on child labour—are missing. The right of access to employment without discrimination, free choice of employment, and a supportive structure that aids access to employment, which includes appropriate vocational education, right to fair wages, safe and healthy working conditions, reasonable limitations on working hours, prohibition of dismissal on dubious grounds and equality of treatment in employment, are less valued. We seriously lack a basic framework for the protection of labour rights and an enabling rights-based environment for equity and development. In an atmosphere where basic principles of freedom of association—the right to organise and the importance of collective bargaining—have been comprehensively cornered by employers and sectors in the past decades, the strength among workers and their organisations has considerable diminished to stop downsising or to protest against anti-union discrimination, though there have been some calls for all India protest actions. No doubt that the primary accountability rests with the governments in whose jurisdiction the present violations are occurring. At the same time, the companies too must be answerable for labour rights abuses within their premises.

In 1980s and 1990s, we witnessed the economic crisis with structural and policy adjustments under the overall dominance of the World Bank and the IMF and along with it a deep ideological and political crisis—a crisis that manifested itself in the shrinking of the sphere of secular, progressive ideology vis-à-vis the rise and development of communal, consumerist and rightist ideology. A substantial part of the working people, peasantry and small farmers, women, rural population had suffered immensely. Millions of working people participated in strikes and protest actions in 1990s demanding a halt to the new economic policies, but the government was rigid in implementing them. Today, the reality of liberalisation and corporate globalisation is more exposed and the alternatives are clearer. The immediate challenge is the labour redundancy. However, the danger contained in the present trend is determined not only by their immediate direct significance, but also the fact that like before, they will create the conditions for a further onslaught on peoples' democratic rights and for an anti-people restructuring of the economic sphere.

(*The Hindu*, 27 February 2009)

30

Migrant Rights: Mobility with Dignity

They are vilified as 'illegal', 'gate-crashers', 'queue-jumpers', 'invaders' seeking to breach the defences and decorum of Maharashtra and Delhi. They are labeled as security threats or as suspected or potential threats in Gujarat. They are tortured and murdered in Manipur and Assam. The scapegoating of migrants, the deliberate fuelling of fear and the nurturing of discriminatory, casteist and xenophobic sentiments by some politicians and parts of media have been accompanied by regular incidents that are trampling on some of the most basic rights of migrants, including the right to life, liberty and security of the person. The current discourses create the impression not only that migrants have no right to enter, but they have no rights at all. The hatred and violence against non-citizens, non-nationals, particularly migrants, could constitute one of the main sources of contemporary conservatism in India.

In the context of globalising, liberalising and corporatising economy, we have been ignoring the substantial body of labour rights laws and standards which guarantees the rights of migrants. Our governments have no will today to turn these guarantees into practical and meaningful measures to respect, protect and promote migrants' rights. The 'life-cycle' of migrant labour—the decision to leave the village/town of origin, the migratory journey, arrival and work in the place of destination, possible back and forth to the village of origin—is the story of exploitation, invisibility, discrimination, detention, denial of adequate housing, human standard of living and access to health care, abuses of the right to work and rights at work, negation of freedom of association and restrictions on freedom of expression. Overall, it is degrading treatment. Except a few trade unions and labour support groups, there are hardly anybody working and campaigning to pressurise governments, employers and others to make the rights set out in national–international laws into a reality for individual migrants. This silent human rights crisis should shame our conscience.

Whether in poor and rich states, thousands of people are migrating every day in the country, sometimes as a result of poverty and unemployment, as a result of national, regional, global economic processes, and often in uncontrolled and unregulated movements of poor people. Our governments' omission and commission on migrant issues in the recent past are to be seen not only in the sea of humanity travelling from one place to another without any governance. In different spheres like employment, housing, security, the limits of the state sovereignty are starkly displayed. Instead of state and its agencies, the companies, contractors, middlemen, power brokers, politicians exercise exclusive jurisdiction on migrants. They exercise authority over the living and working of migrant labourers. They hire and fire them at their will. Thus, the need is to evoke the state sovereignty in support of migrant people. States like Maharashtra, Assam and Manipur have the obligation to respect their voluntarily assumed legal obligations, including protecting the rights of all migrants.

However, states today assert their sovereignty in paradoxical ways vis-à-vis migrants. As seen in Gujarat, Maharashtra and Delhi at different times, when state sovereignty is impacted by the political, religious, or other narrow consideration and circumstance, migration measures, such as identification, issuing of ration cards or voter identity cards are a visible means of asserting state authority. States claim the sovereign right to exercise power over the migrants, their citizenship, their habitation and territory. There are few areas where this claim is made more forcefully by our governments than in the sphere of migration. In such cases, the need is to say that state sovereignty is not absolute, it is not without limits. Sovereignty cannot be used as a defence for acts that are unlawful and unjust. Advocates for the migrant rights should seek to ensure that the primary starting point of the national migration regime is the rights of migrants rather than the interests of states. This is required more as many politicians and policy makers are increasingly influenced by a perception that a hard line on migrants will boost their popularity with the electorate. Migrants are made an easy target and the political currents can be ignited more by narrow local–regional sentiments and preoccupations about the perceived threats that migrants pose to the identity and security of the state.

Most migration management policies and pronouncements today are getting discriminatory. The governments encourage some selected migration in white collar works while officially discouraging the migration of poor and marginal people. Delhi government that publicly state the absolute necessity of excluding irregular Bangladeshi migrants from their territory are prepared to tolerate the existence and even the growth of informal labour markets for the purpose of Commonwealth Games or Delhi Metros which rely largely on the labour of unregulated migrants. If a regime of 'migration management' is to be effective, not only must it be credible to states, but it must also be credible to migrants. We never hear the participation of organisations of migrant workers, individual migrants and their groups in the making of their laws and policies. To achieve their participation and respect their presence, we must stop putting them at increased rise of physical and mental abuse and violence at any stage of their living and working either in Pune, Mumbai, Ahmedabad or Delhi.

In the context of Maharashtra and Manipur, it is regrettable that the debate on migration and migrant workers continue to be framed in the immediate political contexts, with little or no focus on the rights of migrants. On the contrary, the horror, fear, violence coupled with political leaders and political parties has dominated the discussion of migration issues amongst the decision makers and wider public. There has been a tendency in public debates to treat migrants either as victims or as criminals. Portraying them as criminals or terrorists, parasites or parochial encourage a climate in which abuses against migrants are simplified, passed and even condoned. Strategies need to build upon migrants' agency against the attacks and new conservatism and recognise migrants' capacity to organise, to adapt and find ways out of bad situations.

Migrants cannot put in place an exit strategy before embarking on their journey. Thus, we must focus on those migrants who are most at risk. The voices of some courageous individuals and groups who speak out for migrants' rights must not be silenced as we have been witnessing almost regularly from the slums of different cities. Non-state actors, including private companies and individuals, millionaires and billionaires, constructors and builders have a big impact on the lives and human dignity of migrants, although the primary duty to protect the migrants remains with states. Migrants are part of the solution, not part of the problem.

31

Migration: A Silent Revolution and a Crisis

A silent revolution is in the making. Driven by the need to flee a perilous situation, or the promise of a better life elsewhere, millions of people are migrating to India or moving within India today, outside their area of origin. This is a growing phenomenon, and is increasingly more visible. However, migration is also under more attack than ever before. By assaulting and abusing the people of north Indian origin in the Mumbai city and elsewhere, we are killing the dreams, opportunities and aspirations of millions of people. Hate speeches and violent actions of regional chauvinist forces like the Maharashtra Navnirman Sena should shame our country. The problem is that governments and other actors are lacking the political will to tame the forces responsible for such hatred and violence, and are equally careless in turning the existing laws and standards into practical and meaningful measures, which respect, protect and promote migrants' rights. Thus, a silent revolution is slipping into a silent human rights crisis.

Not only in India, elsewhere too—within countries and across regions—voluntary and involuntary population movements are on the rise, pushed by economic, social, environmental and political factors. Thus, for the first time in the history of humankind, those living in urban areas have outnumbered those in rural areas. In 2008, the world reaches an invisible but significant milestone: more than half its population, 3.3 billion people, will be living in urban areas. By 2030, this is expected to swell to almost five billion. Between 2000 and 2030, the world's urban population is expected to increase by 72 per cent, while the built-up areas of cities of 100,000 people or more could increase by 175 per cent (based on the UNFPA, 2007).

It is further true that with higher levels of migration, more and more regions are confronted with issues of multiculturalism, and the challenges of integration, tolerance and diversity. In such moments, certain public statements arouse parochial and xenophobic prejudices, and incite attacks on migrant population at different times in different countries. However, this can only be challenged by focusing on the rule of law, and the human rights of migrants. Disbanding fear-mongers, dispelling fear, and countering misinformation are vital parts of protecting migrants' rights.

There is nothing illegal about north or south Indians migrating to any part of the country. It is entirely legal to move from one place to another to live and/or to work, either temporarily or permanently. We also already have a substantial body of laws which guarantee the specific rights of migrants. Possibly, in the whole 'life-cycle' of a migrant worker, filled with the decision to leave the place of origin, the migratory journey, wages and working conditions in the new place, and the likely return back, it is the poor worker who is more vulnerable to abuse, and migrant women and children most at risk. However, according to any government policies or migrant regulations, none of these migrants can be ever said to be slipping in and out of irregularities during the course of their journeys or while living and working in any state. Then why should they be left at the mercy of certain non-state actors and individuals, who are trying to force their own authority and regime in allowing people to enter or stay in a particular state? Why should not the authorities, for example in Mumbai, take action at an early stage, by putting in place effective measures to protect migrant people? Why should not the people, who are inciting violence and organising attacks, be brought to justice?

There are at least three disturbing trends that have emerged in our cities vis-à-vis the poor migrant workers. First, even when there are no violent attacks on migrant workers, in their everyday lives they are subjected to grave abuses regarding their civil-political, as well as economic, social and cultural rights. Their living places—the large slums—are the visible symbols of disparity, desperation and human rights abuse in cities. Sprawling urban spaces also bring crime and violence. The affluent middle and upper classes wall themselves in, and pay for private security, which itself becomes a source of increased violence and disrespect for human rights. And our policymakers continue to work against rural–urban migration, using tactics such as house destruction, forced displacement, eviction of squatters, and denial of services. The way our state and society function on a day-to-day basis towards migrant workers can also be held responsible for violence, aggression and attacks, which are big scale occurrences over long time periods.

Secondly, by our commission and omission, we are turning the poor survival migrants into stateless migrants. We know that serious abuses of many rights compel many migrants to leave their homes, and often their families, in search of safety, security and a sustainable livelihood. They move as part of a survival strategy. Desperately poor, they often take hard decisions for basic human security for themselves and their families. However, by the sheer callous and careless attitude of the state, they are often denied ration cards, electricity and water connections, address authentication, residence certificate and so on. Their children are at times school-less, as they lack the birth or residence certificate. They are virtually a stateless person in their place of work—a person who is not considered a citizen by the operation of law. Thus, we see them regularly being crushed either by Raj Thackeray or by the police, by bulldozers or by anti-social elements.

Thirdly, by all means, our state and society is benefiting from the migrant workers and their migration. Companies encourage migration because they get benefits from the economic value of the informal market sector. Others encourage contractors and sub-contractors to get them at construction sites, where mostly migrants are employed. Increasing professional and middle class populations want them for their daily services, not least to maintain their living and work infrastructure, and to find sufficient caregivers. Several sectors and states get massive 'brain gain' through the skilled migrants. States, in absence of any alternative thinking, continue with the formal–informal practices of obtaining the benefits of migrant remittances to their economies. However, when it comes to the migration management polices, none of these parties have anything to offer, except some old labour laws that are hardly implemented, and a political perception that a hard line on migration will solve the problems ranging from petty crime, over crowding to terrorism. Here, coupled with other conservative trends in our society, restrictive migration policies are often suggested that are mostly driven by narrow sentiments and preoccupations about the perceived threats that migrants allegedly pose to regional identity and national security.

We should be celebrating the contributions made by migrants to cities like Mumbai, Delhi and others, in terms of skills, resources and diversity. Whether low or highly skilled, migrants are bringing positive changes to our society, benefits which are not only economic, but also social and cultural. We should be recognising the benefits that migration is bringing to areas of origin in terms of not only remittances, but also new or improved skills and knowledge for those returning home.

Instead of states taking a state-centric approach, and regions getting caught in competing regionalism, there must be a national level initiative, so that the competing state governments build a consensus on broad principles underlying a national scheme of 'migration management'. An inter-state mechanism is required to achieve better management at regional and national levels through better inter-state cooperation. States cannot pick and choose which rights it will apply in case of migrant workers. Further, the current data on migrants, and on violations of their rights, remains quite limited. This lack of information, including the absence of a comprehensive and authoritative statistics, is an obstacle to policy development as well as to effective campaigning for the protection of migrants' rights. In the present context, we need to know various things— how many migrant workers are arrested, detained and attacked; the number of migrants engaged in low skilled employment sectors; the implementation of labour laws; which women and children have been victims of trafficking; the new non-state actors and the impact of their practices, *et cetera*.

Speaking about the rights of migrants against multiple odds of violence, exploitation and poverty is, in fact, not about looking for a 'solution' to migration. Migration is a phenomenon, not a problem, and it will grow further. There is a need to place the migrants at the centre of regional and urban policies and planning.

(*The Hindu*, 27 March 2008)

32

Immigrants' Rights under Economic Crisis

The US and many European countries are considerably hardening their policies towards immigrants and their employment. As currencies tumble, stock markets collapse and growth rates are constantly forecasted downwards, the champions of free trade and markets are pulling back their protectionist strategies. From opposing the idea of inviting overseas nurses, including from India, to issuing a 30-day deadline to benched H-1B visa workers for returning to their homes, immigrants are at the receiving end and have become easy targets. While the designing of policies on immigration is fundamentally a matter of individual governments, any such policies must be compatible with international human rights laws and standards. Politicians, public officials and the media should not use public perceptions of immigrants as scapegoats for economic recession, or as solutions to the global economic downturn, which is turn further fuels discrimination, racism and xenophobia. This is also a time for governments to engage in multilateral, regional and bilateral processes to mainstream migration, which can provide for varying degrees of mobility and security to citizens of member states.

People cross borders everyday—sometimes as a result of bilateral agreements between states, or due to global and regional economic processes, and often as uncontrolled and unregulated movements of people, based on demand and supply. Even though we accept that states have a sovereign right to exercise authority over their borders, such rights are not absolute. Sovereign power is not without limits. Owing to global recession and economic meltdown, termination of jobs without notice, retaining employees' visas and not renewing them on time, thus making them illegal immigrants, requirements to leave within 30 days or otherwise becoming 'out of status' and 'illegal', proposing of amendments to visa legislations and many such measures are unlawful under international laws. A state cannot pick and choose people as and when it wishes, and throw away some or the other rights at will. It must exercise its legitimate powers responsibly within the labour rights framework, and there should not be any unilateral actions by one country. Attempts to restore economic stability in one country by closing its borders to labour is bound to generate even more substantial income and employment losses in many countries.

In the past, the US and other developed countries have been encouraging selective migration, while officially discouraging other types of migration. Many European governments that publicly state the absolute necessity of excluding irregular migrants from their territory are prepared to tolerate the existence and even the growth of informal labour markets, which rely largely on the labour of irregular migrants. Others encourage migrants to work in industries which face labour shortages. Ageing populations and dramatically reduced fertility rates in the developed world are also influencing governments in favour of migration, not least to maintain their pensions and social security systems, and to find sufficient caregivers. On the other hand, Asian and African governments favour migration because of the economic value of remittances to the sending country, as well as the social and economic benefits of a migrant worker population to the receiving country. However, in these times of financial turmoil, many politicians, including the US President Barack Obama, and other policy-makers are heavily influenced by an understanding that a hard line on immigration will boost their population with further employment.

The world has evolved some migration management systems over the course of time, and the US and other countries should not resort to unjust unilateralism, at the cost of bilateral, regional and international understandings. See, for example, the agreements of the Economic Community of West African States (ECOWAS), which give citizens of those states the right to 'enter, reside, and establish' in any member state. In the European Union (EU), full mobility is permitted to citizens of EU countries, including for employment purposes. Mobility within the common markets of the southern cone of South America (MERCOSUR) focuses solely on the movement of professionals. In Asia, where binding agreements on migration issues have been rare, states that comprise the Association of South East Asian Nations (ASEAN) have agreed in principle to open up certain sectors to workers from other ASEAN countries. In addition, under the 2004 Vientiane Action Program, member states of ASEAN have committed to elaborating an instrument for the promotion and protection of the rights of migrant workers. The Middle East region has similarly been characterised by a lack of binding agreements on migration. A series of meetings of the 5+5 Dialogue on Migration in the Western Mediterranean, hosted by the International Organisation for Migration (IOM) between 2002 and 2004, aimed to enhance coordination, and identify relevant responses to the complexity of migration patterns in this region.

At the international level, governments have sought consensus on broad principles underlying an international regime of 'migration management'. One recent example is the Berne Initiative, an inter-governmental consultative process aimed at 'achieving a better management of migration at regional and global level through enhanced inter-state cooperation'. Another example is the inter-governmental consultative process within the International Labour Organisation (ILO). The 92nd session of the International Labour Conference called on the ILO to carry out a plan of action on migrant workers designed to ensure that migrant workers were covered by the provisions of international labour standards and benefited from the applicable national labour and social laws. To bring this about, a non-binding Multilateral Framework on Labour Migration has been adopted by the Governing Body of the ILO. The IOM is an intergovernmental organisation which has taken a leading role in discussions on migration management in the international sphere, and plays an increasingly important role in the development of inter-national migration policy. This is most evident in its 'International Dialogue on Migration', which is aimed at strengthening cooperative mechanisms between governments in such areas as migration and trade, labour, health and development. However, the IOM has no formal protection mandate or any responsibility to supervise an international treaty to protect migrants.

According to the ILO, an estimated 90 million workers live and work outside their country of origin. Nearly 200 million people out of a global population of 6.4 billion live outside the country in which they are born (International Organisation for Migration, 2005).

Women now constitute almost half of the migrant population. One can well imagine a situation in which countries are allowed to put in place protectionism as the core of the new regime of migration management, and the impact it would have on the well-being of the vast population of the world as a whole. If a solution to economic recession involving immigrants is to be effective, not only must it be credible to the states, but also to the migrants themselves. To achieve this, states must respect the immigrants. Politicians and parliamentarians of the US and Europe have a choice today. They can either make decisions that ensure the security, dignity and continuity of the immigrants or their resolutions can leave the migrants vulnerable to dislocation, vulnerability and abuse. The first set of choices will bring the world together in addressing the problems of the present economic downturn and will lead to a collective coming out of the crisis; the second would virtually make nations fortressed and to the continuation of the crisis at large.

History, especially the experiences in the aftermath of the stock market crash in October 1929, reveals that protectionist strategies are likely to make matters worse. Solutions to the global economic downturn that we are facing today do not lie solely in financial policies. They require integrated economic, social and environmental strategies at different levels. The great depression of the 1900s prompted the establishment of world governance institutions of today. The 1997 crisis in Asian countries saw many of them introducing or extending social security schemes, including unemployment insurance, and doing away with the IMF loan conditionality. The present crisis should also be seen as a catalyst to new ways of thinking and creative alternatives.

(*The Hindu*, 17 March 2009)

33

Labour and Health Rights: Mines of Misery in Rajasthan

Behind the growing profits of Rajasthan's mine fields emerges a grim picture of human suffering—of hunger, death, disease and fatal accidents. Millions of mine workers and their families are impoverished. According to the Mine Labour Protection Campaign, headed by Justice V.R. Krishna Iyer and comprising a number of voluntary organisations and individuals, the mines have proved to be virtual death-fields, with over 95 per cent of them being worked in an unscientific and unsafe manner, without any restrictions.

Rajasthan is rich in mines and minerals. With 42 varieties of major and 23 varieties of minor minerals mined, the state has earned the epithet the museum of minerals. The state has minerals like wollastonite, jasper, zinc concentrate, fluorite, gypsum, marble, asbestos, soapstone, lead concentrate, phosphate, rock, ball clay, calcite, sandstone, flaggy limestone and felspar, which account for 70 per cent or more of India's total production of these minerals. According to the Mineral Policy issued by the Mines Department, Government of Rajasthan in August 2005, 2,780 mining leases for major minerals, 18,854 for minor minerals and 27,306 quarry licenses are in force. The state has the largest number of leases for small mines in the country.

However, such details are not available about the mine workers. There are no reliable figures about their number and composition. They belong to a workforce that is largely unaccounted for, with the government figures widely contested by trade unions, voluntary organisations and researchers. The Mine Labour Protection Campaign, on the basis of a survey of mining and mine workers in

Jodhpur, Alwar and Makrana areas, estimates that over 1.8 million workers are engaged in variety of mining operations throughout the state. Fifteen per cent of these workers are children, 22,000 of them in the age group of 10 to 12 years, and 37 per cent are women. The Scheduled Castes and the Scheduled Tribes constitute a majority of the workforce.

In the Jodhpur, Udaipur, Rajsamand, Ajmer, Jaipur, Alwar and Makrana areas of the state, mine workers have been victims of ruthless exploitation for more than two decades. The Gramin Vikas Vigyan Samiti, an NGO working among mine as well as rural and agricultural workers, and the School of Dessert Sciences, Jodhpur conducted surveys among the mine workers in 1994 and 1995. Prahalad Singh and Rahul Dev of the Grasim Vikas Vigyan Samiti, giving an account of the lives of sandstone mine workers of Jodhpour, say,

> Over 60,000 workers are engaged in sandstone mining, majority of them in the age group of 16 to 40 years, the most productive period of their lives. Most of the mine workers in the Jodhpur region belong to either the Scheduled Castes or the Scheduled Tribes or to the poor strata of society, which includes the landless or those who have marginal or unproductive land. Because of lack of resources, they have taken to working in the mines.

A sample survey of 300 mine workers conducted by the Samiti in the Jodhpur area revealed that 189 workers suffer from respiratory problems. Accidents are frequent, as most of the work is done manually with the help of heavy hammers, chisels and other primitive tools. Often heavy slabs of stone fall on the workers, resulting in serious injuries. Ninety-four per cent of them received neither wages nor leave during the recovery period and 89 per cent had to pay from their pockets for medical help. Even when an accident occurred at the workplace, 72.7 per cent reported that no medical expenses were provided by their employees.

The Udaipur region (this includes Udaipur, Rajsamand, Banswara, Dungarpur and Chittorgarh districts) is one of the prime mining fields of the Dtate, where, from a population of over 6.4 million, about 6,00,000 are engaged in mining. Madan Modi of the Samayik Sudhar Aur Manavaidhikar Suraksha (SASUMASU), Udaipur says,

> According to government records, there are 750 leases issued for major minerals, 3,500 for minor minerals and over 5,000 quarry licences.

But in reality, many more mines are in operation, covering a very large area in the Aravalli belt. In Udaipur, from Bhuwana to Chirwa, a stretch of about 5 km is full of these units. No land is left unmined in the 25-km Rajsamand–Gomati Chauraya region. Male workers make about Rs. 25 to 35 a day and female and child workers about Rs. 20 to 30 and Rs. 10 to 15 a day respectively. The mine workers of this region are totally unorganised.

The condition of the workers in the Jaipur region is no different. The Institute of Environment Studies, Jaipur in a study conducted on the environmental impact of mining in the Bijolia area, noted that 70 per cent of the mine workers and their family members suffered from numerous diseases.

Mining, as practised in the state, has not only had an adverse impact on natural resources, but has killed a large number of mine workers. Speaking to me, workers recounted various accidents: in Udaipur district, a softstone mine near Parsola witnessed a serious accident Workers said that, Rupe, 32, was buried under mine debris that came down. In Rajsamand district, 40-year-old Nana Lal was killed in the Dholi marble mine. Mohan Lal, who works in the Dhula mines in Udaipur district's Kherwara block, said, 'I receive meager wages for working in such unsafe and unhealthy conditions. Everyday when I go to work, I think I am not going to come back again. In the last five years I have seen so many accidents, injuries and deaths of fellow workers. They always haunt me.'

Government officials confirm the mine workers' complaint that these mines have no written records of employment. They are either contract labourers or daily wage workers. There are no health schemes, group insurance, Employees' State Insurance, Provident Fund, gratuity, bonus or pension for them. The laws regarding minimum wages, overtime, welfare, health and safety simply do not exist as far as these areas are concerned. Even in the case of serious accidents, deaths and injuries, no compensation is given normally. Government officials say that not a single case for compensation or for providing any other facility to which these workers are entitled, has ever been made out or filed. Not a single case of silicosis or any other occupational disease has ever been reported. Rarely, when a worker dies, a small amount is given to his or her family.

In this 'jungle raj' where brute force and terror rule and trade unions have a very minor presence, the state and its machinery have almost abdicated the responsibility of safeguarding the interests of the workers and implementing the labour and social welfare laws.

At the same time, the Central Government and the state government are keen on increasing the mining activities, through corporate groups, joint ventures and multinational companies.

Although the Directorate of Mines Safety has a tremendous responsibility, it is practically non-existent in a majority of the mining areas in Rajasthan. Director of Mines Safety says, 'There is a lot of mining activity going on in this region. But we know very little about most of them. We don't think that it is possible to monitor the mining activities in this whole region with our limited resources.' He asks: 'When all other concerned parties are interested only in raising production, who is going to care for the workers' health and safety?'

He also accepts that 'there are a large number of small mines that operate without any control. They have strong political connections and patronage. These mines operate in very congested areas. There is no proper space left between two mines. There are no benches, stairs or roads in these mines. There are no records maintained here.'

He adds,

> Most of the mining areas in Rajasthan are dangerous today. A large number of accidents and deaths take place in the mines. But we get very little information regarding them. We come to know about an accident and visit the site only if some mine gives us notice regarding the accident. Recently, the local police and the Mines and Geology Department informed us about two accidents in the marble mines of this region. We have filed cases, but nothing has been done in similar cases filed by us two years ago.

He justified the Directorate's role in the present state of affairs:

> Everybody knows that there are large-scale violations of safety regulations in these mines. Then what purpose do our inspections serve in this situation? Our office goes to the mining area and finds out violations in the safety laws. He prepared the report and asks the mine owner to undo the wrongs. If the mine owner does not follow his instructions, then he can do another inspection or start prosecution. But what is the use of going for a prosecution on safety violations when prosecution proceedings regarding fatal accidents are not proving to be of any worth? And even if the case is decided, the penalty will be a maximum of Rs 200, Rs 300 or Rs 400. In such a situation, violations continue. We neither do first or second inspection, nor go in for court cases. The problem continues. Our department also continues to work, but without any result.

Labour Commissioner, Udaipur division, adds, 'We don't have even a single case regarding the mines. Neither do we have a single claim. So far as our jurisdiction goes in this field, there are no problems at all. We are concerned only with the processing units.' He admits that mafias run the mines in the State. Their armed guards keep an eye on the workers and the minefields. 'Nobody dares to enter the mining area. Actually, there are no laws of the state applicable here. However, for the first time, we convened a meeting of all the state departments concerned with marble mine. We have decided to do a comprehensive survey of them in the Udaipur region,' the Labour Commissioner said.

The Labour Enforcement Office, Ministry of Labour, Government of India, is another department in charge of implementing various labour laws other than on health and safety. Their problem, according to its official spokesperson, is that 'there are a large number of mines in the Udaipur region, but we have no list of them. We have no infrastructure to inspect them. The mining activities of Udaipur, Banswara, Dungarpur and Rajsamand districts come under our jurisdiction and we have only a three-member staff here. There are four major labour laws—the Minimum Wages Act, the Payment of Wages Act, the Equal Remuneration Act and the Payment of Gratuity Act, which are to be implemented in these mines. Every year we file an average of 300 cases regarding violations of minimum wages and payment of wages. However, they take a long time to decide. Even if there is a decision, mine owners get Rs 500 as penalty under the Payment of Wages Act.' He emphasises that 'there is no coordination between the state department, the Mines Safety Directorate and the Labour Enforcement Authority. 'All work independently of each other,' he says.

However, the Mines and Geology Department, Government of Rajasthan, which issues leases and licenses for mining and is the sole administrative authority for all the mining activities in the state, gives a rosy picture. Its Director says, 'We want to maximise the use of the vast mineral wealth. We do not want to harp on safety aspects because there is a separate department for this. When we receive any complaints regarding violations of the standards, we refer them to the Mines Safety Directorate and the Labour Enforcement Authority. It is for them to inspect and follow it up with necessary action.' He adds,

Most of the large-scale mining activity in the State has very few health and safety problems. Most of the mines have resorted to safe and scientific mining. In the marble mines there has been a revolutionary change in the production process in the last 10 years or so. Systematic use of automatic devices has reduced the accident rate drastically. Apart from the Makrana mining area, all the other mining regions are by and large safe today.

The Mines Safety Directorate, however, has a different story to tell. Placing the responsibility for mismanagement at the door of the state government, the spokesperson of the Directorate says,

> It is the Mines and Geology Department of the Rajasthan Government which is primarily responsible for the health and safety hazards. They have their own interest in issuing leases in a reckless manner. We had written to the director, Mines and Geology Department, saying that leases for small mines are granted in a dangerous manner. There is no 15-metre open spade between two mines as required by the Act. The space left for roads is very narrow. There is no provision for bench-making. Sometimes one mine is just below another, so stones from one go down to another and hurt the workers. We suggested that leases should not be given to mines smaller than 500 metres. There should be enough space for roads, benches, first aid and there should be a qualified mine manager as per the Act. But no response came from the Mines Department. In spite of our reminders, they are not taking any action.

In such a situation, only hope for the workers is community service organisations, which are playing an increasingly active role in some regions. Although there were a few successful attempts earlier to raise the issue of the environmental impact of indiscriminate mining in Sariska and elsewhere in Alwar, and the Supreme Court had given directions to stop environmentally hazardous mining, the issue of workers' health and safety was not taken care of. However, after the Mine Labour Protection Campaign came into being, there has been an effort to shift the focus to labour issues as well. The Campaign has formulated detailed recommendations concerning the health, safety and welfare of the mine workers. As a group, it is trying to highlight the sufferings of the workers and initiate a process to organise them into a group.

Madan Modi, a social activist and a main organiser of the Campaign in the Udaipur region, suggests that the permission of the village panchayat be made mandatory for any mining activity on village land.

The village's share of the profit should be determined and this should be used for the village's development. A proper place should be identified for waste disposal. There should be strict enforcement of mining and other laws.

The health and safety of the mine workers is another major area of concern. For this, Madan Modi suggested that adequate fencing be done in the mining areas to prevent accidents and time-bound afforestation should be done in the left-out areas. There should be proper and regular medical check-up of the workers. The use of explosives should be heavily restricted, he said.

34

Panchayats: The Making of Peoples' Power and Right to Vote

I

Booth, Boat and Vote

Udangharari

'We need a polling booth right in our village, so that our 100 houses can cast their votes', was the prime concern among the 40-odd women-men gathered on a scorching April noon in Udangharari village of Khagaria district in Bihar. They all sat in the shadow of the village panchayat house and argued as to why their panchayat house or the primary school of their village should be made into a polling booth.

Udangharari has 90 Musahar and 10 Mallah families. They realised in early January 2001 that the polling booth for the forthcoming panchayat elections was not only far, that is, at a distance of 2–2.5 kilometre and that too by boat through some of the way; but was also situated in a Kurmi-dominated Khairi village, from where a Kurmi landlord was contesting for the Mukhiya post. The villagers soon gave a written complaint to the Gram Panchayat Supervisor and the Block Development Officer.

The villagers had enough reasons to be alarmed, as the same had happened in 1978 when the panchayat elections were last held in Bihar. 'None of us could vote in 1978. Our polling booth was in Khairi village. When few of us reached to cast our votes, we were beaten up. After this, others did not dare to go', recalls Ramvilas, who was one of the ones beaten. The result, a landlord-cum-petty-trader from Khairi, Rajendra Teli, won the election.

Election or no election, nobody seems to care for Udangharari. 'We have never seen our MLA or the MP, even during the election times. The MLA Pashupati babu has been winning from this constituency since 1977, but has not visited us even once', claim the villagers. This small dalit village is very difficult to access for six months of the year, since rivers Ganga, Buri Gandak and Bhagmati surround it. The village is regularly affected by floods and land erosion, because of which 30 Musahar families have been living on the high embankment area since the last five years. Only one family has 1.5 *bigha*s agricultural land; the rest are agricultural labourers. Twenty families are also sharecroppers. The agricultural labourers and sharecroppers work on the land mostly owned by the Koeri-Kurmi landowners from Khairi and other nearby villages. Disputes over wages and sharecropping have been continuing in courts since many years. Women have much less employment opportunities and most of them work in the fields for a maximum of two months in a year. The daily wages are Rs 50 for men and 25 for women. The majority migrates to cities, factories and brick kilns for their survival. The village has a primary school which has two teachers, both of whom are always absent—one is not to be seen for years and the other has hired an unemployed youth for Rs 400 to teach in his place.

However, in the panchayat elections, the candidates are coming and campaigning in the village. The number of candidates is also high and the competition is tough. There are 13 Mukhiya candidates for Dahma Khairi Khutha panchayat, to which Udangharari also belongs. In most of the villages, there are candidates for notified or reserved posts. From Udangharari, there is a candidate for Mukhiya, there is a candidate for the SC reserved post for panchayat samiti, and there is Surendra Sadai elected unopposed for the reserved post of ward member. The candidates are promising many things, immediately and deeply felt by the voters.

For a Musahar candidate like Chamaru, the road and the boat are the two most important things worth fighting for by a *Mukhiya*. 'From the Khagaria to the Sonebanki ghat, until the point one can come by bus–jeep, there is no pucca road. There is no boat even for the flooded and rainy days. The boats belong to the landlords of Khairi village. What I stand for is the road and the boat, so that we can move and live in a medical emergency', says Chamaru. The unopposed elected ward member Surendra Sadai emphasises the need for the boat and the presence of the teachers in the primary school.

Ramvilas has a strong hope that with the onset of the panchayat elections, the villagers will be able to interact with the officers, who are otherwise difficult to access. The villagers themselves will solve the problems of the village and the officers will listen to the villagers.

Various concerns and hopes have made Udangharari rather alert and active. Who will win? Who will vote? Who will build the road for whom? Who will make use of government schemes and for what? Who will have this new power, coming out from a rather new exercise?

Even when the panchayat elections were just announced, the villagers wrote to the district administration that the polling booth should be placed in the village primary school. They apprised the administration that even last time, their Harijan candidate could not win because of booth capturing. They demanded that their area be announced sensitive, especially keeping in mind the record of the previous panchayat elections. However, the District Magistrate hardly has any clue of the issues crystallised in the placement of a particular booth, or the basic facts of this village. Deepak Kumar Singh, DM, Khagaria, has been prompt in identifying three levels of sensitive booths, that is, those which are Naxalite-affected, those which are ridden by caste tensions and those which are inaccessible by roads. He claims to have made all the arrangements for the safety of these booths. However, Udangharari does not figure in any of his categories, and thus is virtually left on its own.

It is unlikely that the booth for Udangharari will be relocated. It is also unlikely that the police will come to this remote area to give the villagers electoral justice. What next? 'We are holding our meeting soon to chalk out our strategy in this situation. Unlike 1978, we will make all efforts to cast our votes this time. It is very much possible that the landowners will remove their boats on the Election Day, to prevent us from voting. We are arranging our own boats', informs Sabo Devi, who runs a small shop in the village, in the absence of her migratory husband.

II

Flag Hoisting

Latha

Mahadeo Singh, a Rajput landlord, became the Mukhiya of Nariyar panchayat in Saharsa district in 1978. He owns approximately 90 bighas agricultural land, and tractor, taxi, jeep. In his house are located the primary health centre, the post office and the panchayat ghar. In April 2001, he is again contesting for the *Mukhiya* post.

Another contestant is Amarnath Sardar. A Tanti (basket weaving caste), who no longer weaves, he owns 2.5 bighas agricultural land and has been a sharecropper.

Shivaji Singh, another Rajput, is also in the fray. He is said to have a vast area of urbanised, highly priced land, close to the Saharsa town.

Nariyar panchayat has a sober look. The houses, roads, wells, hand-pumps and cattle are in a better condition. Being adjoining to the Saharsa town, the village has access to electricity, water and such basic infrastructure. A keen contest is in the offing: the panchayat has 1,600 Tanti, 1,200 Muslim and 400 Rajput votes. The Rajputs have land, money, muscle; the Tantis have numbers. Other than the numbers game, in the recent past, they have started growing vegetables by introducing new farming methods and by catering to the urban market, and have thus improved their economic situation.

However, the relative freedom from the landowner and the marginal improvement in their economic situation is not sufficient for the Tantis to take a complete break from the multiple relations of dependence. They have very less land or no land of their own, and as sharecroppers, they are tied at many places. 'I have 10 *kattha*s of land. And the rest is sharecropping on the land owned by the babu sahebs', narrates Ramdeo Sardar, who is also living on a piece of land given by the landowner since generations, but is now facing the threat of eviction.

Keen contest is not a clean contest since Babu Mahadeo Singh has openly announced that he wants to continue with his services to the village. He would not allow his adversaries to caste their vote and for this purpose, 60–70 Rajput musclemen are seen camping in his house.

What if Amarnath Sardar is a graduate and is the one who has prompted the Tantis to take up vegetable cultivation in a new way? How does it matter that most of the Tantis together with the Muslims have decided in a meeting that Amarnath Sardar will be their lone candidate for the post of *Mukhiya*? What difference does it make if he has taken the initiative to organise the Tantis and is now the district president of the Tanti Samaj and panchayat president of the Rastriya Janata Dal?

Mahadeo or Shivaji Singh do not care for all this, but fighting an election makes a hell of a difference to Amarnath Sardar. He is campaigning tirelessly on his motorbike and his brother Jagganath is leading a group of cyclists. His supporters include people like Mantu Singh, a Rajput, who has been beaten up for supporting a Tanti. 'I am a poor person. What did I get from the rule of a fellow-caste in all these years? Not even a proper school and a hospital are ensured. Some people of Mahadeo babu caught me one day and beat me up. I was threatened as well', tells Mantu Singh. Now-a-days, he leaves his house early in the morning, avoids crossing the Rajput tola in fear of a physical attack, takes a longer route to reach the Tanti tola, and comes back late at night.

Amarnath Sardar is overwhelmed by the response he is getting from the poor of various communities. His most lively memory of this phase is how they all joined him in a procession, with their hands folded. What makes him contest for the *Mukhiya*? He puts forward his point simply, 'We have no right to live with our head raised. We have no right to speak out'. He further substantiates, 'I am contesting so that the poor-dispossessed can live and speak with confidence. The developmental schemes are able to come to us as well'.

Nariyar panchayat is sitting on a volcano of conflicting claims, especially concerning government plans and schemes, which have become a public issue. The most recent incident pertains to the constitution of a Block Education Committee, to oversee the functioning of the schools within the panchayat. As recalls Jagganath Sardar, 'A 12-member committee was to be constituted. The erstwhile *Mukhiya*, with the connivance of the District Magistrate, filled the committee with his people. That too after the fact that we had demanded beforehand that the committee members should be taken from the broader sections of the society and the members should be educated. Our protests made two inclusions possible from our side. They were Amarnath Sardar and Mantu Singh.'

A place in the committee did not guarantee dignity or activity. The most humiliating experience came at the celebration of the Republic Day on 26 January. Amarnath recounts, 'We were invited for the flag hoisting in the Nariyar Madhya School. However, we were stopped outside the gate of the school by the musclemen and were allowed to enter only after the hoisting ceremony was over.'

What could be a fitting reply to this humiliation? What could be a match to it? How to undo an insult? Nothing could have been better than something done at the Independence Day on 15 August, at the same place, and at the same event. 'There was the flag hoisting ceremony in the school. The flag, the place, the tent, all were in the right position. We, the people, went early, hoisted the flag on our own and started celebrating the Independence Day', says Amarnath, who was there all along at the centre of this planning.

Incidentally, Amarnath's election symbol is a flag. Will he be able to unfurl his flag in the election? Will he be hoisting the national flag as a Mukhiya?

III

Small World, Whole World

Hardia

A woman sitting in the backyard of her mud house in Hardia village of Chautham block of Saharsa district could be understood for anything, but for an election candidate. However, Poonam Devi, a mother of two girls, is a candidate for the panchayat samiti member. She is keenly fighting against her husband, Rajballi Paswan, who is standing for two posts, panchayat samiti member and mukhiya.

In an evening of mid-April, Poonam Devi is sitting quietly with her brother. Both are arranging the voting slips with the serial numbers, to be given to the voters, for the day of the voting. The sister has especially called her brother from her *maika* (mother's place), to help her in the election arrangements, as her husband refused to co-operate with her.

'Matric fail' Poonam Devi, as she calls herself, speaks out slowly and quite hesitantly. Though she is the president of the DRDA women's group for the last two and a half years and has been instrumental in arranging loans for all the 15 members of her group, she does not claim it for herself. At the same time, it is also true that she is harping on the support of these 15 people for her campaigning.

'Why are you fighting against your husband?' I ask, and she questions me instantly in her reply, 'Why can't I fight the elections, husband or no husband? Why can't a woman and a man be candidates from the same family?'

Rajballi Paswan looks an angry man. Like most husbands, he does not consider it worth it to talk about the candidature of her wife. After all, she is an insignificant, weak candidate in front of him! His contest for the *Mukhiya*'s post is a token one, as this is not a reserved constituency, and he is concentrating his energies for the post of panchayat samiti member. Rajballi confidently claims, 'I am an educated person. I have 1.5 *bigha*s of land. I do tutions and can teach the students up to matric (secondary) class. As an educated, young, unemployed youth, I am a competent person to be a *Mukhiya* or a panchayat samiti member.'

Two stories go around the village regarding the duo candidature. Story One: In the beginning, Hardia panchayat was supposed to be a reserved constituency for women. Poonam was initiated to be a candidate, in consultation with her husband. When finally the constituency turned out to be a non-reserved one, Rajballi wanted to contest himself and asked his wife to withdraw. She however, refused to oblige. Story Two: Poonam Devi is a distant relative of Mr Ramvilas Paswan, a seasoned leader of Bihar, whereas the husband is an active member of the BJP. The political affiliations and the backing tore them apart.

In a discreet fashion, Poonam confirms both the stories, 'My husband pressurised me not to contest. That is why, I decided to contest. My relatives and parents are supporting my candidature.' Without hesitation, she acknowledges, 'Rs 1,500 have come from my mother's place for this purpose.'

Poonam is not very articulate, but in her own way she expresses her concerns for problems like unemployment, non-disbursal of old-age pension, and the insecurity faced by single, widowed women, in her election manifesto.

Like Poonam, there are a large number of women candidates, both for the reserved and the unreserved constituencies. The panchayat elections in Bihar seem to be giving women a beginning to come out in the public political domain in many unexpected ways. Women are seen to be here, there, everywhere.

Nirmala Devi is another example of this. She is the only woman candidate for the mukhiya's post in the panchayat of Rahimpur Madhya village in Khagaria district. Belonging to a non-governmental organisation working in her area, she was encouraged to file her nomination by the organisation. 'My husband is a government schoolteacher and we have a big family to look after to. When I asked my husband and other relatives, they all advised me not to think of contesting the elections. I decided against their advice because within the home, it is a small world and outside the home, there is a whole world to see.'

What is Nirmala Devi's vision for her panchayat? 'A proper road, nala and electricity', answers she, in a clear-headed manner. Where does she want to go from here? She has her role model, 'After winning the mukhiya's post, I can take the place of Renu Singh, the Member of Parliament.' What are her chances? Nirmala Devi has her assessment, 'I have banners, posters, and photos ready for the campaigning. We have begun canvassing. However, the panchayat area is big and it is difficult to get women to go around at all the places. There are hardly any men coming with us. If a woman becomes a *Mukhiya* then what will the man do, is the heart-burnt feeling prevalent here.'

Sometimes a woman's candidature or her being elected unopposed, has left its impact on campaigning in an entire area. Enter the Maksudpur village of Shahjahapur panchayat in Patna district and notice a wall-writing:

> *Ankhon mein ansu chalak rahe, manma jo hai bhari.*
> *Kyon abhi tak nahin mili hai, mukhiya ek bichari?—Lakho Devi ko vote dijiye.*
>
> (Tears are flowing from our eyes, our heart is heavy.
> Why do we not found a mukhiya till date?—Vote for Lakho Devi.)

Herd is Kanti Devi, who has been elected unopposed as ward member. She is actively campaigning for the woman mukhiya candidate. For Kanti Devi, '*Vidya* (education) is the most important thing for the village. Children drop out after II-III standard. Men-women, old—most remain uneducated.' A social activist claimed in Patna that in one Supaul block, 13 women have been elected unopposed for several posts, and altogether 63 women are in the fray.

Majority is from the reserved post, but a few are standing from unreserved ones. A minuscule of them are contesting for unreserved mukhiya and other posts. A clever, convenient argument has gained ground in most places that 'those posts that are not reserved for women are reserved for men'. This is only one example of the slip between the cup and the lip. For the women of Bihar, such slips are many.

IV

Waiting for Their Turn

Maina

It is a voting day in mid-April in a few blocks of Saharsa district. The Kosi embankment areas/villages like Maina, Mahpura, Naharwar, Mahesi (north), and Mahesi (south), comprising the Naharwar panchayat, are to choose their candidates for multiple layers of the village panchayat. The day ostensibly progresses peacefully. There are no reported incidents of attacking, killing and booth capturing, and there is regular police patrolling. Also are to be seen clusters of people collected around their booths in the village in queues, verifying and voting. The absence of physical violence is declared as an ample proof of prevalent peace. No killings or looting make ground for claims to a free and fair election.

Sitting in the block office with his wireless and telephone, the District Magistrate Mr D.S. Gangwar, claims, 'Polling is going on very smoothly here. There is no complaint of any kind whatsoever from this area. We have a regular force at our command to ensure free poll and new Cheeta Mobile Commandos have also been introduced. In the entire area, we are altogether successfully monitoring 249 booths, out of which 141 are in between the Kosi embankment areas.'

However, things seem to move much more discretely and covertly, at least in this part of Bihar. Violence has new faces; peace is somewhat illusionary. As we are approaching Ward No. 11, we encounter a group of 30–35 men, women and children in a desperate state. They are Kumhars, Kanus and Tantis of Mahpura village. Their votes are listed in the nearby Mahesi (north) and they are coming back from the outskirts of Mahesi, without entering the village and of course without even seeing their polling booth. Says Hariom Kamat, a part of the group, 'As we reached close to the village, we were told not to enter it and not to cast our votes if we wanted to live. We were asked to leave the place peacefully. There were many musclemen. What else could we have done, except to leave?'

In several villages of the Naharwar panchayat, spread over several flash points of the Kosi river, Brahmins, Thakurs, Yadavs, Mallahs, Chamars, Kumhars, Kanus—all had been living in somewhat the same boat. Regular floods, land erosion and water-logging have turned the entire region into a deprived and degraded state. However, the forward, land-owning classes have, in the last two decades, gone increasingly into new power-grabbing fields, and are regularly benefiting from an all round criminalisation of the entire area.

Power grabbing has many forms in the Kosi region, be it cornering the government contracts, or running the transport and shops, or taking part in the elections of MLAs and MPs. In the absence of broader democratic alternatives, panchayat elections in this particular area are providing the traditional power-owning people an opportunity to be at the centre of local politics, and they want to grab this opening in any way they can. There is cut-throat competition among them, but with a difference.

Vijay Singh, Madan Singh and Rajuvendra Singh—three powerful Rajputs from three different villages—are fighting vociferously against each other for the mukhiya's post. They together rule Naharwar; they set the rules. Others—the backwards and the dalits—have to follow them. Comes the voting day and nobody is allowed to go out or enter their village or their respective areas of dominance. They are the kings; their people cast the votes for all. No blood is spilled; no tears are shed. In Mahesi (north), the people of Rajuvendra Singh cast the votes for all the Rajputs, Yadavs, Musahars, Chamars and Tantis. In Maina village, the people of Madan Singh do the same.

All the ward numbers (11, 24, 28, 29, etc.) are in a way fortified by yes-men, muscle-men, caste-men. When Radhe Shyam Ram and his two family members went to their polling booth at Lahta Bathan in their own village, they were cold-bloodedly told to go back and stay in their house, as they were not considered to be reliable voters. 'What could we do in such a situation when this is happening in front of the eyes of *masterjee* (polling officer), police and guard, we better save our lives', says Radhe. He could only do one thing: to complain to the erstwhile mukhiya Inderdeo Singh, who ironically is leading the operation on behalf of one of the Singhs.

Singhs are also not fully safe. It was an angry and much confident Madan Singh who dared to enter the domain of another Singh and he was hit on the head in front of the police post. Madan Singh, a law graduate, alleges, 'It is the Rajput and Yadav combine against me in some villages that is to be blamed for all the mischief. I am not the initiator.'

Having been told about this stage-managed peace and the new violence in the Naharwar panchayat, the DM and the SP sitting in the same panchayat, could only express their willingness to look into the matter. They had neither the information nor the inclination to unearth a stage-managed peace or undo a stabilised power. 'We read between the lines when we get complaints. Often the losing party complains of electoral malpractice. We received a complaint that a section of voters were not allowed to vote and that the opposite party had fired bullets to scare them away. Our investigations revealed that the complainants were the real accused', claims Gangwar.

As we are coming back in the afternoon from Ward No. 11, we see a group of poor people sitting beneath the shadow of a tree, away from the booth. They are voters, but are not allowed to sit near the booth. Innocent, hopeful and quite eager they are still waiting for their turn to vote. A long, endless wait indeed!

V

Will There be Alternative?

Sarthua

In Kharkhawa panchayat of Patna district, a street play is being enacted by a group of youth and teenagers. The message, simple and loud, is being conveyed to the villagers: vote and vote correctly; identify different seats and colours of ballot papers earmarked for those seats.

This is a noble effort by Suswajas, a voluntary organisation, which has also got some cycles fitted with hand-mikes, tapes and batteries to move into the villages, distributing leaflets and pamphlets on various aspects of elections. A Mahila Chetna Vikas Mandal in Latha is focussing on women candidates and voters, to enhance their participation. Kaushal Kishore of Bharat Gyan Vigyan Samiti in Teghra block of Begusarai district is busy in organising street meetings, women polling agents and booth committees.

Here, meet a Panchayat Raj Chunav Jagrukta Abhiyan Samiti, established in November 2000 in the wake of panchayat elections. The Samiti consists of 326 organisations spread over 33 (out of 37) districts of Bihar. Arun Kumar, regional convenor of the Samiti, claims in Patna, The Samiti has intensively worked in 18 districts in a coordinated fashion, and organised campaigns and awareness materials. Two NGOs—PRIA in Delhi and CENCORED in Patna—have gone all out in their campaign programmes: setting up information centres at the district, the block panchayat and the gram sabha levels; undertaking various activities like cycle rallies, mobile information centres, puppet shows, wall writings, audio cassettes and newspaper; pre-nomination, post-nomination activities and many more.

A new development is unfolding in this panchayat election. A large number of voluntary, social, dalit organisations and activists are getting involved with the panchayats all over the state. Many of them are from the organised traditional NGOs network. However, an even larger number constitutes of groups and people coming into this kind of activity for the first time. They are entering the life reality and polity of a village, and are attempting to raise various issues and concerns of village life, poor, women, dalits, and their stakes in local governance. It is a unique opportunity to activise many, with an unleashing of tremendous energy.

It has become increasingly clear that political parties are not there to carry on panchayat campaigns for broader democratic objectives. Renu Singh, MP from Khagaria tells, 'I am not going to my area now-a-days because of the panchayat elections. Everybody has turned political; everybody wants to come to power. Whosoever will ultimately win, I will garland that person.' It is a simple, practical and an opportunistic consideration.

The state government is present in so far as facilitating and organising the electoral process is concerned. Beyond this there is not much to their account. They did not think of going among the people, to keep them informed of the many intricacies involve in the elections. Upendra Prasad Verma, Panchayat Minister, Bihar Government, takes the credit for his government to make panchayat elections a reality. Leaving aside the dubiousness of his claim, he has only few words to say on the pre-post election scenario: 'The state government has spent 75 crores on the elections. After the results, we will call the mukhiyas and other elected representatives to Patna to be addressed by Laloo Yadav.' This kind of a poor statement is nothing to be surprised at, seeing the pathetic arrangements for the elections, before or on the polling days.

'No political party is visibly present; even then the election is highly political', comments Mani, a leading activist of Samta, a social organisation in Khagaria. Village and district people know their needs, problems and priorities. They invariably state these in clear terms. Given the charged socio-political atmosphere in Bihar, where expectations, aspirations, hopes and demands are always in the air, the future need will be to transform these 'positive' times into a thorough, concrete planning and action. Upendra Prasad Verma wants 'the Kerala model to be followed in Bihar, where every panchayat has its office, and each mukhiya sits in the office for an hour to solve various problems'. Will there be an effort to better understand and spell concretely the Kerala model in the context of Bihar?

During our discussions with social activists and NGO workers in Patna, Ram Narayan Kumar from Musahari, which has witnessed Naxal protests, underlines that having a large number of candidates in the panchayat elections is not a positive development, as most of the people are after power, money and chair. Power, in different forms, remains the key to the search for development. However, it is precisely the use of state, money and muscle power that has disillusioned a majority of the people, in their search for a just and equitable life. If power is the only way, will there be any alternative?

An apparently non-political election has taken a distinct political dimension, thanks to the presence of the poor, their burning issues and associations. It is in this context that the work on panchayats in the future should be located. The pre and post election campaigns, the trainings and the workshops are commendable in a vacuum. However, without thinking of questions like wider socio-economic realities and macro-support and alliances, there will always be a concern of many support organisations getting de-politicised, though action for grassroots democracy is essentially political.

After a gap of 23 years, Bihar Panchayat elections were completed in six phases in May 2001. In 37 districts, the electorate exceeded 40 million in 1,11,029 polling stations, choosing amongst 4,36,232 candidates.

35

The Social Forum Phenomenon: Peoples' Experiments in Politics

R ecent years have seen the rise and spread of regional, national, thematic and global Social Forums (SF), inspired directly and indirectly by the World Social Forums (WSF). Any SF, influenced by the WSF, is conceived as an open space that facilitates the coming together of people to oppose neo-liberalism and the domination of world by any form of imperialism. They are committed to building a planetary society directed towards fruitful relationships among Humankind and between it and the Earth. The Indian social and political activism has shown tremendous energy for the SF in these years: Activities of the WSF process in India were initiated in early 2002. Asia Social Forum was hosted in Hyderabad in 2003 and the WSF in Mumbai in 2004. And now, the proposed India Social Forum (ISF) in Delhi from 9 to 13 November 2006 marks an initiative to further advance the movement against neo-liberal globalisation, sectarian politics, casteism, patriarchy and militarisation.

The phenomenon of SFs is surprisingly absent in a majority of the countries of Asia and South Asia, even though active civil societies and anti-globalisation movements exist in countries like Indonesia, Philippines and South Korea. This seems to suggest that the coming together of the SF is not a necessary colliery of the most favourable circumstances in a country. Instead, it more or less depends upon a felt need of enough number of people and organisations for such a space that is not there in letter or spirit in any given socio-political situation. Thus, it is understandable that the SF processes began in India at a time when the neo-liberal and the Hindu conservative forces were looming large.

Other interrelated strands give a push to the SF process. Opposition to the neo-liberal economic policies has not been new. However, the novelty of WSF was that it was virtually the first global civil society event that was conceived, and took place, in the South. The location of the South, and its political antecedents, has a continuing relevance to Indian activism. ISF is also being conceived as a space for deepening the unity of movements in the developing world, and especially in forging African–Asian solidarity. The event itself is timed to take place a few months before the WSF in Nairobi, Kenya, in January 2007, where for the first time a global WSF event travels to Africa.

Indian social and political activism still draws some of its sustenance from the legacy of anti-colonial struggles, where ideas of a New International Economic Order, active role of the Third World governments and self-reliance had been emphasised. Moreover, in the post-emergency era, Indian democracy has seen not only a survival, but a dynamic growth of socialist and communist party activism of all stripes, and the rainbow 'new social movements', which are often associated with women's movements, environment movements, and assertions of Dalits and Adivasis. In the same period, NGOs dealing with environment, human rights, gender and development issues mushroomed in the country and some of them connected to several United Nations Conferences. Even though different from SF phenomenon, they have contributed in relating to wider civil society activities at the international level.

Since the unleashing of the neo-liberal economic policies in the 1980s, India has also been witnessing diverse anti-globalisation movements. These have also been the times of the street uprising at Seattle in America, the Zapatista uprising in 1994, the growth of the Workers Party in Brazil, the Ogoni struggle and its solidarity network, and many such movements in various places, which have enhanced the imagination of social movements. In a way, the WSF-India was an idea waiting to happen. Approximately 10,000 participants were expected in Hyderabad; more than 30,000 showed up. And the WSF 2004 in Mumbai had 130,000 participants, with eight conferences, eight panels, 1,400 seminars, along with numerous marches, songs and dances, adding to the dynamism of the event.

An open space inspires thousands of people and groups to connect with each other, but the SF's open space is not a neutral space. It clearly sets out as being against neo-liberal globalisation, and for social justice. The Charter of Principles of WSF further states, 'Neither party representatives nor military organisations shall participate in the Forum. Government leaders and members of legislatures who accept the commitments of this Charter may be invited to participate in a personal capacity'. However, politics is integral to SF, which raises questions on neo-liberal institutions, BJP and the Hindu Right, war, Bushism, Manmohanomics, and the new political dispensation in the country. Today when the ISF is being held under a Congress regime, a party which came to power on a combined platform of pro-poor economic policies and anti-communalism, there will be many deliberations on peoples' issues and struggles, and their relationship to the present state of governance in contemporary India.

In a vibrant democracy, a utopian thinking has to interact with grounded social and political activism. The utopian in the Indian scenario can be seen in different forms of Gandhism, socialism, Marxism, Ambedkarism and others who negotiate with, as well as negate, the current course of development and politics. They all explore new modes of human possibility, and use their imagination to confront the apparent inevitability of whatever exists, with something radically better. The uniqueness of the Indian democracy is that different utopias have managed to find space for themselves in it. There are of course some radical discursive differences, translating into diverse manifestations, be it violence of the armed groups, or collective urge of autonomy from the Indian State, or an abandonment of parliamentary democracy. Yet there is a strong propensity among almost all to continue participating in the democratic institutions and covenants. The open process in India is there to strengthen these democratic processes, by creating an atmosphere of inclusion of, and respect for, divergences, making this space more attractive, even greater than its capacity to deliver. Even those who are critical of the journeys of WSF have not been far away from its processes and events. We may suggest that in the realm of broader alliances and campaigns on peoples' issues in the country, the desire to highlight what the movements have in common prevails over the desire to underscore what separates them.

The dominant issues in Indian democracy from a people's perspective, like caste, class, gender, liberalisation, displacement, war, religious fundamentalism, environment, labour and work, have been appearing prominently in different editions of the WSF in India. Issues and strategies, however, are only a part. Another world is possible when we also work on ways in which people approach organising and decision-making. Experimentations with forms, where the practice of politics is more network-based, horizontal, participative and democratic has not been very successful in Indian polity. Vicious confrontation, fragmentation and individualism are the prevalent rules of the game. Amidst this, in spite of conflicts and contests, the politics of an open space opens up new possibilities for organising and sharing of common goods. A process involving more than 200 organisations in India, compared to eight in the Brazilian Organising Committee (the originator of the WSF), or a panel of all women speakers opening the ISF event on 9 November are milestones in processes of democratisation and change. However, the jury is still not out on this key issue and it is quite likely that the SF phenomenon in this country will continue to oscillate between different ways of organising. A contest-ridden process of continuous challenges to different hegemonic tendencies, but also one of cementing together, may in fact be the best possible way forward for SFs in India.

Against the global onslaught of capital, our experiences show that the SF phenomenon will continue to flourish. A large number of events, participants, local-regional SFs, more than one SF: all are possible. Because SF is still such a child phenomenon, concrete examples of its actual accomplishments are difficult to cite. It is also problematic to attribute specific results to specific forums. If the SF is conceived as a space rather than a movement, then, by its very nature, success can be attributed not to it but to the various groups and movements within it. They are the ultimate takers and users of this space.

(An earlier version of this chapter was published in *The Hindu*, 3 November 2006. It has been expanded and revised.)

Section VI

New Paths of Human Rights

36

India, Brazil, South Africa:
Human Rights Footprint

Mid-April (7–18 April 2008) witnessed the unfolding of a new international mechanism, when the UN Human Rights Council's Universal Periodic Review (UPR) began the process of examining the human rights records of its member states. Selected by drawing lots, the UPR working groups, in their first session, started with the human rights records of 16 countries: Algeria, Argentina, Bahrain, Brazil, Czech Republic, Ecuador, Finland, India, Indonesia, Morocco, Netherlands, Philippines, Poland, South Africa, Tunisia and UK. This new device is aimed at addressing one of the main criticisms of the Council's predecessor, that is, the Commission of Human Rights, which was accused of scrutinising only a small number of countries.

In the context of the positive emergence of IBSA (India, Brazil, South Africa) Summits, the Brasilia/Tshwane Declaration, and the coming together of the Heads of State and Governments of these countries, the UPR gives us an opportunity to see the human rights footprints of these three countries together, which are not only important in the regions of which they are part of, but which also have an emerging role in the making of a new international world order. After analysing the length and breadth of national reports, official UN documents regarding the adherence of treaty bodies, special procedures and other human rights mechanisms by governments, large number of reports submitted by civil society organisations, presentation by the states and the subsequent questioning by other states, 'key issues identified' and the 'final adoption', it can be said that India, Brazil and South Africa are today finding themselves at crossroads, or caught in a crossfire, of a tension between individual and state rights. Issues of state killings, torture, disappearances, and ill-treatment in an era of terror/counter-terror are becoming central, and they need to transcend political debate and policy choice, for the emergence of a decent political system. The Brazilian detention system and the recurrent accusations of police abuse, torture and extrajudicial killings in the country, and the growing police violence and prison population in South Africa, are as important reference points in the UPR, as the concerns over Armed Forces (Special Powers) Act and related concerns of impunity in India. There has been a steady increase in human rights violations, committed in the name of security, and not every abuse can be attributed to the 'war on terror'. However, there is no doubt that it has given a new lease of life to repression in IBSA.

IBSA in UPR also shows the successes and the limitations of the state and its civil society attempts to frame access to food, housing, health and education as individual human rights; and hunger, malnutrition, homelessness, inadequate housing, and lack of access to health and education as violations of human rights. The UPR further demonstrates the diverse initiatives in India, Brazil and South Africa in the realm of peoples' rights. These countries need to also promote a trilateral exchange of information, best practices, institutions and skill, as well as to compliment each other's individual strengths and collective synergies. The way IBSA Forum has formed working groups and joint programmes on trade, defence, climate change, energy, science and technology, information society, tourism, culture and education, to develop South-South solidarity; it needs to also form a working group on human rights.

IBSA and the International

India, Brazil and South Africa are aspiring for an international role, and are integrated closely to the neo-liberal and the corporate world. However, they also have a cautious and, at times, closed approach to the international scrutiny on human rights. India has yet to ratify two of the seven main human rights treaties: the UN Convention against Torture and Other Cruel, Inhuman or Degrading Treatment or Punishment, and the UN Convention of the Rights of All Migrant Workers and Members of Their Families (ICRMW), as well as the two Optional Protocols to the International Covenant on Civil and

Political Rights. India has also yet to sign the Rome Statute of the International Criminal Court, and instead has signed a bilateral impunity agreement with the United States. It continues to display an unwillingness to cooperate with the UN Special procedures. For example, Special Rapporteur on Torture or Special Rapporteur on extrajudicial, summary or arbitrary executions has not been given permission to visit the country since 1993 and 2000 respectively.

Brazil is not a party to many core treaties, like the International Covenant on Civil and Political Rights— Optional Protocol (ICCPR-OP1 & OP2), Convention on the Protection of Persons from Enforced Disappearance (CED), and Convention on the Protection of Persons with Disabilities (CPD). Core treaties, to which South Africa is not a party, are Optional Protocol to Convention against Torture and Other Cruel, Inhuman or Degrading Treatment or Punishment (OP-CAT), International Covenant on Economic, Social and Cultural Rights (ICESCR), CED and ICRMW. This is when all these three countries are elected members of the UN Human Rights Council and at the time of their elections, had made voluntary pledges to sign and ratify the international instruments and special procedures.

Tensions in Rights Frame

The UPR considers variously issues of poverty, inequality and discrimination, displacement and evictions, hunger, homelessness, preventable disease, migrants and refugees, land distribution, HIV and AIDS, and attacks on freedom of expression, association and peaceful assembly in India, Brazil and South Africa. Within the UPR framework, there are deep tensions inherent in the economic and social rights structures of the IBSA governments. First strain is that the rights violations are found in abundance here, alongside conspicuous government powers and pronouncements. There are old and new policy measures in place, with or without implementation systems. The second friction is that the normative systems—laws, international treaties and their implementation—are developing in tandem and are partly dependent on each other, but are not going well together. The third tension finds expression in the reports of civil society organisations, surrounding various violations. The Human Rights Council says that 'States are encouraged to prepare the information through a broad consultation process at the national level with all relevant stakeholders'. Leave aside consultation, South Africa had not even submitted its State report until the day of the review. India did not provide any details regarding inputs or consultations with civil society organisations. Brazil had a national consultation and a public hearing in the Brazilian Senate. (Altogether 23 organisations in Brazil, the South African Human Rights Commission, the University of Pretoria and 16 other organisations in South Africa, and 37 organisations in India have submitted their reports to the UPR working group). The notion and norm that non-state actors, including non-governmental organisations, might have legal human rights obligations is very underdeveloped. Thus, there is still an exclusive reliance on the states for addressing the social justice and peoples' rights issues in a corporatised and privatised world.

Best Practices

India's Right to Information Act 2005 and National Rural Employment Guarantee Act 2005 are cited as great achievements in the interactive dialogue of UPR. Several innovations in Brazil, in the realm of economic and social rights, are widely referred to: 'Fome Zero' (Zero Hunger), 'Direito a Memoria e a Verdade (Right to Memory and Truth, which presents the results of the work performed by the Special Commission on Political Dead and Disappeared People), land distribution and 'Bolsa Familia' (Family Allowance). The establishment of Equality Courts in South Africa, where an individual can file a discrimination complaint without legal counsel is an innovative way to deal with racial segregation and discrimination. Extending invitation to all UN special procedures in future by South Africa has been lauded.

The world is now witnessing new challenges and opportunities on the human rights front from countries like India, China, Brazil and South Africa. Based on their best and worst practices, it is time to assess their human rights footprints in the continent, amongst themselves and in the world at large.

37

South Asia: Towards a Human and Peoples' Rights Agenda

I

As the 14th SAARC (South Asian Association for Regional Cooperation) Summit draws nearer to April 2007, it seems a good time to raise certain issues and questions, designed to draw lessons for the next stage of regional institution building, in particular and the future of South Asia, in general. Where are we? What issues, practices and policy changes can be proposed to improve the quality of peoples' lives and of regional policy making and implementation? What are the challenges for civil society organisations and citizens? How can SAARC be made more open and transparent to South Asian citizens? The vision of South Asia today should be that of a South Asia that is integrated, prosperous and peaceful; a South Asia driven by its own citizens; an anti-colonial, democratic and dynamic force in the global arena; and human and peoples' rights the cornerstone of its political programmes.

Wars and killings in the name of nations; violence, often on a massive scale; boundaries and borders creating major elements of conflicts between the nation states; trans-border crime, narco-terrorism, illegal and informal transactions; illegal migration and large-scale refugee infiltration; trade and transit barriers and trade imbalances—we can find all this and much more in serious proportions in these times of South Asia. However, they are not the core of our assessment, as nobody had believed that these issues could be resolved soon amidst the vast sea of humanity. The core is that even though some significant spaces have been opened up for greater and more sustained regional cooperation and some significant democratic struggles have made their impact felt, the overall mood is not optimistic regionally, and the prospects of a people-driven region remain largely unfulfilled. Lack of vision, initiative and will, inadequate institutional capacity, and inappropriate policies and procedures have totally negated any thought and practice that we should build a partnership between governments and all segments of civil society, to strengthen solidarity and cohesion among our people in South Asia.

Three developments—terror and counter-terror, corporate globalisation, and political violence—have been deeply impacting the South Asian region in recent times. A few random examples from any region, be it Bangladesh, India, Nepal, Pakistan or Sri Lanka, reveal that blatant violations of human rights and fundamental freedoms are immense. In Bangladesh, politically motivated misuse of institutions of the state, including the police and the judiciary, and the frequent use of violence against political opponents has had a grave impact on respect for human rights. An increase in human rights abuses purportedly committed in the name of political and religious ideology, high incidences of extreme poverty, and the inability of so many Bangladeshis to enjoy adequate access to basic economic and social rights, are of continuing concern. The human rights situation in Sri Lanka has deteriorated dramatically and there is no end to unlawful killings, recruitment of child soldiers, abductions, enforced disappearances, destruction of homes, schools and places of worship. The Pakistani government is committing numerous human rights violations as a result of its cooperation in the US-led 'war on terror'. Hundreds of people have been arbitrarily detained. Many have been subjected to enforced disappearances, held secretly, incommunicado and in undisclosed locations, with the government refusing to provide information about their fate and whereabouts. More than 85 per cent of detainees at Guantánamo Bay were arrested, not on the battlefield by the US forces, but by the Afghan Northern Alliance and in Pakistan, at a time when rewards of up to US$ 5,000 were paid for every 'terrorist' turned over to the US The continuing saga of the Bhopal Gas Tragedy and the Armed Forces Special Power Act, the disappearances in Kashmir, the massive displacements and repression in the wake of Special Economic Zones and other corporate projects, violence against women and children loom large on the face of the Indian government, readying itself to take a lead in SAARC and other regional–international forays, including the UN Human Rights Council.

In this context, South Asia and its several initiatives at the governmental–non-governmental level need a paradigmatic shift today. For example, SAARC came into being with the basic aim of accelerating the process of economic and social development amongst its members through joint action in the agreed areas of cooperation. However, today SAARC requires each of its member states to promote and protect human and peoples' rights, consolidate democratic institutions and culture, ensure good governance and rule of law, promote peace, security and stability in the region, and base its actions on essential principles like respect for sanctity of human life, promotion of equality between men and women, and condemnation of impunity and unconstitutional changes of government. The principle of non-interference in internal affairs should be replaced by a principle of non-indifference to the problems facing South Asian States, and the right of the Association to intervene in respect of grave circumstances, namely wars, pogroms and crimes against humanity. The Association is required to promote democratic principles and institutions, popular participation and good governance. It should be a sum total of democratic states, respectful of human rights and keen to build equitable societies. This vision should be implemented at the institutional level by the creation of new organs, like a South Asian Parliament and an Economic, Social and Cultural Council, designed specifically to increase the voice of South Asian people in SAARC's decision making procedures.

Everyone has certain human rights and fundamental freedoms that South Asian governments must uphold and respect. This is required even more today, as the governments in the region are also being shaped through military dictatorships, ethnic and religious conflicts, emergencies and political violence. Human rights and fundamental freedoms that are universally recognised have developed over the decades. There are a number of treaties, declarations and resolutions to this effect. Despite this, if our governments today continue to violate human rights and justify their actions on grounds of 'security' or 'sovereignty', it is up to the regional community as a whole to protect these rights on behalf of the people all over South Asia.

We can look up for some good practices from the African regional systems like the African Charter, which was unanimously adopted by the Organisation of African Unity (OAU) in 1981. The Charter laid out a range of rights and duties that should always be respected. It also established the African Commission to oversee its implementation. However, the Commission was not a judicial body and could only make recommendations, which were often ignored by governments. This lack of an effective enforcement mechanism led to calls for the establishment of an African Court on Human and Peoples' Rights and in 1998, the OAU adopted a protocol to establish such a court. It took six years for the Protocol to enter into force and it was in January 2006 that African Union Assembly of Heads of State and Government elected the 11 judges to serve in the Court. Other Protocols have been adopted, among them are: the Protocol to the African Charter on Human and Peoples' Rights on the Rights of Women in Africa (2005), the AU Convention on Preventing and Combating Corruption (2003), and the African Charter on the Rights and Welfare of the Child (1999). The African Commission itself has adopted several guidelines and declarations. Any individual or organisation can make a complaint to the African Commission concerning a violation by a state party of any of the rights guaranteed by the African Charter. The Court can consider cases of human rights violations brought by the Commission, by states and, in some cases, directly by the victims themselves or their representatives, including NGOs.

We need to remind ourselves now of the late K.R. Narayanan's address, titled 'SAARC 2000 and Beyond': 'SAARC must place emphasis on non-governmental and people's initiatives and participation. It is perhaps on a wave of peoples' interest and enthusiasm that SAARC could carry the governments and fulfil its destiny.'

II

How does SAARC deal with human rights issues? What are the prospects of a South Asian Human Rights Charter and an accompanying regional mechanism? What are the other current regional systems?

The world presently consists of three regional human rights regimes. They are the European, Inter-American, and African systems. The Southeast Asian region is just beginning the process towards a regional regime. The three current regional regimes differ in their organisational structure, and in their scope of human rights recognised. The differences are said to exist because of the historical and cultural context in which they were formed and in the environment in which they operate. For this reason, many believe that the regional level of human rights implementation is most important and effective, as it is the centre between the international level, viewed conceptually as universalism, and the domestic level, which is viewed conceptually as cultural relativism.

Europe

The harsh realities of totalitarianism, notably the Nazi Holocaust, were indeed the driving force behind the creation of the European regional human rights system. This dark period of history, coupled with the fear of Communism, spawned a serious reflection and reexamination of the fundamental question as to what human rights really is. Contemplation and dialogue persisted. The conviction that human rights were a domestic problem to be remedied only with domestic solutions transformed, and in May of 1948, European leaders met at The Hague and made the following statements when the meeting concluded:

We desire a united Europe, throughout whose area the free movement of persons, ideas and goods is restored;

We desire a Charter of Human Rights guaranteeing liberty of thought, assembly and expression as well as the right to form a political opposition;

We desire a Court of Justice with adequate sanctions for the implementation of this Charter;

We desire a European Assembly where the live forces of all our nations shall be represented.

With the inception of the 1948 Universal Declaration of Human Rights, the European human rights system, now considered the most comprehensive regional human rights system, has as its foundation two treaties: The European Convention on Human Rights of 1950 (referred to as the European Charter) and the European Social Charter of 1961. The Convention focuses on civil and political rights, while the Social Charter guarantees economic and social rights. Although the Social Charter was revised in 1996, the main focus of this regional regime is political and civil rights. The convention entered into force in September of 1953 and thus was to serve as the framework that would effectively implement the 1948 UN Declaration.

The European Convention established two institutions: the European Commission of Human Rights and the Court of Human Rights. In 1998, the Commission of Human Rights and the European Court of Human Rights merged into a single institutional governing body when Protocol 11 entered into force on 1 November 1998. All 47 member states of the Council of Europe recognise this court system; Belarus and Kazakhstan are the only exceptions as they are not part of the Council of Europe. Also, the European system has as an executive organ of the Council of Europe, The Committee of Ministers. The members of the Committee are the Ministers of Foreign Affairs of the member states. They serve as government representatives and oversee the Court's ruling. Although it has no formal means of using force against countries who do not comply, this committee can request expulsion from the Council of Europe. Also, the European Union seriously considers the judgement of the Court and Committee, and therefore can be seen as monitoring body as well.

The admissibility criteria outlined below is similar in all of the current regional human rights systems. The individual petition must meet some admissibility conditions:

1. All domestic remedies must be exhausted. 2. The petition should not be of a matter which has already been examined by the Commission or has been submitted to anther procedure of international investigation or settlement. 3. The petition should be well-intentioned and not violate the right of petitions. (European Charter, Article 35)

If the complaints are considered admissible, the Court opens a thorough examination and investigation of the case at hand. Since the consolidation of the system, individuals can refer a case to the court. In addition to individuals, NGOs can refer a case to the Court. In system prior to Protocol 11 entering into force, NGOs did not have the right, independently, to refer a case to the Commission unless they themselves were victims of abuses relative to the Convention. In 1954 the Committee of Ministers adopted guidelines for granting consultative status to a group of NGOs. To date, many

NGOs have been granted the consultative status. Some of the significant contributions NGOs have made to the European human rights system are the following:

- The European Torture Convention was prepared jointly by the International Commission of Jurists and Swiss Committee Against Torture.
- NGOs helped applicants to complete the application and provide legal assistance before the Court (for example, the National Council for Liberties, Justice, the National Association for Mental Health, and the Advice on Individual Rights in European Centre).
- NGOs provided legal advice to the victims, assisted them in formulating applications and in finding adequate arguments, and suggested competent lawyers capable of representing the victims.

The Americas

Like the European system, the Inter-American system of human rights was created out of the shadows cast from World War II, and soon after, the anxiety stemming the preconceived notions many had regarding Communism. The system and its initial declaration, The American Declaration of the Rights and Duties of Man, were intended to truly define human rights along with the Universal Declaration of Human Rights, which it pre-dates by a few months. And like the UDHR, although it was not meant to be legally binding, it is indirectly legally binding through the creation of the OAS Charter, Commission, and Court system which are the cornerstones of this human rights regime. It is important to note that the ideologies behind regional and international human rights regimes at this time were a deviation from modern international relations theory, sometimes referred to as The Westphalia System, whose key characteristics included state sovereignty, self-determination, and non-intervention of one state in the internal affairs of another state.

The legal basis for the Inter-American system is The American Declaration of the Rights and Duties of Man (1948), The Charter of the Organization of American States (1948) and The American Convention on Human Rights (1978).

Like the Council of Europe, the Organization of American States (OAS) is a regional organisation whose purpose is to achieve peace and promote solidarity amongst its people. Its charter covers the rights of the child, the right, to nationality, and the right to asylum, in addition to civil and political rights.

An independent body, the Inter-American Commission on Human Rights, was created in 1959 and is composed of seven nationals of member states. One state cannot have more than one member on the commission and are elected by the General Assembly of the OAS (American Convention, Articles 34–40). The commission is to promote human rights in all OAS member states, assist in the drafting of human rights documents, work as a mediator over human rights problems, handle individual complaints, raise awareness of human rights issues, and prepare country reports (American Convention, Articles 41–43). It is important to note that the commission receives less than two percent of the OAS budget.

The Inter-American Court of Human Rights

In 1978, the American Court of Human Rights came into force after the ratification by the eleventh state (Grenada). Individuals are not allowed to bring their case to the Court directly; the Commission has this as its duty. Judgements of the Court are binding on the parties and not subject to appeal. Also, the Court has advisory jurisdiction, which empowers the Court to interpret the Convention and other human rights instruments at the request of OAS member states and other OAS bodies (American Convention, Articles 52–69). Active NGOs contribute to the Inter-American system. These NGO activities include collecting information, visiting countries, disseminating information, and intervening in cases directly and indirectly.

Africa

The Organisation of African Unity (OAU) was created in 1963. The OAU is a regional inter-governmental organisation which was formed around the concept of sovereignty. African nations desperately wanted to be the architects of their future, and free themselves from the chains of colonial and imperial exploitation. This organisation provided Africa with a spirit comprised of solidarity and strength, hoping to regain what it had lost and moved forward as an independent, united Africa. The rights included in the African Human Rights Charter reflect this sense of sovereignty, as the Charter was specifically designed with concerns, traditions, and social conditions that were uniquely African.

Like the European system, the African regional human rights regime has as its nucleus one main instrument: the African Charter on Human and Peoples' Rights (also known as the African Charter or Banjul Charter). The Charter was signed in 1981 and entered into force on 21 October 1986. The distinguishing feature of the African Charter is the recognition of human rights through the African lens. It was the first charter to include social, economic and cultural rights, commonly known as second generation rights, in addition to civil and political rights. It is also the only current system which includes individual duties, such as one's responsibility to family, community, society, the state, and the international community. (African Charter, Article 27) Duties also include a mutual respect without discrimination to others, and to work at serving his or her community in a way to promote solidarity, and unity amongst African nations. (African Charter, Articles 28, 29) In essence, the Charter was making a point that communal and societal institutions as political bodies also had rights, which needed to be recognised as they were important to the balance and harmony of rights in general (individual rights on one hand and societal rights on the other). The Charter also addresses the third generation of solidarity rights, referred to as peoples' rights, with particular emphasis on the right to development, the right to national and international peace and security, and the right to a satisfactory environment. (African Charter, Articles 22–24)

The African Commission on Human and Peoples' Rights

In 1987, the African Commission on Human and Peoples' Rights was established, approximately one year after the African Charter entered into force. Essentially, the Commission functions to promote and protect human rights outlined in the Charter. More specifically, the Commission's main responsibilities include examining state reports, researching African problems in relation to the field of human and peoples' rights, communication and network sharing through conferences, symposia, and workshops, and raising awareness of rights at the local and national level consider violations brought to the Commission, and explaining and interpreting the Charter (African Charter, Article 45). These aforementioned responsibilities are the general responsibilities inherent in all current regional human rights systems today. It is also said that the African Commission was greatly influenced by the rules and procedures of the UN Human Rights Committee and other international human rights bodies.

The African Court on Human and Peoples' Rights

Historically speaking, African customs and traditions favour mediation, conciliation, and consensus over the adversarial and adjudicative procedures common to Western legal systems. As a result, the establishment of the African Court on Human and Peoples' Rights was largely due to the lobbying efforts of NGO and the academic world. In 1995, a draft of a prospective African Court was produced in South Africa, the OAU adopted the draft protocol in 1997 which opened for ratification in 1998, and entered into force on 25 January 2004. On 2 July 2006, eleven judges were sworn in to mark the beginning of the newly established African Court on Human and Peoples' Rights.

NGOs play an integral role in the functioning of the African human rights regional system. NGOs can submit communications to the African Commission act on behalf of groups and individuals who in all likelihood do not know how to receive assistance from the system. The Commission also allows NGOs to attend public sessions of the Commission, and therefore can directly influence to the internal functions of the system. Also, NGOs can acts as consultants and bearers of important input that have direct influence on the system as well. NGOs have also played a significant role by heavily influencing the Commission in other ways, including lobbying. It was NGOs lobbying that prompted the Commission to appoint Special Rapporteurs on Prisons and Other Conditions of Detention, on Summary, Arbitrary and Extrajudicial Executions and on Women's Rights, and NGO's have been essential to their functioning.

Initially, the African Charter was seen as overly ambitious, with its inclusion of both second and third generation of human rights. Functioning without a regional court system until 2004, many believed that the system has failed to reach its lofty goals in relation to the inclusion of these rights. For many years, the Commission was said to only focus on cases which dealt with civil and political rights while avoiding cases that focused more on the progressive aspects of the Charter, namely second and third generation rights. Only recently has this regional system begun to work with the social, economic, and cultural rights, as well as the right to development, the right to peace and security, the right to education, and the right to health. This aspect, coupled with the African concept of reconciliation (the traditional non-justiciability of disputes, hence the reason it is said why it took a very long time to establish a court system) and its inclusion of individual duties, made it a system that was many believe was setting itself up to fail.

In the same breadth, these same far-reaching characteristics make the system truly unique and relevant to African culture, tradition, and identity, a quality which is at the core of what a regional human rights system ought to be.

The Art of Giving and Taking Away: Clawback Clauses

Language such as 'within the law' (African Charter, Article 9), 'provided that he abide by the law' (African Charter, Article 10), 'for the protection of national security' (African Charter, Article 12), and 'in accordance with the law' (African Charter, Article 12) are clauses contained in many of the articles of the African Charter which have the potential to restrict the very rights that are explicitly stated in the Charter. When examining jurisprudence as it relates to clawback clauses, many believe that these clauses are not of significant concern as the word 'law' has come to be interpreted as international law. Still, many believe otherwise; the word 'law' can be interpreted as domestic law, thereby forcing people to abide by draconian laws from the colonial times that restrict even the most basic human rights.

The African regional system has been marred with serious organisational problems, notably budgetary concerns, and a lack of political independence as Commissioners are appointed by the political Assembly of Heads of State and Government of the OAU, and until recently, members of the Commission have been a mixture of former government persons and members of the judiciary and academic legal profession. These problems, along with the lack of a Court system for much of its history, is said to have created a system that lacks clout, unable to enforce the rights of the Charter and the recommendations and advice of the Commission. Even with the recently established Court system, it is ambiguous as to what mechanisms actually enforce compliance with Court decisions; compliance is still essentially voluntary, as the Council of Ministers is responsible to oversee the execution of the decision, but has no enforcement power. Looking at the issue with optimism can be encouraging though as positive critics point to the fact of progress made since the Charter and Commission was realised many years ago. Going forward, the idea of merging the African Court of Justice, which deals with resolving inter-state conflicts, with the African Court on Human Rights has surfaced and is believe to strengthen and further develop the role of enforceability within the overall system.

South Asia

After years of existence, no attempt has been made by SAARC to discuss human rights issues. Indeed, the promotion of human rights is not a goal listed by the SAARC Charter. The SAARC member governments are wary of the very words human rights, even though their representatives in international fora vouch for their commitment to promote and protect human rights. The SAARC countries have, for instance, signed the Convention on the Rights of the Child, and all except Maldives have signed the Convention on the Elimination of All Forms of Discrimination Against Women. Every SAARC member state's constitution guarantees fundamental rights for its respective citizens, but such constitutional rights are laden with contradictions and exceptions.

The human rights debate in South Asian countries often revolves around concepts like the South Asian perspective or South Asian views. The most important distinction, however, is between the interests of the government and the people. In the context of public debate, only the interests of the government have been projected. Each year for the past several years, government officials convene at the SAARC summit, and yet the most glaring human rights problems are never mentioned. The existence of significant ongoing human rights abuses simply is not acknowledged by the South Asian governments.

Regional bodies have developed in recent history, as is evident in the three current systems (and the announcement of the fourth in Southeast Asia) and now act as the centrepiece of international relations theory and practice, providing synergy between international and domestic theory and institutions.

Unfortunately, South Asia is one of the only remaining regions in the world which lacks a human rights charter and mechanism. Even more disheartening, as evidenced in the sentiment of major human rights organisations is the notion that the regional organisation of states in South Asia, SAARC, which represents one sixth of the world's population or the most populated regional active bloc (see Table), has done little in the way of promoting and protecting human rights issues.

On 8 December 1985, in light of the Declaration signed by Foreign Ministers in New Delhi on 2 August 1983 regarding regional cooperation, SAARC was officially established originally by 7 member states: Bangladesh, Bhutan, India, Maldives, Nepal, Pakistan, and Sri Lanka (SAARC Charter). In April 2007, Afghanistan became SAARC's eighth member. Ultimately, SAARC was created to promote regional cooperation through the acceleration of economic and social development amongst its member states. This regional bloc is also to act as a bridge between the international and regional level, which is also a goal of the charter, as stated in Article 8 of the SAARC Charter. The key components, which form the foundation of SAARC can be found in Article 1 of the SAARC Charter:

1. To promote the welfare of the peoples of South Asia and to improve their quality of life.
2. To accelerate economic growth, social progress and cultural development in the region and to provide all individuals the opportunity to live in dignity and to realise their full potentials.
3. To promote and strengthen collective self-reliance among the countries of South Asia.
4. To contribute to mutual trust, understanding and appreciation of one another's problems.
5. To promote active collaboration and mutual assistance in the economic, social, cultural, technical and scientific fields.
6. To strengthen cooperation with other developing countries.

Table 37.1

Most Active Regional Blocs

Regional bloc1	Area (km²)	Population	GDP (PPP) (US$) in millions	Per capita	Member states1
Agadir	1,703,910	126,066,286	513,674	4,075	4
AU	29,797,500	897,548,804	1,515,000	1,896	53
ASEAN	4,400,000	553,900,000	2,172,000	4,044	10
CACM	422,614	37,816,598	159,536	4,219	5
CARICOM	462,344	14,565,083	64,219	4,409	(14+1)3
CCASG/GCC	2,285,844	35,869,438	536,223	14,949	6
CEFTA	298,148	28,929,682	222,041	7,675	(7+1)3
EU	4,325,675	496,198,605	12,025,415	24,235	27
EurAsEC	20,789,100	208,067,618	1,689,137	8,118	6
EFTA	529,600	12,233,467	471,547	38,546	4
GUAM	810,506	63,764,600	456,173	7,154	4
NAFTA	21,588,638	430,495,039	15,279,000	35,491	3
PARTA	528,151	7,810,905	23,074	2,954	(14+2)3
SAARC	5,136,740	1,467,255,669	4,074,031	2,777	8
Unasur/Unasul	17,339,153	370,158,470	2,868,430	7,749	12

Source CIA, 2005; International Monetary Fund.

Notes
1 Including data only for full and 'most active' members.
2 Including the largest five countries by area, population and GDP (PPP), but not #4 in population or #5 in GDP (PPP).
3 Including 'non-sovereign autonomous areas' of other states.
4 Members or 'administrative divisions'.
5 Data for the People's Republic of China does not include Hong Kong, Macau, or regions administered by the Republic of China (Taiwan).

7. To strengthen cooperation among themselves in international forums on matters of common interests.
8. To cooperate with international and regional organisations with similar aims and purposes.

With these eight core objectives, one can reasonably assume that the main objective of SAARC was and is clear: to bring unity and peace to a region of the world that is heavily populated and plagued with the unfortunate realities of poverty and oppression.

SAARC has not completely ignored human rights. Below is a brief timeline outlining SAARC and its acknowledgement of human rights:

- Established in 1985
- Foundation—Charter of the South Asian Association for Regional Cooperation
- Bangalore Declaration (1986)—'the needs of all children are the principal means of human resources development. Children should, therefore, be given the highest priority in national development planning'. The Declaration recognises peace, security, and respect for international law are essential for growth and stability.
- Male Declaration (1990)—'there has been integration of national economies into the world economy. There is the trend of increasing integration of the pattern of global production, consumption, trade, and integration of markets. SAARC is convinced that their mutual cooperation can be a critical factor in enabling them to face new challenges.' Human trafficking was addressed for the first time.
- The Colombo Declaration (1991)—which recognised the interdependence and equal importance of civil, political, economic and social rights. The Declaration reaffirms their commitment to democracy, human rights and rule of law. The Declaration accords the highest priority to the alleviation of poverty in all South Asian countries.
- SAARC Convention On Terrorism (1987/1998)
- SAARC Convention On Drug Abuse (1990/1993)
- 1991–2000: SAARC Decade of the Girl Child
- The Delhi Declaration (1995)—which reaffirms the realisation of the rights of all, in particular those of the poor, to food, work,

shelter, health, and education. Considering that the exploitation of the Girl Child is a direct reflection of the status of women in society, the Leaders reaffirmed their resolve to take necessary measures to eliminate all forms of discrimination against women and female-children.

- 1991–2000: SAARC Decade of the Girl Child
- The Delhi Declaration (1995)—which reaffirms the realisation of the rights of all, in particular those of the poor, to food, work, shelter, health, and education. Considering that the exploitation of the Girl Child is a direct reflection of the status of women in society, the Leaders reaffirmed their resolve to take necessary measures to eliminate all forms of discrimination against women and girl children.
- 2001–2010: SAARC Decade of the Rights of the Child
- SAARC Convention on Human Trafficking (2002)
- 2001–2010: SAARC Decade of the Rights of the Child
- SAARC Convention on Human Trafficking (2002)

One can reasonably conclude that within the context of this timeline, SAARC has dealt with human rights on a case-by-case-basis. Following the SAARC Convention on Human Trafficking in 2002, SAARC reaffirmed its original objectives via the SAARC Social Charter, which also reiterates the method of dealing with human rights on a case-by-case-basis.

In 2004 January, the SAARC Social Charter entered into force, reaffirming the original objectives of the initial charter. Key social issues addressed in the SAARC Social Charter are stated in Articles 3–9: Article 3: Poverty Alleviation, Article 4: Health, Article 5: Education, Human Resource Development and Youth Mobilisation, Article 6: Promotion of the Status of Women, Article 7: Promotion of the Rights and Well-Being of Children, Article 8: Population Stabilisation, Article 9: Drug De-Addiction, Rehabilitation and Reintegration.

Article II, XII of the Principle, Goals, and Objectives section specifically addresses human rights in a broad context, further reaffirming its case-by-case approach:

XII–Promote universal respect for and observance and protection of human rights and fundamental freedoms for all, in particular the right to development; promote the effective exercise of rights and the discharge of responsibilities in a balanced manner at all levels of society; promote gender equity; promote the welfare and interest of children and youth; promote social integration and strengthen civil society. (SAARC Social Charter, Article II, 2XII)

SAARC is the driving force behind the crucial concepts it recognises in its original Charter and the recent Social Charter, namely that of unity, cooperation, and trust. Its goal is to progress economically and to develop socially by using these concepts as fuel which serves as the indispensable energy and spirit that gives life to its vision. Without this fuel, that is, without these concepts, the idea is only but a dream.

South Asia has taken a more sub-regional approach towards human rights. SAARC has made progress in the name of human rights, as noted above with the creation of the SAARC Social Charter and its explicit recognition of human rights in Article II, but the progress may be short-lived without moving the issue to the forefront of its agenda, thus pushing the objectives outlined in the original SAARC charter further and further away. Given the deplorable state of democracy, human rights, and the rule of law in the South Asian region, a regional human rights charter and mechanism, properly drafted, enacted, and enforced, would prove to be of paramount significance to the SAARC and the region alike. On the one hand, a regional system would work to strengthen the national institutions imperative to the solidarity of SAARC, while, on the other hand, it would work to create synergy with the international institutions absolutely necessary to the overall health of the region, and thus SAARC as well.

III

The ASEAN Charter: Window of Opportunity or Window Dressing?

The ASEAN Charter, signed by the Association of Southeast Asian Nations (ASEAN) in November 2007, is the first Asia-Pacific regional treaty that, once ratified, will legally oblige states to respect and protect human rights. If fully implemented, the Charter, together with other human rights instruments adopted by ASEAN in recent years, will herald a new era for human rights in the region. We should strongly supports civil society organisations and others throughout the region that are working to ensure the Charter does not become a lost opportunity.

We should highlight the human rights provisions in the ASEAN Charter and set out our position on the establishment, composition and mandate of the ASEAN human rights body.

The ASEAN Charter

There have been a few other ASEAN human rights initiatives and mechanisms: In June 2004, ASEAN adopted the Declaration on the Elimination of Violence Against Women in the ASEAN Region, which includes, a commitment to adopting 'an integrated and holistic approach to eliminate violence against women', to 'gender mainstreaming' and to 'take all necessary measures to eliminate all forms of discrimination against women and to empower women'. In January 2007, ASEAN adopted the ASEAN Declaration on the Protection and Promotion of the Rights of Migrant Workers, which includes a provision to establish an 'instrument on the protection and promotion of the rights of migrant workers'. In 2004, ASEAN leaders agreed to 'the establishment of an ASEAN commission on the promotion and protection of the rights of women and children', but this, along with other human rights related initiatives, has yet to materialise.

The ASEAN Charter was adopted at the ASEAN Summit in Singapore, November 2007. It will become legally binding when ratified by all 10 ASEAN member states. To date, six member states have ratified. The ASEAN Charter contains several provisions that either directly, or indirectly, address human rights, including:

Article 1: ASEAN should 'promote and protect human rights and fundamental freedoms'.

Article 2: ASEAN should act in accordance with 'respect for fundamental freedoms, the promotion and protection of human rights, and the promotion of social justice' as well as 'upholding the United Nations Charter and international law'.

Article 14: ASEAN should establish a 'human rights body'. A body of experts has been set up to draft the human rights body's terms of reference.

While the inclusion of these provisions are welcomed, concern remains that some member states may view these commitments as little more than a window-dressing exercise, and will try to make sure that the human rights body has no real 'teeth' and is under the control of political interests. This is compounded by the fact that commitment to human rights in the ASEAN Charter is couched in very general terms, a weakness which could be remedied by a strong, professional and representative human rights body applying international standards.

The ASEAN Human Rights Body

Regional human rights bodies are an effective means of ensuring international standards are applied effectively. In the ASEAN region, where there are serious, ongoing human rights violations, a human rights body is no less essential to guarantee the implementation of the human rights commitments in the Charter.

Regional and international human rights monitoring mechanisms often rely on co-operation with, and information from, human rights defenders and civil society. They provide information on the general human rights situation as well as on individual cases, and they facilitate contact with victims of human rights violations and outreach to communities and individuals. Participation by civil society in the process of establishing a human rights body, in determining its composition and in supporting its work, is central to the body's success.

The provision for the establishment of the ASEAN human rights body offers no detail as to its nature, powers, composition or remit. There are calls on ASEAN to follow these general principles:

Establishment

The human rights body must be established within a reasonable timeframe that allows for meaningful participation. It should follow broad and substantive consultation with human rights defenders, women's organisations, minority groups, Indigenous communities, trade unions and other sectors of society within all member states. Draft terms of reference for the body should be made widely available, for example on the ASEAN Secretariat website, to allow for comments by all interested persons and organisations well in advance of their finalisation.

Composition

The human rights body must be, or must have the power to appoint, an independent, impartial, competent, well-resourced, professional, expert body, whose membership reflects the region's diverse peoples and cultures and has gender parity. Members should be nominated and elected in a transparent process involving civil society at every stage of the proceedings.

Mandate

The human rights body must encourage ASEAN member states to guarantee the level of human rights protection that is required by international law and standards.

It must have the authority and the resources to carry out:

A monitoring role, including the investigation of specific human rights situations, in response to submissions by individuals, organisations or states, or on its own motion. It must work to ensure that states allow human rights defenders to carry out their work unhindered. The human rights body must be authorised to determine that a state's human rights violations amount to 'a serious breach of the Charter or non-compliance', in which case the Charter provides for the ASEAN Summit to decide on the matter;

An advisory role, including on the ratification and implementation of international human rights and otherrelevant treaties, the implementation of recommendations of UN treaty bodies and special procedures, and on the establishment and operation of national human rights institutions in accordance with international standards. In addition, the human rights body should provide advice to national and regional human rights defenders;

A promotional role, including urging member states to ratify international human rights treaties, to report to human rights monitoring bodies and to invite UN special procedures to visit;

An educational role, including the development of tools and materials for human rights education and helping member states to provide human rights education and training, for state officials, vulnerable groups such as detainees, and for the public as a whole.

The human rights body's mandate should be phrased in such a way that it allows for the future development, expansion and elaboration of ASEAN and other regional human rights prevention, protection and promotion mechanisms.

A New Era for Human Rights?

The human rights commitments within the Charter are a tribute to the vibrant, active and dedicated civil society in the region that has been at the forefront of efforts to push forward an ASEAN Charter with a strong human rights component. But, whether the Charter will translate into real change, with a strong human rights body capable of transforming ASEAN into a truly human rights-friendly region remains to be seen.

38

Towards a Millennium Movement

The Indian Government has almost buried it. The Indian Parliament and polity have shown no clue of it. And the diverse ranges of public activisms, which are being displayed regularly in case of several developmental issues, have not taken it up till now. The UN Millennium Development Goals (MDG), the goals that India and all the other United Nations Member States have pledged to meet by the year 2015, need to be vitalised today from the vantage point of people's needs and the common minimum programme of the government. Of all the regions in the world, Asia and Africa face the most challenging task to fulfil people's basic needs and they are the ones where once again, many MDG targets will be missed. A political process has to be evolved by which the MDGs can be framed in our government policies and programmes in the coming five years. The issues and goals, especially related with public health and universal primary education have to be taken as important strategic entry points by the people's organisations, to sharpen their struggles. It has to be ensured that the voices of the poor are heard in the economic deliberations and the policy making.

It was in September 2000 when the member states of the United Nations unanimously adopted the Millennium Declaration and the General Assembly recognised the MDGs as part of the road map for implementing the Declaration. There are eight goals that comprise 18 targets and 48 indicators. They are like ABCs of any progressive society: Eradicating extreme poverty and hunger, and here the target is to reduce by half the proportion of people living on less than a dollar a day and the people who suffer from hunger; achieving universal primary education and ensuring that all boys and girls complete a full course of primary schooling; promoting gender equality and women's empowerment in such a way that gender disparity in primary and secondary education can be eliminated preferably by 2005, and at all levels by 2015; reducing child mortality rate by two-thirds among children under five; improving maternal mortality ratio; halting and beginning to reverse the spread of HIV/AIDS, malaria and other major diseases; and ensuring environmental sustainability by integrating the principles of sustainable development into country policies and programmes, by reducing by half the proportion of people without sustainable access to safe drinking water and by achieving significant improvements in lives of at least 100 million slum dwellers by 2020. The goal of developing a global partnership for development has to go through many posts, as this might be the most contested one for evolving a consensus. It talks about the need to develop an open trading and financial system that is rule-based, predictable and non-discriminatory. It has also the target to address the special needs of the least developed countries, landlocked and small island countries, and developing countries with debt problems.

Some would say, it is too little too late. One can also rightly say that every single person on this earth should be free from hunger and must get safe drinking water and a house of his/her own. Seeing the track record of the partnership with the private sector, international financial institutions and the rich countries, one would also be suspicious of the intention of some stakeholders involved in this. However, the crucial significance of the MDGs lies in its ability to challenge and change the current paradigm of globalisation, by taking into account concrete people's needs and demands. In this sense, this is an important paradigmatic shift: Whereas the whole of 1980s and 1990s were dominated by the interests of the Washington Consensus, with its emphasis on the neo-liberal economic reforms; the MDGs comes out with a new global consensus that emphasises on human, social, political and environmental values. It is true that the Washington Consensus has long been challenged in the sufferings and struggles of millions of people all over the world. However, the MDG Consensus is somewhat of an institutional manifestation and recognition of what was already happening in the streets.

The international and national development machineries are huge monoliths, working like bulldozers: An infrastructural development project will think of their roads, dams, bridges, never in relation with the schools, hospitals or water. Environment and labour will not be a part of the mainstream trade agenda. Forest, water, flora-fauna are not thought of as part of health and environment, as they are conceived of the agricultural development strategy. The MDGs try to make a coherent developmental agenda, in which a single goal is achieved only with the other. This interconnected imperativeenvironment with education, education with gender equality, gender equality with access to health and poverty reduction, poverty reduction with economic growth—poses new challenges for our institutions and governance. One set of institutions like the WTO, the IMF, and the World Bank have to come to terms with another set of institutions like the ILO, the WHO, and the UNEP. If the intersectional synergies are not being identified, acted upon and fully exploited by the organisations committed to people's needs, it will create a vacuum. Those forces that might want these goals and partnership to protect the policies of free trade and neo-liberal economic policies will hegemonise this kind of vacuum.

The new nature of developmental discourse in the official arena, as characterised in the formalisation of the MDGs, demonstrates the readiness to go for an integrationist and intersectoral approach to policy and programme design in every sector and institution. This also poses a challenge to the infinite terrain of our social and political activism. They too will have to organise around finite focal points, and converge around some common needs, demands and goals. The 1980s and 1990s saw the emergence of many alliances and fronts in our country around specific themes and issues. The politics of the Asian Social Forum and the World Social Forum have provided an opportunity to these many alliances and fronts to know each other and sometimes share their experiences. However, in the new global reality, working for better labour standards, or for primary health care, or for education, or for elimination of HIV and AIDS: each by itself is insufficient and not necessarily the need of the hour. Environment groups need to support actions necessary to advance the health agenda, which inevitably will advance the environment agenda, if health policies and programmes are designed effectively. Health groups should support actions necessary to advance the environment agenda, which without doubt will benefit the health agenda. Groups supporting poverty reduction should encourage both health and environment agendas as integral to there own. Environment and health groups should buttress the poverty reduction agenda. Education is key to all three of these agendas, as is gender equality. The networks of networks is the need of the new millennium, and if MDGs leads us to this one goal in our present-day activism, then Asia and Africa will surely be a much better place to live in for the millions of the poor.

The Asian governments are slow to wake up. The MDGs were not presented in the Indian Parliament. For that matter, not a single South Asian country has placed it before their Parliament. The previous NDA government had taken the position that it is not the MDGs, but our new five year plan that remains the centre of our policies, and thus the MDGs will be merged in our plan goals and objectives. Simply, if you want to kill an idea, keep it in a cold storage, so that there is no set of targets, no quantified or time-bound values for specific indicators, and no monitoring or evaluation. More importantly, there is no need to generate a momentum for creating a policy framework and a political will, with the necessary budget allocation. The priority of all the groups and leaders associated with the common minimum programme of our new political formation should be to see to it that the MDGs are definitely placed in the Parliament. Our Parliaments have been under-informed and less engaged in the globalisation debates than many other institutions of the society, and they are the bodies that to a large extent decide the fate of our future. The Ministry of Finance must be engaged thoroughly in the implementation of the inter-sectoral agenda, with adequate budget allocation for meeting the goals. The financial stability, exchange rate stability, export–import growth, duties and concessions that frequently dominate and continue to dominate our finance ministry should be counter-posed with much broader and higher criteria of meeting the basic needs and aspirations of people. Changes are required not only in the realm of the finance ministry; an inter-ministerial coordination mechanism is also necessary to identify and exploit the inter-sectoral synergies embodied in MDGs, to generate higher yield results.

Right to food, Right to education and Right to health constitute the core of the MDGs. Goal 4, 5, and 6: all focus on health. We need a Millennium Mobilisation Movement, bringing different move-ments and campaigns together, to harness the energy necessary to push the governments towards achieving these goals by 2015. Up till now the top-to-bottom mechanism of monitoring has been evolved. The United Nations system is charged by the Secretary General to assure that every five years between now and 2015 individual country reports are prepared, assessing the degree to which each country is on track or not in achieving the MDGs by 2015. In the UN General Assembly in the fall of 2005, the Secretary General will provide his first of three assessments of global progress towards the MDGs, based on these national reports. There could be multiple channels of mobilisation and monitoring. One of the most important channels is a set of sectoral monitoring and evaluation exercises, undertaken by public bodies, institutions, intellectuals and groups themselves. Another is an immediate identification of the actionable issues of the highest priority, on which all major secular and progressive forces can rally. The future of the goals of people's needs is secured only when its polity is in people's hands.

39

Agenda for Food Rights

The demand for a 'Fundamental Right to Food for All' is a volatile issue. It has several contexts: Corporate globalisation, privatisation and planned destruction of agricultural production since the 1990s, and its impact on agriculture and food security; establishment of the WTO and particularly, the Agreement on Agriculture (AoA) under it; the phenomenon of hunger amidst plenty; the right to food campaigns; monitorable targets under MDGs on poverty, women and child nutrition; large corporations and their profits; and also the policies followed by nations and nation states. There are, of course, all kinds of players in this field: from NGOs, INGOs, struggling organisations and networks, with their immediate and along terms concerns on the one hand, and multinational corporations, national governments and regional and international bodies of governance on the other.

To realise the fundamental right to food through the prism of access to land, water and seeds for small scale and subsistence farmers, requires a multi-dimensional strategy, which combines key elements of the Four A's: *Availability, Accessibility, Advocacy* and *Assertion* of the goods, services and people relating to food.

- *Availability* is related to the growth of economy in general, and of agriculture in particular in this case, and therefore to the policies that engine the growth of material and human resources, with macro-economic stability.
- *Accessibility* is linked to the ownership and distribution of resources, and ways in which these reach the most vulnerable and marginalised sections of society.

- *Advocacy* means relating with the national, regional and international governance structures of nation states, to direct towards policy changes.
- *Assertion* is the people's power that lies in their numbers, and in their different ways of social and political mobilisation.

The working principle should be to 'think globally, while acting locally', and organisation's strategy should be to 'take pro-active initiative, while act in alliance'.

At the International level, the campaign should draw *positive energies* from the Universal Declaration of Human Rights (UDHR); the Preamble to the Constitution of the Food and Agriculture Organization (FAO), 1965; Article 11 of the International Covenant on Economic, Social and Cultural Rights (ICESCR); the United Nations Convention on the Rights of the Child, 1989; World Food Summit's Plan of Action adopted in 1996 (aimed at reducing the number of undernourished people, estimated to be about 800 million in 1996, to half that number by 2015); NGO Forum's proposed Code of Conduct on the Right to Adequate Food; a set of voluntary guidelines by the FAO Council Inter-governmental Working group, and the like. In terms of availability and accessibility, these give enough sites of intervention to demand policy measures to satisfy the basic dietary needs of millions of hungry people, and culturally acceptable, safe and good quality food.

The campaign should draw 'negative energies' from the global destruction of agricultural production, and small and subsistence farmers; appropriation by MNCs; and the onslaught of the WTO. This onslaught is so severe and overwhelming that people's demands can be articulated in a sharp and an assertive manner.

At the National and Local levels, the campaign should work on reclaiming agriculture, farmers' security, and community rights. Agriculture is a way of life. Local communities all over the world strive to live sustainably and meaningfully. There is no food security without farmer security, which in turn is linked to the maintenance of biodiversity. Maintenance of biodiversity and enhancement of genetic resources has been carried out by farming communities, particularly women, all over the world, wherever localised food production prevails. People also rely on common property resources—forests, lakes or even roadside areas, which are owned by the community or the state—as vital means of survival. However, these are also areas of intense conflicts, and questions of survival, of farmers and communities, of distribution and ownership of resources, are appearing upfront. Thus a *Demand for the Social Security of Farmers, and Community Distribution Systems of Land, Water and other Natural Resources* has the potential to mobilise farmers and village communities. *Right to Work* and *Right to Employment* can also be anchoring points to build the right to food campaign.

To *make a connection between the international and the national,* and to *create a rallying point internationally* for campaigns, we can propose four issues:

- *Recognising Rights to Freedom from Hunger:* Incorporating them into national laws. The Indian experience provides a good example.
- *Establish a World Commission on Hunger.* Modelled after the World Commission on Dams, which concluded its mandate in 2000 and has been a unique experiment in global policy making. Representations from communities, NGOs, business, and governments should review past experiences in eliminating hunger, and identify areas for time-bound future tasks, guided by a human rights framework.
- *Recognise Rights to the Natural Habitat:* The rights of local communities to their resources should be integrated into the national and the international law. The OAU Model (2000) on community rights provides a good example. It is a matter of fundamental human rights that local communities can enjoy the right to resources such as land, water, fishing grounds, forests and seeds. They should not be dispossessed of these resources without prior consent, nor fair compensation.
- *Initiate a Convention for Community Resource Rights*: Resource conflicts are frequent/intense between communities, state agencies and corporations. Fair access and equitable benefit sharing are fundamental cornerstones of any international agreement. We should launch a campaign process, to commence negotiations for a UN Agreement on Community Resource Rights. The starting point for such an approach includes the two main human rights instruments: the International Covenant on Civil and Political Rights, and the Covenant on Economic, Social and Cultural Rights.

40

Arms Trade Treaty and India

Over 1,000 people are killed every day by arms. Eight million small arms and light weapons are produced every year. Each year, at least a third of a million people are killed directly with conventional weapons and many more are injured, abused, forcibly displaced and bereaved as a result of armed violence. Based on an evaluation of the value of total exports for 2005–07, as officially reported by the authorities of each country, listed for deliveries of all military equipment and services, the top-ten arm exporters in the world—the US, UK, Russian Federation, Israel, France, Germany, Italy, Sweden and Spain—value for US$ 72,917 million. To date only about 40 states have enacted laws and regulations for controlling the business of arms brokering, including or excluding related financial and transport services, and extra-territorial provisions.

Anybody would suggest in such a situation that states should reduce and regulate arms trade. Governments must prevent arms transfer, especially where there are substantial risks that they are likely to be used for serious violations of human rights. People, tired and fearful of terror-counter terror, insurgency-counter insurgency, armed and violent groups, would like to immediately go for reducing the risk of diversion of arms to unauthorised users, unlawful use of arms, and for minimising the risk of loopholes and weakness being exploited by unscrupulous arms dealers. Arms trading is a multi-billion dollar industry globally. Seeing the range of politico-geographical circumstances, both of armed conflicts and repressive situations, and reflecting on the current weakness and loopholes in the poorly regulated arms trade, and its horrific consequences on human rights, a more informed opinion would suggest that a global problem requires a global solution.

In fact, this is what has been happening since the beginning of October 2003: A new Control Arms campaign had gathered the support of over one million people worldwide. It is in the form of a popular Million Faces Petition, calling for a global, legally binding agreement, an Arms Trade Treaty (ATT), to ease the suffering caused by irresponsible transfers of conventional weapons and munitions. Escalating global wars propelled by the arms trade industry, and increasing realisation about how UN arms embargo violations continue in Somalia and Darfur because of loopholes in national laws and lack of commitment and capacity by some governments, has made the campaign fast forward. Fifteen Nobel Peace Prize Laureates, including Dalai Lama, Desmond Tutu and Oscar Arias, have called on governments to work for a Treaty, in order to stop irresponsible arms exports 'which are causing the peoples of the world so much pain and destruction'. A substantial number of parliamentarians from African countries came out in support of an international treaty. Thus a historic vote at the UN General Assembly in December 2006 saw 153 governments vote for a resolution to start working towards a global arms trade treaty. The following year, over 100 states submitted responses to the UN Secretary General's consultation on the proposed Treaty, one of the rare success stories of civil society organisations in recent years!

The proposed Arms Trade Treaty would be incorporated into the national law and regulations of every ratifying nation, and reinforced through rules such as regular public reporting. Consequently, it would be illegal for any supplier government to ignore the Treaty's criteria, when supplying arms. Any decisions that break the terms of the Treaty could then be challenged and potentially overturned in the national courts. Under the proposed treaty, governments would be required to report their arms transfers in an open and transparent way, which would lead to greater public and parliamentary scrutiny.

However, this is what some countries, deeply involved in the arms trade, do not want. The United States was the only state to vote against the 2006 UN vote in favour of working towards a treaty. There were 24 abstentions, including China, India, Israel, Iran, Pakistan, Russia, Saudi Arabia, Syria and Zimbabwe. In the run-up to the crucial October UN discussion to concretise moving towards negotiations on ATT, a few states, including China, India, Egypt, Pakistan, Russia and the US, are attempting to block, delay and water down proposals and thus make the treat defunct, which would allow continued unchecked trade in arms.

Look at the case of Iraq. Prior to the 2003 invasion which overthrew Saddam Hussein, there were an estimated 15 million small arms and light weapons in Iraq, mainly AK-47 assault rifles, circulating among a population of about 25 million. Since the invasion, the new authorities in Iraq have agreed contracts with the US and its partners to import at least one million infantry weapons and pistols with ammunition, as well as other munitions and military equipment. Amnesty International has identified 47 US Department of Defense contracts, dating between 2003 and 2007, for the procurement of small arms, light weapons and associated equipment for the Iraqi security forces. These contracts comprise at least 115 delivery orders to Iraq, totaling almost US$ 217 million. Many of these imported weapons remain unaccounted for. Stocks have been diverted to, and captured by, armed groups, militia and individuals. There is no clear US audit trail for approximately 370,000 infantry weapons supplied to the Iraqi security forces. An arms trade treaty could address this, by setting out common provisions that require states to establish effective, accountable and transparent systems for all international arms transfers.

In our neighbourhood, we have witnessed arms supplies to Myanmar. Further, China, Serbia, Russia and Ukraine have between them supplied armoured personal carriers, military trucks, military weapons and munitions that have crushed people's movements for democracy. India has also at times offered to supply more arms, despite persistent patterns of human rights violations committed by the Myanmar forces.

India has been one of the worst affected countries due to the illicit and irresponsible transfer of arms, weapons and explosives, and its use by non-state terror groups. It had been supportive to the idea of an arms trade treaty and international arms registry in early 2000. However, its present response is that 'it is premature to begin work on a comprehensive, legally binding instrument establishing common international standards for the import, export and transfer of conventional arms. India encourages the United Nations and member states to continue the process of consultations and consensus building on the issue of conventional weapons transfers. Regional efforts could be encouraged as part of this process so as to act as building blocks for an eventual international effort' (Ministry of External Affairs, 2007). This is an argument primarily to maintain the status quo, business as usual. Huge illegal, irresponsible arms transfers will continue as usual, rendering arms control and embargoes weak and ineffective.

It is also disturbing that while opposing the idea of ATT, the Indian government is underlining 'the right to self defense... This right also implies that states enjoy the right to engage in trade of arms, including export to another country'. India has not been a big arms exporter country, and like in economic and political spheres, it must not develop an aspiration to follow the big global arms leaders like the US and China.

Globalisation is changing the way in which arms trade is carried out. Arms companies, operating from an increasing number of locations, now source components from across the world. Their products are often assembled in countries with lax controls on where they end up. Too easily, weapons and munitions get into totally irresponsible hands. Each year, at least a third of a million people are killed directly with conventional weapons and many more die, are injured, abused, forcibly displaced and bereaved as a result of armed violence. Rapidly widening loopholes in national controls demonstrate that this global trade needs global rules. Hence there is an urgency of an effective Arms Trade Treaty. State-to-state transfers, state-to-private end-user transfers, commercial sales, leases, loans, gifts or surpluses, imports, exports, re-exports, temporary transfers, transits, transshipments, re-transfers—all should be publicly scrutinised, and legally accountable.

In today's world, there is a grave need for enforceable multilateral and global restraints to reduce the arms trade, as it is a direct impediment to the achievement of peace and international security. It requires a political will on the part of India to come forward in support of the Arms Trade Treaty, as in the absence of it, we will be confronted with more arms race and an increasing global arms trade, without regard to its long-term consequences.

(*The Hindu*, 30 September 2008)

One hundred and forty seven states at the United Nations voted overwhelmingly to move forward with work on an Arms Trade Treaty on 31 October 2008. The vote was particularly strong in Africa, South and Central America and Europe indicating strong demand for arms control both from countries severely affected by armed violence and from major exporters. Only the US and Zimbabwe voted against, ignoring increasing global consensus for an ATT. India abstained.

References

Amnesty International. 2007. 'Indian Helicopters for Myanmar: Making a Mockery of Embargoes?', 16 July. Available online at http://web.amnesty.org/library/Index/ENGASA200142007

Central Intelligence Agency. The World Factbook. Available online at https://www.cia.gov/library/publications/the-world-factbook/

Dick Marty. 2006. 'Alleged Secret Detentions and Unlawful Inter-State Transfers Involving Council of Europe Member States, 7 June 2006: Draft Report—Part II [Explanatory memorandum]'. Available online at http://assembly.coe.int/CommitteeDocs/2006/20060606_Ejdoc162006PartII-FINAL.pdf

EUbusiness. 2007. 20 July. Available online at http://www.eubusiness.com/news_live/1184580002.08

The Guardian and AFP. 2007. 'Myanmar May Still Get EU Choppers', *Taipei Times*, 17 July. Available online at http://www.taipeitimes.com/News/world/archives/2007/07/17/2003369968

Himal SouthAsian. 2007. Available online at http://www.himalmag.com/2007/february/cover2.htm

Hina Jilani, Human Rights Council. 2007. *Report submitted by the Special Representative of the Secretary-General on Human Rights Defenders.*

India Defence. 2007. 'Defense Relations With Myanmar Surge; Progress Made During Vice Admiral Thane's Visit', India Defence, 3 April. Available online at http://www.india-defence.com/reports/2996 (accessed on 03.04.2007).

Indian Express. 2006. 'Tyagi in Myanmar to Push Arms Offer', *Indian Express*, November 22. Available online at http://www.indianexpress.com/story/17045.html

International Monetary Fund. World Economic Outlook Database. Available online at http://www.imf.org/external/pubs/ft/weo/2009/01/weodata/index.aspx

International Organisation for Migration. 2005. 'World Migration 2005: Costs and Benefits of International Migration'. Available online at http://www.ilo.org/dyn/migpractice

Ministry of External Affairs, Government of India. 2007. *Indian Mission to UN.*

Official Gujarat State Portal. Available online at www.gujaratindia.com

Thomas Paine. 1776. *Common Sense*. Republished 2008. Forgotten Books. Available online at www.forgottenbooks.org

UNFPA. 2007. 'State of the World Population 2007—Unleashing the Potential of Urban Growth'. Available online at http://www.unfpa.org/upload/lib_pub_file/695_filename_sowp2007_eng.pdf

UN Human Rights Council. 2008. *Report of the United Nations High Commissioner for Human Rights on the Protection of Human Rights and Fundamental Freedoms while Countering Terrorism*. Available online at http://www.unhcr.org/refworld/docid/484d121a2.html

Index

About the Author

Mukul Sharma is a journalist, a writer, a trade unionist and a developmental professional. He writes on environment, development, labour and media issues in English and Hindi and has published extensively, including the books *Landscapes and Lives: Environmental Dispatches on Rural India*, *Defining Dignity* and *No Borders: Journeys of an Indian Journalist*. He is the editor of *Improving People's Lives: Lessons in Empowerment from Asia*. He has recently co-authored a book, *Contested Coastlines: Fisherfolk, Nations and Borders in South Asia* (2008). He has received 12 national/international awards for his writings, the most recent being the Award for Excellence in Asian Print Media Writing by Singapore Press Holdings and Asian Media Information and Communication Centre, Singapore. He is closely associated with the World Social Forum and the World Dignity Forum. Mukul Sharma was the Director of Heinrich Boll Foundation, India. He was then the Asia Campaigns & Advocacy Coordinator at ActionAid International. He was the Director of Amnesty International in India. Presently based in Bangkok, Thailand, Mukul Sharma is the Executive Director of AIDS Society of Asia and the Pacific (ASAP) and is also associated with the Faculty of Public Health, Mahidol University.